A PARENTHESIS
IN ETERNITY

By the same author

A
PARENTHESIS
IN ETERNITY

Joel S. Goldsmith

HarperSanFrancisco
A Division of HarperCollins*Publishers*

FIRST HARPER & ROW PAPERBACK EDITION IN 1986

LIBRARY OF CONGRESS CATALOG CARD NUMBER: 64-10368
ISBN: 0-06-063231-3

RRD(H) 20 19 18 17 16 15 14 13 12

Except the Lord build the house, they
labour in vain that build it.
—Psalm 127

Illumination dissolves all material ties and binds men together with the golden chains of spiritual understanding; it acknowledges only the leadership of the Christ; it has no ritual or rule but the divine, impersonal universal Love; no other worship than the inner Flame that is ever lit at the shrine of Spirit. This union is the free state of spiritual brotherhood. The only restraint is the discipline of Soul, therefore we know liberty without license; we are a united universe without physical limits; a divine service to God without ceremony or creed. The illumined walk without fear—by Grace.

THE INFINITE WAY

CONTENTS

PART TWO

RISING OUT OF THE PARENTHESIS
Attaining the Mystical Consciousness

PART THREE

LIVING IN THE CIRCLE
Living the Mystical Life

A PARENTHESIS
IN ETERNITY

INTRODUCTION

Somewhere in consciousness there lies a land undiscovered, a land not yet revealed by religion, philosophy, or science. I know that it exists for it continually pushes itself into my awareness. I know that when it discloses itself, it will change the nature of mankind: wars will be no more, and the lamb will lie down with the lion. I know its name, for it is revealed as My[1] kingdom or My grace. Christ Jesus spoke of this Kingdom, but neither the spoken word nor the manuscripts so far discovered have revealed its full significance.

In my high moments I have lived and experienced this Kingdom, and sometimes its atmosphere clings to me for days, but then again it eludes me. Sometimes in healings I have witnessed its action, but have caught only glimpses of it. It has shown me the human mind of mankind and its operations, and how men can use the mind for evil purposes as well as for good.

This spiritual kingdom, this inner world, is as real as the world we see, hear, taste, touch, and smell—if anything, more real. What we become aware of through the senses eventually changes and disappears, but this inner world, these spiritual glories that are revealed to us, these spiritual lights with whom we learn to tabernacle—they never disappear.

[1] The word "My," capitalized, refers to God.

This is the world the Master Christ Jesus revealed, a Kingdom which exists right here where we are if we will but receive the Spirit of God within us. It is already established here on earth, only awaiting our recognition and realization.

Finding that Kingdom will in no wise take us out of the world. It will leave us in it, but not of it. We will enjoy all the things that go to make up a full and rich life; we will not become ascetics, but we will no longer desire *things* or long for them, and even though the riches of life will be a part of our experience, inwardly we will be so free of them that our whole inner being will be lived in and of God.

The mystical world is a real world. It is a world of people and a world of things formed of the illumined or enlightened consciousness. But how do we become the illumined or the enlightened? How do we find this mystical world? What is mysticism?

Mysticism is "the experience of mystical union or direct communion with ultimate reality reported by mystics." It is "a theory of mystical knowledge; the doctrine or belief that direct knowledge of God, of spiritual truth, of ultimate reality, or comparable matters is attainable through immediate intuition, insight, or illumination and in a way differing from ordinary sense perception."[2]

The mystical message of all times is the same. The language and the mode of approach may be different, but the message and goal—the attainment of conscious union with God—never change.

No one can become a seeker of God in his humanhood, but when God touches a person to some measure of awakening, he is led to some kind of a spiritual teaching. He may remain on that one path to the end of his search, or he may go from teaching to teaching until ultimately he finds that which meets his unsatisfied need and brings him to God-realization. Although revealed in different languages, different terms, and different forms, the inner unfoldment leads unerringly to the one goal.

Nothing can equal the fascination and adventure of the mystical life. It is a life of discovery, discoveries which forever lie ahead of us, never behind. We may have had an experience yesterday that lifted

---

[2] Merriam-Webster's *Unabridged Dictionary*, Third International Edition (Springfield, Mass.: G. and C. Merriam Company, 1961).

us to the mountaintop, but we cannot live on yesterday's "pearl" or on yesterday's manna because the experience of yesterday, regardless of how great and soul-stirring it may have been, is only a preparation for the greater ones that lie ahead. Always there is the challenge of the intangibles awaiting our discovery here and now.

The kingdom of God is without limitation or boundary, and all the truth that has been given to the world in the past thousands of years is but a thimbleful in comparison with what there is yet to be discovered. No one has yet experienced even one-millionth of what has already been revealed.

Can anyone ever reveal the last word of spiritual truth? Can anyone ever penetrate the depths of God? Can anyone ever discover the allness of God? True, the mystics of all ages have given us glimpses of truth, and their words carry conviction because behind the words is the experience itself. But how much of what we have read of spiritual revelation have we actually experienced? How much of it still lies between the covers of a book? How much of it have we actually witnessed? How much truth has come as an inner unfoldment with the renewing strength and power of revelation?

Every aspirant on the spiritual path should be constantly alert for some original revelation of truth. If he is content, however, to dwell merely on words without drawing forth the deeper and richer meanings of which the words are but the symbol, he is not being fed from within, but from the pages of a book. Black ink does not taste good, nor is there any sustenance to be found on the printed page, and those persons who are living on the printed word are going to be just as hungry as those who suffer from malnutrition. The sustaining substance to be found in words, printed or voiced, lies in the truth that can be drawn into consciousness.

The truths that are revealed in spiritual literature are seeds planted in consciousness, and if those seeds are planted in an active and fertile consciousness, they spring up and bear fruit; but if they are taken into the sleeping consciousness—the unconscious or dead consciousness, the consciousness that is living on form, ritual, or yesterday's thoughts —they cannot break open, sprout, and mature.

Every word of truth that we hear or read should be taken into our consciousness as if it were a seed, and there nourished and fed. It should be fertilized with meditation and by pondering and putting it into practice, until in a moment of stillness and silence the seed can break open, take root, and begin to bear fruit.

What we read, then, cannot become stale. Always there is the expectancy that the very next paragraph may contain the "pearl of great price" for us. The next paragraph, or the one we read tomorrow, may be the "pearl" to our neighbor or to someone else. There is no such thing as only one "pearl."

The spiritual life is a necklace that would fit around this entire globe —so many pearls are there in it. Every statement of truth is a pearl, every single principle is a pearl, every experience, almost every meditation, is a pearl, if only we search for it deep enough within our own consciousness.

Each grain of truth should be used as a steppingstone or bridge to lead to a deeper awareness, letting more and more truth come to the fore as we travel further and higher. If we are not alert, however, and do not keep the ear and mind wide, wide open to see what lies ahead, it would be the same as trying to cross the ocean in a boat while asleep at the steering wheel.

Spiritual literature and spiritual principles are certainly stepping-stones or bridges over which you and I can travel, but they are steps or bridges leading where? Always to our own consciousness! That is the only place where a truly spiritual teaching can ever lead—to our own consciousness.

"God is no respecter of persons," and whatever is possible to one is possible to all, but only to those who seek. Seek and find; seek and find; but seek within the realm of your own consciousness. Your consciousness and my consciousness are just as infinite as the consciousness of any spiritual seer, and whatever degree of unfoldment any illumined soul has had, we can have in an equally deep degree. We may not express that Infinity in its fullness, but nevertheless that is the truth about us.

Regardless of how much truth reveals itself to us, however, or how many experiences we may have of a spiritual nature, as soon as these have served their purpose, we let them slide out of memory and look forward to the next because the next one will be greater. If we should write a hundred books on truth, or heal a hundred thousand people, let us never believe that we will have come to the end of our consciousness, because our consciousness has a depth far beyond that of the ocean and a circumference greater than that of this entire universe and of all the other universes yet unknown and undiscovered. There is no limit to the depth of our being and the richness of our consciousness, but we must dive deeply into ourselves to bring forth the revelation of the nature of God, and eventually the nature of our own being. Then we shall discover that God is in truth our very being and our very life.

To seek, to find, and to experience this inner glow, this inner realization of the Presence, this inner communication with God, and then realize that each time that it is repeated it becomes a deeper, richer experience, and a more fruitful one, so that there can never be an end, or a sense of dullness, monotony, or boredom in it—therein lies the real adventure of the spiritual life.

God is infinite; truth is infinite. It is for us to rise into that Infinity, explore new avenues of truth, open new areas of our consciousness because all this truth is our consciousness, our very own! At one level of consciousness we can bring forth literature, art, inventions, or discoveries. At a deeper level of consciousness we can bring forth spiritual experiences up to, and including, the final one, which is known as the marriage, or union, with God. It all depends on what we are seeking.

And what is it that we are seeking? Is it merely a healing of some nature? Is it merely more comfort in the human world? Is it merely a little happier companionship or a little more money? It is right to enjoy health; it is right to have an abundance of supply; it is right to have satisfying human companionships. And all these things inevitably do follow, but if they alone are the goal of our search, we are debasing truth. The goal itself is discovering the essence of spiritual wisdom, exploring every corner of the spiritual kingdom, every depth of it, every height of it. Therein lies spiritual adventure.

Who knows what great truth will be revealed to us? Who knows what wonderful things lie ahead of us an hour from now? Who knows what startling revelations of truth may come to us? It is marvelous when they come; it is wonderful when they happen, but they cannot come if we permit some particular message to become crystallized in us, or if we go to bed tonight thinking we know the truth or wake up tomorrow morning believing we have reached the ultimate in spiritual wisdom. Every day of the week must be a fresh day. With each day there should always be an inner longing, not to recall or remember something that was revealed the day before, but an acknowledgment of our emptiness and a reaching out: "Father, Father! Come, come, reveal Your message! Give me a vision today; let me know You aright; let me go deeper into Your consciousness."

There are greater truths buried in our consciousness than any that have ever come forth. Just as truth came through a humble shoemaker like Jacob Boehme, so can world-shattering truth come through you or me, and if it does not, it may be because we did not want it as desperately as have the great mystics of the world, or because our interest has been more on the surface of life than in its depths.

Sometimes students who have been studying for only a year write me of their dissatisfaction, disappointment, and even discouragement over their lack of unfoldment and progress. Often my response is, "In just a year, just a year? There are another thousand million years ahead of you, and no one is ever going to accomplish the transition from that 'man, whose breath is in his nostrils,' to the man who has his being in Christ merely by studying or meditating for a year." If the kingdom of God were that easily attained, everyone would attain it. But how few have done so!

Make no mistake, this is the most difficult of paths; this is the most difficult life there is. It is far easier for a person to become a Croesus with fabulous wealth or to attain great fame than to succeed in attaining the spiritual life. It is far easier to accomplish anything in the human world than in the spiritual because in the spiritual world you and I are called upon to "die" before we can attain what we are seeking.

The spiritual life is not gained by giving up smoking or drinking or the eating of meat, or by studying for a few years, or by attending church or classes. If only it were that easy! The Kingdom is attained by "dying daily." Every day of the week, as a part of our involvement in the life of the Spirit, we must see to it that some trace of humanhood either leaves us or is sent about its business. Every problem must be viewed as an opportunity to rise above whatever the situation may be, and if that sounds too difficult, it is better not to begin. But if there is a drive in us that compels us to go forward, then we must be patient and persist until we do attain.

Attainment is possible to everyone who sets out on this spiritual adventure, and it is possible without price—except the one great price. There *is* a price: "Sell all that thou hast." That is the price, and it is paid in the coin of our devotion. It is the price the Master demanded of his followers when he told them, "He that loveth father or mother more than me is not worthy of me. . . . Sell all that thou hast. . . . Follow me, and I will make you fishers of men." From this we can understand how difficult spiritual attainment is and why our progress is slow, and we will not complain. We will be satisfied, realizing that if the followers of Jesus in his day had to walk those steps, so do we.

But although we may plumb the depths to the limit of our capacity and fail to reach the goal, the search is still worthwhile, even if we have to go on for years and years and years believing that we are not making any progress. The truth is that with every effort, with every expedition, with every search, with every meditation, we are moving slowly and inexorably toward the goal of all life—union with God.

Problems and circumstances affect the lives of different people in different ways. They can make or break a person, or they can leave him where they found him. There is nothing tragic or disgraceful about being broken or about being a failure, nothing at all. A person who fails has tried, usually very hard, and there is a satisfaction in that, and there is a hope in it because if a person continues to try, he can never be kept down, and even though he may be broken, he will rise up again. The tragedy, if there is one, or the disgrace, lies in being willing to go on day after day, waking up in the morning and going to bed at night, and being nowhere tomorrow that he was not yesterday.

Think of the unlimited opportunities there are in every large metropolitan area for gaining a knowledge and appreciation of the great art, literature, music, religion, and natural sciences of the world, and then think of the thousands of aimless people walking the streets of those cities without even being aware of these opportunities, and more often than not, not even caring. There is tragedy!

Is it not the same, only more so, with any truly spiritual teaching or message? Are there not countless people in the world who are exposed time and time again in some manner or by some means to truth, and yet who pass "by on the other side"? That is sad because finding a spiritual message could and should be the beginning of a life of adventure. True, it does not always happen that way. It could even leave us where it found us. It cannot break us—that it could never do—but it can make us, and it should open life to spiritual joy and excitement, to seeking and finding. It should spur us to turn round and round and then to start all over again to see how much further we can go on this Path.

There is no God out here in space. The God there is, is hidden within us, waiting for each one of us to discover for himself. We do not have to go any place in time or space. The spiritual journey, the greatest of all adventures, is not made in time or space. It is a journey in consciousness—and this journey no one can make for us.

PART ONE

THE CIRCLE
OF ETERNITY

The Basis of Mysticism

CHAPTER I

THE TWO WORLDS

There are two worlds. There is "this world," and there is "My kingdom." There is the world that we see, hear, taste, touch, and smell, the world that we live in, in our business and in our home with our family; and there is the world within, where we live when the Christ has been raised up in us, the world inside our consciousness where we are alone with God and where we tabernacle with the son of God in us. On one hand, there is the mortal man, and on the other, the spiritual son of God.

Paul, who was spiritually and inwardly taught by the Master, described mortal man as the "creature," the "natural man" who "receiveth not the things of the Spirit of God: for they are foolishness unto him: neither can he know them, because they are spiritually discerned"; and explained that "as many as are led by the Spirit of God, they are the sons of God."

Until we learn about the man who has his being in Christ—the man we must become—we are that "natural man," that "creature," that mortal who must put off mortality, that man who must "die daily."

Progress on the spiritual path will be much more rapid once it is understood that this human or mortal man, this "creature," the "natural man," is entirely cut off from God, is never under the law or protection of God, and is never governed or sustained by God. If he were, could there be murder, rape, arson, or war? Could there be death if man were God-governed? Could there be disease? Could an airplane go hurtling out of the sky to kill all the people in it?

If man were God-governed, would not disease have diminished? But has it not rather increased? For every disease that has been brought under control, have not two new ones, more deadly than the old, made their appearance? Yet every day millions upon millions of prayers go up to God; and then when a solution to the problems of the ills of the flesh comes, does it come from God or from a bottle of medicine, an antibiotic, or a new surgical discovery? Do not human beings die of the most horrible diseases and tragic accidents? Does God interfere?

Human beings suffer terrible injustices at the hands of others: they are governed by tyrants; wars are fought, and the righteous do not always win those wars. In every age there are those in slavery, there are those in bondage. We have only to look at history to know how many thousands of years this world has suffered from war, even though every generation has felt, as we do, that war is wrong, that it does not solve anything, and that no lasting good comes from it. Has not every generation prayed to God to end war, and in all these thousands of years, has there ever been an answer to such prayers? Are not nations whose history goes back thousands and thousands of years and whose people have been praying to God all those years still in slavery, ignorance, and poverty?

God never has been known to do anything for a human being as long as he is immersed in "the things of the flesh." A lack of understanding of this point causes many aspirants on the Way to miss the mark, because they are forever trying to get God to do something to, or for, a human being, but this He does not do. Regardless of how much humankind suffers or enjoys, regardless of whether men are sick or well, poor or rich, they are not under the law of God; they are not fed, sustained, or protected by God; and for that reason the tragic things that happen to the human race keep right on happening generation after generation, with only a few escaping the common fate.

This need not be, for both Christ Jesus and Paul, as well as others before them, taught that these experiences of the human race can be avoided, and they also taught how it is possible to "come out from among them, and be . . . separate," and bear fruit richly. That was the whole purpose of the ministry of the Master—to reveal to the world how to come out from among the masses and avoid the strife, the lack, the sins, and the diseases that beset mankind.

Human beings think they can add spirituality to their humanhood and thereby attain God's grace. This cannot be: there has to be a "dying daily"; there has to be a putting off of "the old man"; there has to be a putting off of mortality and a clothing with immortality; there has to be a transition from the man of earth to that man who has his being in Christ; there has to be repentance. God has no pleasure in "the death of him that dieth . . . wherefore turn yourselves, and live ye." There must be a turning before we can live again.

Most of us think that we can turn to God and persuade Him to add something good to us, without our losing, giving up, or changing anything. We expect to add immortality and divine Grace to our human self. But it is only as the old man in us "dies" that the new man can be "born"; it is only as we change our outlook that spiritual harmony can begin to function in us and as us.

It is not that God, Spirit, is going to do something for mortal, material man: it is that mortal, material man is to put off his materiality that his spiritual identity may be revealed. It is nonsense to believe that human beings are under the law of God when all the prayers that the human race has ever invented have never brought God into human experience: they have never brought peace on earth, eliminated disease, nor have they overcome the sin or the poverty of the world. Have the prayers of the Christians, the Jews, the Hindus, or the Buddhists been answered? Why not? What is wrong? Is God a respecter of persons? Is God a respecter of races or religions?

For thousands of years there have been human beings who have observed every kind of ritual without ever approaching the kingdom of God. Jesus made that clear when he cautioned his disciples that their righteousness must exceed that of the scribes and the Pharisees who of all men were the most scrupulous in their rigid following of the Mosaic law. And yet Jesus said that the righteousness of those who seek the kingdom of God must be greater than theirs. They must enter into the silent sanctuary of their own being and pray where men cannot see them. They must not merely support the temple or the church: they must do benevolences without letting anyone know about them.

It is easy to be a human being full of trouble—that seems to be the easiest thing in the world to be. But it is not easy to be the child of God, spiritually free of troubles. Anyone who tries to live the Sermon on the Mount or to give up this eye-for-an-eye and tooth-for-a-tooth business, anyone who seriously tries to "resist not evil," anyone who earnestly attempts to resist the temptation to return evil for evil, finds such a way difficult at first. This is because, as human beings, we are not children of God, nor are we under the law of God. If we would be children of God, there is a price to pay, and the price is to "resist not evil"; the price is to learn to pray for our enemies, to forgive seventy times seven; the price is to dwell in the realization that we of our own selves are nothing.

Gaining the kingdom of God has to be accomplished inside of our own being. Something must take place within us; there must be a conscious remembrance that the Christ abides in us. Through this conscious remembrance of our oneness with God, the grace of God becomes active, a Grace that brings things and experiences to us that humanly would be improbable, if not impossible. There is a lessening of dependence on our mind, our education, or our pocketbook, and a greater reliance on the Infinite Invisible. Consciousness is being opened to receive the invisible things of God, of which all things that are visible are made.

The whole of the spiritual life has to do with an activity of consciousness, an activity of your individual consciousness and of mine. To live as the son of God and not as a human being means to dwell consciously in the realization of an invisible Presence; it means to live consciously in the awareness that God is the guiding and sustaining principle of our life. There must be a change of base; there must be a change of consciousness. It is not God who comes to the human experience: it is the human being who has to give up the human experience, exchanging it for his spiritual identity.

Whether a person is good or bad is not the determining factor in the descent of Grace upon him. There have been, and are, millions of good people who have never attained their spiritual estate because human goodness does not bring it about. What really counts is the degree of devotion there is to the search for God. How much hungering and thirsting after truth is there? How much longing is there for an understanding of God, for coming face to face with God?

It is not what our outer life is. We do not prepare for the acceptance of our spiritual identity merely by trying to change ourselves into good human beings. Being good humanly has no relationship whatsoever to "dying daily." "Dying daily" is a realization that we are dissatisfied with our present mode of life, dissatisfied even if we have economic sufficiency, good health, or a happy family. Still there is that dissatisfaction, that sense of something missing in us. There is an inner unrest, a lack of peace, an inner discontent.

Without this hunger and this inner drive, there is no "dying." But as soon as we make the decision that we are going to walk the way that leads to spiritual fulfillment, we have begun the necessary transformation of mind; we have begun our spiritual journey. First must come the clear-cut realization that we cannot go on being just human beings, and attempt to add God's grace to our humanhood. There must be a turning; there must be an inner transformation. This has nothing to do with our outer life. The change takes place within us. The whole experience is an inner experience; it is one of consciousness, but when it takes place, it affects our entire outer experience.

No one of himself has the power to receive God's grace. Grace comes through an evolutionary progressive unfoldment of consciousness. To illustrate that, let us go back in memory to our own life-experience, and as we recall our childhood, youth, young adulthood, and our thirties or forties, we may be able to pinpoint a time—possibly even a specific date—at which a change of consciousness took place within us which caused us to turn and look in another direction. It may have been a disease that compelled us to reach out and up to a new and higher dimension of life; it may have been a sin or a false appetite; it may have been lack, limitation, or unhappiness; or it may have been just a natural unfoldment that led us to the place where we were dissatisfied with life as it was being lived and wondered if there were not something better, something higher. It was then that our consciousness began to change, and even though we could not observe any noticeable progress, progress nevertheless was being made gradually from day to day and month to month.

Anyone far enough along on the spiritual path to be seriously pursuing a study of this nature was undoubtedly on the Path before he was born into this experience. Whatever his former state of existence may have been, had he not been on the Path in some previous life-experience, he would not now be ready for a mystical teaching, nor would he have been led to the reading of this book. Once a person touches a mystical teaching, he is drawing closer and closer to the ultimate realization of the name and nature of God and of his true identity. Throughout all time, it has been true that when an individual realized the name and nature of God, that individual was free; and furthermore, in proportion as that individual could impart this realization or revelation, those who could accept and receive it were made free.

In every age, when there has been a great religious teacher, there have been those able to receive the imparted word of wisdom, to respond to it, and to demonstrate divine sonship, but in that very same age and very same country, there were also those who rejected the Word, who were unwilling to accept the principles. Living side by side were the saved and the unsaved, those who were able to rise above the discords of the flesh, and those who could not receive the spiritual word in their bosom.

No one who believes he is man or woman has even begun to suspect spiritual truth. No one who believes that there is a power somewhere that can operate on him for good and a power that can operate for evil has come even close to touching the hem of the Robe, for there are no such powers. There is no power of good; there is no power of evil.

No one can be prepared to receive this knowledge in one lifetime, nor is anyone capable of assimilating this wisdom in one lifetime. It takes many lifetimes of living and of spiritual unfoldment to prepare an individual for the final revelation of his true identity. Only those who have been prepared have the capacity to receive such truth.

Do we have eyes and do not see? Do we have ears and do not hear? We cannot see spiritual identity with physical eyes or hear the still small voice and its impartations with physical ears. Every individual has a Soul-faculty which has no relationship to the physical senses of sight, hearing, taste, touch, and smell, nor even to the intuitive sense which is the seventh sense. It is this spiritual faculty which becomes our power of discernment, the power to discern the nature of the two worlds in which we live.

With such discernment this outer world becomes only a symbol, a shell, almost a "suffer it to be so now." The real world is the world of Consciousness and Its forms, not the forms created by nature, not the forms created by the imagination of man or the forms we see with the eyes, but the forms that Consciousness assumes, the forms that we behold in the kingdom of God within us.

The lessons that we learn in the interior world become the basis of our conduct in the outer world. The spiritual grace we learn within becomes our life without. Without the impetus of this spiritual grace, the life as lived on the outer plane is an animal life. It has its periods of good and its periods of bad, its periods of health and its periods of disease. It never knows the peace that passes understanding; it never knows the life that God gave us, the life that is God. This life is discerned only through inner grace. Through this power of discernment we glimpse the Spirit of God and then behold It[1] in others; we witness that Spirit living in what we call human form, and just as the Spirit of God lived as the human form of Jesus, so It lives as individual you and me when we are animated by It.

Ah, yes, there are two worlds—the outer world of the senses and the inner world of the Spirit, and once we have been touched by this inner world of the Spirit, the "natural man" becomes less and less that the son of God may be more and more.

[1] In the spiritual literature of the world the varying concepts of God are indicated by the use of such words as "Father," "Mother," "Soul," "Spirit," "Principle," "Love," and "Life." Therefore, in this book the author has used the pronouns "He" and "It," or "Himself" and "Itself," interchangeably in referring to God.

CHAPTER II

RELEASE GOD

Only the very courageous can embark on the spiritual journey, and only those of great strength and vision can hope to continue on this Path. Nearly twenty centuries ago, the Master made it clear that the way is straight and narrow and few there be that enter. That this is true is borne out by the fact that up to the present time very few have been able to remain on the spiritual path and continue to go forward. It is not easy to surmount superstition, ignorance, and fear, and, despite prejudice and previous failures, to set forth in search of new horizons.

We cannot adopt new ideas while still clinging to the outworn beliefs of the past: we must be willing to relinquish our old concepts. That is where the courage comes in, and the daring. It takes courage to leave behind that which has proved to be unsatisfactory in our experience. It takes courage to look at ourselves objectively and ask: Have I sincerely worshiped God? Have I in some measure lived up to my convictions about God?

When we turn to the search for God, we should be bold enough to ask ourselves: Am I satisfied with such answers to prayers as have been given to the world? Do I believe that such truth as has been revealed is all the truth there is, or am I seeking for something yet

18

unknown except to those few mystics who have experienced the truth, tried to impart their knowledge, failed, and gone on their way?

Man's heritage is spiritual freedom, and if the revelation of Jesus Christ has taught us nothing else, it is that we are entitled to live in the full freedom of the Spirit as children of God, not as prisoners of the mind and body.

Freedom is not a condition of mind or of body: freedom is a condition of the Soul. If we do not find our freedom in Soul, we will find only limitation and bondage in our experience. Freedom cannot be given to a nation or to a race of people: freedom must first be realized in individual being, and then some measure of that freedom can be shared with those who are in need of it.

Nothing external to us can limit or hinder us because our freedom must first take place in our consciousness, and this, no one can prevent because fortunately no one can read our thoughts, look into our consciousness, or know what is going on in our Soul. So it is that wherever we are—at home, on the street, or at business—we can make a transition from the slavery of the senses to the freedom of the Soul. It all takes place within our consciousness.

There are those who complain that they cannot find this freedom because of a lack of time, but there is no lack of time: that is merely an excuse that one person uses; another uses as his excuse his lack of money; a third, his lack of sight or of hearing. All these are just alibis and excuses.

Some persons complain that they cannot study spiritual wisdom because they cannot afford to buy books. Just another excuse! The public libraries of this country and many countries of the world are filled with books and teachings of every nature. It would take only a few minutes to pick up a telephone and learn how many informative and inspiring books there are in the library or in a nearby second-hand bookstore. The person who uses his inability to buy books as an excuse for not studying is merely trying to hide from being taught or trying to ensure that he will not be taught.

Freedom is attained within us, and it is not at the mercy of time, money, health, or relationships—not even at the mercy of those countries that have made laws against religion.

The point that I am making is this: if we are bound by sin or disease, or by any form of limitation, physical, mental, moral, or financial, freedom is ours if only we have the desire to break through. It cannot be a mild desire; it cannot be just the hope, "Oh, I wish I were free; I wish I were like other people; I wish I knew what other people know; I wish I had their education."

These are excuses, alibis. There is education available for everybody, from elementary schooling on up to courses in universities, and this, without even attending classes in person. There is physical, mental, moral, and financial freedom for anyone who has a sufficient drive for freedom. Without that drive, it cannot be attained. There must be such a desire for freedom that it is virtually a passion if we are to attain the heights that we sit around wishing for, hoping for, and complaining that we do not reach. No person and no condition external to us are binding upon us. They may bind us for a year, or five, or ten, while we struggle, strive, work, and pray for freedom, but eventually freedom must come from every form of limitation.

The only thing essential to freedom is the desire to be free—nothing else—because with the desire to be free, the means toward bringing it about reveal themselves. It has been said that when the student is ready the teacher appears, sometimes externally as a person, sometimes as a book; but if in no other way, when the desire is sufficiently deep, the teacher will appear inwardly because there are just as many spiritual teachers on the inner plane as there are on the outer, if not more.

Freedom comes only when we can break through the limitations of our mind, when we do not try to pin everything down to a meaning or confine every statement to meaning the same thing always. Words sometimes seem to be contradictory, but that is because they mean one thing today, and something different tomorrow, when they are used in different ways.

The real things of life cannot be restricted. Freedom will not limit itself to a word. It is like joy; it is like peace: we know what they are, but we cannot describe or explain them because they cannot be confined to a word or a phrase. How can anyone explain what the Psalmist meant by "the secret place of the most High"? What is that? Where is it? Is it a place? Is it up high somewhere? Can "the secret place of the most High" be located in time and space?

Paul said, "For in him we live, and move, and have our being." How can we describe the place where we live, when we live in God? Where is that? What is its climate?

We are instructed to open our consciousness. How do we open our consciousness? What does it look like open, and what does it look like closed? When we speak of going within, closing the door, and entering the sanctuary to pray, where is that sanctuary? Is it in our home? Is it in a church? Is it anywhere except in consciousness?

Those are just words, and if we try to break them down into their meaning, we lose them. We might say that they are poetry. They are, but we are never going to find the kingdom of God without poetry. We must let imagery and poetry have their way with us, and not try to confine ourselves to the literal meaning of words. Let us be free from the limitations of made-up words and made-up prayers and accept the poetry and the imagery of our Soul, accept our freedom in God—not lose it by trying to analyze and dissect every word.

For years I have been seeking for a word in which I could imprison what I am trying to teach, and so far I have not succeeded in finding that word. What comes nearest to expressing my meaning is the word Christ, but if we try to pin down that term and find a meaning for It, we will lose It because what the Christ stands for cannot be limited within the confines of a word or a term.

The Spirit, or the Consciousness, of man cannot be restricted. We cannot confine God; we cannot understand, analyze, or dissect God; we cannot even name God. God eludes us when we try to put God into the letters G-o-d. The Soul of man is free; the Spirit of man is free; the consciousness of man is free. That is why we cannot put God into a religion; we cannot put the Christ into a religion; and we cannot put religion into a man. We cannot confine, restrict, or limit God, the Christ, or religion. These are free, and if we ever try to contain them within a form, we lose them.

One thing we do know: there is God, and the nature of God is omnipotence, omnipresence, and omniscience. These do not limit God, but the reason they do not limit Him is because we certainly cannot claim to know the meaning of omnipresence, omnipotence, and omniscience. Those are just words we use that have a special meaning for us.

If we can accept the Christ, if we can open ourselves to receive and rest in It, It will function in and through us. If we try to understand or explain It, or have It explained, we will lose It. We cannot bring It down to the confines of our mind. Nobody has ever had a mind big enough to hold the Christ; nobody has ever had a mind big enough to embrace It, and yet the Soul of man can experience It.

But we must be willing to experience It, and then let It go. The experiences come, over and over, and they go. When they go, we let them go because it is not possible for anyone to sit on Cloud Nine twenty-four hours a day. Those to whom much has been given, of them much is expected. So, when we receive even a ray of this spiritual light, we have to come down to the valley and share it with others who are seeking it.

Spiritual freedom is attainable by any one of us. It is our birthright. Every person on earth, be he white, yellow, or black, friend or foe, Christian or Jew, Moslem or Buddhist, is entitled to the fullness of life. But the attainment of that spiritual fulfillment does not come lightly or quickly. The whole point is whether the desire for it becomes the ultimate meaning of life, or whether we are hoping to achieve it in our spare time. It cannot come that way. It will involve effort and struggle.

Why, then, are we not enjoying it? Only because of ignorance, an ignorance of God and an ignorance of prayer, for when we know God as He is, when we understand how to pray and to pray without ceasing, we find that none of the evils of the earth come nigh our dwelling place.

It requires boldness and daring to release God, to acknowledge that we do not know God and that we do not know how to pray. It takes courage to be done with the old and to seek the new, to prove that we can live as children of God, as the very temple of God, glorifying Him.

The first bit of courage required is to acknowledge that we have never really prayed to God. Instead, we have prayed to some concept of God, a concept that came either from our parents, a church, or from books. Nevertheless, it was not God that was revealed to us, for if God had been revealed to us, we would now be living as children of God, and all our prayers would long ago have been answered.

No one can deny that in the presence of God there is fullness of life. Who would be presumptuous enough to deny that "where the Spirit of the Lord is," there is fulfillment and freedom, freedom from all the discords of the earth? Unless we deny this, we must be willing to admit that it is true; and if it is true, we will have to confess to ourselves, "I have not known God: I have known some concept of God which I have accepted and to which I have prayed, and this concept of God is really an image in my mind, a thought, a belief, or an idea." Such an admission takes courage.

If God is infinite, it must be self-evident that God cannot be contained within the mind, yet we go on believing that some concept of God in our mind is the infinite God. If the Spirit of God were as close to us as to be within our mind, we actually would be children of God, and as such would be set apart from this earth. But, instead of having the Spirit of God, what we really have is only a concept of God, a concept which may envision God as a man with a long white beard sitting up on a cloud, as a man hanging on a cross, or as a hundred other different concepts. And what do we do? We pray to these images in our own thought and expect to receive answers from them. Is that sensible? Is it reasonable?

No image that can be conceived in the *mind* can ever be God; no concept of God ever entertained by man has the power to answer prayer. Then, is not the acknowledgment that God is too great to be bound by the mind and body the very first step that a seeker must take?

"Thou shalt not make thee any graven image . . . Thou shalt not bow down thyself unto them, nor serve them." What difference whether the graven image is external to us or an image in thought? It is still a graven image which we ourselves have carved out of our own thought. Let us do away with graven images; let us have no image of God; let us have no belief of what God is.

No one knows *what* God is, but if we think of God as Omnipresence, we are free of concepts because since God is, God must be here, there, and everywhere. There is no place where God is not, or God would not be infinite Being. If we think of God as Omnipotence, we are not building any image of God: we are merely stating that God is the only power there is, the all-power and the omnipresent power. If we think of God as Omniscience, then we also are not building an image in thought: we are merely realizing that there could not be a God if Its nature were not infinite intelligence. Infinite Intelligence, All-power, All-presence! And still there is no picture in our thought, still no image in thought, still no creating of a God in our image.

Ultimately, every concept of God we have ever had must be dropped—every image, every belief. The moment we think Omnipotence, Omnipresence, Omniscience, we have no time, no space, and no place, nor is there any time, place, or space where there is an absence of God.

This may cause some to shout, "Oh, you have taken my Lord away from me. Where have you buried Him?" Yes, yes, we have, and that is a very healthy place to come to—where our Lord has been taken from us. But was it our Lord, or was it our concept of Lord that was taken away?

Do not think for a minute that every one of us is not guilty of having created a God, and then going to Jerusalem to look for Him —to Rome, to Mecca, or somewhere else. We have all done that: it is part of human nature; it is part of the belief that we are man and that somewhere there is God—and if we could only get the two together! Originally, this was part of paganism, this making a mental image of what God is, and then going out to try to find Him. Later, this sense of separation from God was made a part of the teaching of Christianity.

The beginner who thinks of God as something far-off, perhaps only half believing that there really is a God, should be guided into acknowledging that there is a God and that it is His good pleasure to give him the Kingdom. But that is really a trap into which we are leading him, for when he believes that there is a God and that God is within him, then afterward, when he is ripe, we tell him, "Now, throw it away. That image was all right for yesterday, but today let us throw all images away."

"You mean there is not a God, that God is not within me, that there is no God above me, that there is no God here with me?"

"No, that is not what I mean. I mean that God is both within and without, up there and down here."

We are now making a transition, having gained a better image in mind than we had before, but only for the purpose of leading us step by step up to the moment when we can say, "Now be still, be still and know." That is all—just be still and know, but we are not to know anything because anything we know will be incorrect, only an object of sense, an object in mind.

God is: that is enough to know. No images! No concepts! In the moment of not knowing, of unknowing—not in a moment of blankness, dullness, or of falling asleep—in a vibrant aliveness, God is experienced. Then we find that through this experience we live and move and have our being in God, and God in us.

Mind and body cannot contain God, and He is so far beyond our imagination that no one can draw pictures of Him or hold mental ideas or concepts of what He really is. All we can do is to declare with all our heart and soul that God is. Only God can maintain and sustain the heavens, and hold the sun, the moon, and the stars in their orbits. Only that which is beyond man's ability to conceive could bring forth such wisdom as is evidenced by man's ingenuity in his discovery of the principles underlying the inventions resulting in the manufacture and use of the automobile, airplane, radio, telephone, television, space rockets, and atomic energy. Only out of the storehouse of God could these emanate.

Who can stretch his imagination sufficiently to conceive what God is, God that is the Source of all that exists in the sky and in the air and in the earth and in the waters beneath the earth? We earthbound creatures are aware of only one tiny corner of the universe, one little speck called the earth, but what must the wisdom of God be that encompasses the countless planets, suns, moons, and stars of this and all the other universes?

Think of the discoveries and inventions of past centuries, and then remember that an entire century is of no more importance or significance in the mind of God than is one grain of sand on all the beaches of the world. Think of what is yet to be revealed! Think of the marvels which already exist and have existed since time began, only awaiting to be revealed!

After we begin to see how foolish it is to cling to a concept of God will come the second piece of wisdom, and we will see how foolish it is to tell God what we need or think we need, or to try to influence Him through our prayers to give us our desires, as if He were capable of withholding good or as if He were some kind of human being with power to give and to withhold. How limited is our concept of God if we believe that we have the power to influence God to do for us what He is not already doing, and how finite our sense of God must be when we go to Him with our picayunish desires or approach Him in any way except to ask for light, grace, and wisdom, for an understanding of His ways, His laws, and His life.

When we pray, we should release God from any personal obligation to us, release Him in the awareness that we are trusting that which created this universe to maintain and sustain Himself and His creation, that we are trusting God in His infinite wisdom to be about His business and God in His divine love to care for His own. When we do this, we are releasing God and no longer trying to channel Him in the direction of our personal desires. Actually, we shall find that we cannot release God, for God never was imprisoned in our mind or in our desires, nor was He ever obedient to our will.

God will not change His ways to benefit or bless us: we must change our ways in order to receive God's grace. We cannot bring God to our disobedience and ignorance, but we can become obedient and spiritually wise.

Let us give up every attempt to use God and every expectation that God will do our will or fulfill our desires, and yield ourselves to Him:

Not my will, but Your will be done in me. I do not ask You to fulfill my desires, my hopes, or my ambitions: let me fulfill Your will, Your grace, Your direction.

You have never failed me, but now, Father, I ask in what way I have failed You. Nevermore will I ask You to do my will; nevermore will I pray that You do something for me. Use me; fulfill Yourself in me; let Your will be done in me.

Release me, Father, from all desires, hopes, wishes, and plans. Let me be obedient to Your plan for me. Show me plainly the way in which I am to go, and I promise to follow the light as it is given to me.[1]

We must let go of God and let God use us. We must release Him from our mental clutches, stop hanging on to God, and let Him hang on to us. If we are in ignorance of God and His ways, let us become spiritually wise. If we are willfully disobedient to the laws of God, let us correct ourselves and bring ourselves into attunement and alignment with His laws that the finger of God may touch us to His will and His grace. The moment we relax and stop trying to bring God to our mind or body, that moment we shall find that God has always been there.

God has made a covenant with His own image and likeness:

Fear not! Fear not! If you walk through the fire, the flames will not kindle upon you; if you walk through the water, you will not drown. Fear not! Let go and be confident. In quietness and in confidence shall you realize your spiritual sonship.

My peace, give I unto you. Do you not see that there is no need for you to struggle, no need to exert mental effort, or to attempt to mold My will to yours? My peace, I give to you. That is My gift to you, a spiritual gift of spiritual peace. Only let go!

And still with some there is a mental strain, as if it were not true, as if we had to make it come true, or as if we had to woo God. The

[1] The italicized portions of this book are spontaneous meditations which have come to the author during periods of uplifted consciousness and are not in any sense intended to be used as affirmations, denials, or formulas. They have been inserted in this book from time to time to serve as examples of the free flowing of the Spirit. As the reader practices the Presence, he, too, in his exalted moments, will receive ever new and fresh inspiration as the outpouring of the Spirit.

mind struggles to *get* God instead of to *let* God, while all the time the gentle Presence envelops and enfolds us.

We cannot make God do our will, but that does not leave us hopeless. Rather does it give us added courage and strength because we know there is no need to reach God in order to sway, influence, or persuade Him. When we learn that, we will realize that instead of releasing God, we have released ourselves from finite concepts of God, from our ignorant superstitious beliefs about prayer, and from the paganistic belief that we know more than God and have more love than God.

When we pray for ourselves or for our neighbors, we evidently think that we know better than God what our need is or what our neighbor's need is, and furthermore that we have the love to want that neighbor to have it, but believe that God neither knows the need nor has the love to want to fulfill it. In our innermost heart we know that that is not true even though that is the human picture.

Human picture or no human picture, however, it is not that way at all. God is not the servant of man and God does not act in accordance with what man thinks God should be or how He should work. If it were left to man to guide the affairs of the world, all his friends and relatives would be blessed and all his enemies cursed. Then, tomorrow when his enemy becomes his friend, this procedure might be completely reversed: he might begin to pray for the enemy who has now become his friend and curse the friend who has become his enemy.

God is not like that. God is not changeable as we are, and we must give up these childish concepts of God and grow into spiritual adulthood, not attempting to tell God what His grace should be or when, but resting in the confidence that His grace is our sufficiency, and releasing ourselves from the absurd idea that we can reach some God who may, if it pleases Him, do something for us.

Let us release ourselves into the rhythm of God and thereby become a part of the rhythm of this universe. The Master gave us explicit instructions as to how to do this: " 'Take no thought for your life. . . . It is your Father's good pleasure to give you the kingdom'—it is your Father's good pleasure to give you life eternal. Take no thought for your supply, for it is your Father's good pleasure to give you supply. Take no thought for peace on earth, for it is your Father's good pleasure to give you peace on earth."

Let us follow the Master's teaching. Let us give up believing that our wisdom is greater than God's wisdom or that our love is greater than God's love, and in *silence* let us accept God's grace. Silence is the only form of spiritual prayer. True, we may use words and thoughts to lift ourselves into an atmosphere where we can be still, but the words and thoughts we are using are not prayer: they are merely aids to lift us to the heights where prayer can be experienced.

If prayer is to be effective, whatever words or thoughts we use in the preliminary stages of prayer must eventually come to a stop, and we must retire within in the attitude of "Speak, Lord; for thy servant heareth." Whether it takes a day, a year, or many years, it is imperative to have those periods of silence until we do hear that still small voice within and feel the Presence and Its power.

We do not have to go anywhere to find God: we carry God within us, not in our mind and not in our body, and yet the kingdom of God is within us. God constitutes our being; God constitutes our life; therefore, our life is as eternal and immortal as God's life, for there is only one Life. God constitutes our consciousness; therefore, our consciousness is the same consciousness as the consciousness of God. There are not two: there is only one. "I and my Father are one. . . . He that seeth me seeth him that sent me."

There is only one Life, infinite Life; there is only one Consciousness, infinite Consciousness; there is only one Soul, infinite Soul. The Soul of God embraces man; the consciousness of God contains man; and the life of God is the life of man—not a part of it, but all of it.

To pray aright, then, means to release God from any obligation to give us more than we now have. True prayer is a realization that God constitutes our being and our life. God is the Father, and God is the Son, and all that God the Father is, God the Son is; and all that God the Father has, God the Son has: all the dominion, the grace, and the glory.

To pray without ceasing is to rejoice all day long that the grace of God is working in us and through us without our telling God or pleading with Him, without our asking or desiring anything from God because He has already given all good to us, and we have only to be still to realize it and show it forth.

We have sought every kind of power in heaven and on earth to meet our needs except one, and that one is the power that is within us. That power is not in heaven, and it is not on earth; it is not to be found in a book, in a building, or in great teachers. True, it is within great teachers, but it is there in exactly the same measure that it is within you and me, and in no greater degree. We are all equal before God, and the grace of God that has given spirituality to one has given it to all. The one difference is that only a few seem to have gained access to it because only a few have learned that the power of God is made manifest in silence and in stillness. It is a power that we cannot use, but which we can permit to flow from us by our recognition and realization of it.

As we walk the earth, realizing that the kingdom of God is within, we are releasing this power and letting it flow out from us to the world, but if we try to use the power of God or push it out into the world, we lose it. It is when we realize quietly, peacefully, and confidently that all the power of God is within us that we have it. We need but be still and know that God in the midst of us is mighty, and then go about our daily work, whatever it may be: housekeeping, painting pictures, building buildings, or ministering to the sick. We do all that we are called upon to do, always realizing that we are just witnesses to God's glory and to the kingdom of God within us.

When we do this, our very presence makes the Spirit of God felt, giving peace and comfort and uplift to others, not because we want to be a blessing to our fellow man, but merely because we have learned to be still and let God's power and grace flow without any help from us, without forcing, begging, or pleading for it, and without any thought that you and I are spiritual. There is only one Spirit, and that is God in the midst of us.

We are dishonoring God if we think that He is withholding wisdom, integrity, loyalty, fidelity, justice, or harmony from us or from anyone else. Whatever qualities seem to be absent will quickly begin to appear as we learn to honor and love the Lord our God with all our heart:

I will rest in the assurance that Thou, God, knowest my need before I do, and it is Thy good pleasure to give me the kingdom.

I will not seek: I will rest. I will release myself from any belief that Thou art separate and apart from me. "If I make my bed in hell," Thou art right there with me. If "I walk through the valley of the shadow of death," Thou art with me. Wherever I go, Thou goest with me, for I and Thou art one.

Our realization and acknowledgment of this bring the presence of God into activity in individual experience. It is important to remember that there is no power in the sky to which we can appeal to save this world from catastrophe. There is no power except what comes from God: there is no power in the whirlwind; there is no power in the storm or the tempest; there is no power in madmen; there is no power in ambition, lust, or greed. Power is only in the still small voice within. Then, as we tell no man what we have learned, but share the truth with those who by their dedication and devotion have shown their readiness for it, we will be releasing this infinite power into the world, and the world will respond.

We do not have to do or think anything to release the kingdom of God into the world: we only have to know that it *is*, and be still. It will do its own work. It may be that the faithful practice of the principles of spiritual living by "ten righteous" men here, and another ten there, will release this power of God on earth. Nobody will be able to take credit for it. God's power has always been available—that is the glory! And no one can brag or boast that he is able to use it. On the contrary, the greater the power that flows from a person, the less the person is as a person and the greater he is as a child of God. Within ourselves, however, we will know that releasing God into the world brings spiritual freedom and spiritual fulfillment to those who are receptive.

God's will, God's love, and God's law are all-embracing truth and universally in operation: for you, for me, for friend, enemy, saint, sinner, for the just and for the unjust. God's activity is not directed to you or me, and yet it includes you and me: it embraces all men because of its all-inclusiveness.

We cannot bring God to our body or mind: God is already the

life of every body; every body is the temple of the living God, whether animal, vegetable, or mineral. We are now under God's law, God's love, and in God's being, not by bringing God to us but by bringing ourselves to God, and by placing every person—saint and sinner alike—in God.

Those who bring themselves to God are the beneficiaries of God's grace. Those who try to "finitize" God and pull Him into their minds and bodies lose Him. Loose Him and have Him.

When we release ourselves from the mental struggle and let God have His will here where we are, and in this whole universe, we have released God and we ourselves are free. The fetters that bind us are in the mind. It is with our mind that we are trying to hold on to God. If we let our mind relax, we will realize that we cannot lay hold of God, but that God can lay hold of us. We cannot use the mind to get God. Our mind has a function, and it can operate constructively in our life, but let us not try to use it to get God.

There is no struggle except in the mind. When the mind is still, there is no strain, and God becomes a living presence: the Christ, the individualization and individual experience of God, has come alive in us. We feel It as a Presence, as a Cloak around us.

Release God from any obligation, and let God perform His work.

CHAPTER III

THE SPIRITUAL ADVENTURE

From earliest times this world with all its magnificence, yet punctuated by untold tragedy, has been a mystery, with man himself the greatest enigma of all. Here a man, and there a man, has sought to penetrate this mystery, but for the most part men have gone about their business, doing all that needed to be done humanly—some with great integrity and some with less, some with great ability and some with less, but all having one thing in common: all that existed for them was what they could see, hear, taste, touch, or smell, or could reason and think about.

They might have looked up at the sky occasionally—a passing glance, a passing thought—but it had no meaning for them except that the sun was up there in the daytime, often very uncomfortable, and the stars and the moon were there at night, very beautiful. These things had no significance: they were just something they saw or felt, things they were aware of, but of which they had no knowledge, and in which, at the moment, no interest.

To these people it was as if there were no world other than the one in which they lived. They saw the horizon, and it was so real that, to them, it represented the edge of the world, and they did not dare to go out to investigate. Had they only known the global nature

33

of the earth and the laws of navigation, they could have sailed all around the world and found continents, islands, and unlimited wealth, but because of their ignorance, they were confined within the limits of their immediate environment.

Similarly, is not the world today filled with people, educated and uneducated, yet knowing nothing beyond what they see, hear, taste, touch, smell, or feel?

The human race, as we know it, is composed of men and women living completely shut off from divine aid, divine sustenance, and divine providence. From the most ancient of times up to modern days, man has not only lived by the sweat of his brow, but has engaged in strife to gain his ends, whether in the case of individuals, or companies under the name of competition, or as nations under the name of war.

Somewhere along the road, man lost sight of his identity and began to look upon himself as a person separate and apart from his Source, under the necessity of earning his living, having to provide for his family, and later being compelled to protect his family and community from neighboring peoples who had also lost the awareness of their true identity and, in seeking their livelihood, cared little whether they gained it by earning, stealing, or by going to war for it. Thus developed this world of human beings, each one of whom looks upon himself as an individual separate and apart from others, with interests of his own and with the responsibility on his shoulders of providing not only for the present but for the future.

Among even primitive peoples, however, there must have been some not earthbound, some able to rise above their surroundings, able to rise in consciousness, and at least begin to question the wonders of this universe. Those who watched the sky out on the desert on a clear night, the stars hanging low, probably a moon close by, or those who were alone on the sea surely must have sensed the mystery of the atmosphere, of the sky, and something even of the incomprehensibility of the desert and the sea.

The awesomeness of this great universe undoubtedly raised questions in the mind of the person who was already attuned to its mysteries, or who for one reason or another had come into this world unbound, not of the earth, earthy, walking the world, but not of it. At nighttime, as he looked up into those wondrous, faraway, unreachable stars, he must have felt that there was a hidden mystery, something not known to the mind of man. Yet here it was; it existed. There must be a meaning to those stars in the sky; there must be a cause.

To him, whether on land or sea, came the inevitable questions: What lies behind this visible world? How did this world come into existence? How did I come into existence? What am I doing on earth? Is this really life—being born, doing a little hunting and fishing, raising a family and carrying on a business, and then getting old and dying? Is this universe the product of something greater than I, or am I just a little bit of protoplasm thrown out here on the earth for a time and for no good reason? Is this an accidental world? Am I here as a victim of chance and change, a victim of a merciless desert, of a tidal wave, a hurricane, floods, fire, or other cataclysmic disasters?

There must have been times in the experience of the men who sought to penetrate the mystery of life when they envisioned the possibility of being the masters rather than the victims, when they really believed that this world had been given to them, and that it was theirs. These may have been fleeting glimpses, but nevertheless they surely were there.

Probably long days and nights of riding a camel across the desert or waiting on board a small ship for a catch of fish led to extended periods of introspection, wondering and pondering. True, this may not have happened often, but someone, somewhere in the dim, dark past, thousands of years before recorded history, caught a glimpse of the inner man, the inner Self, and each one must have interpreted and evaluated it differently.

As the centuries rolled by, the record of these many revelations shows us clearly and unmistakably that these men of the long gone past knew that they, as human beings, were not the men of God's creating. They discovered, centuries before Abraham, Isaac, and Jacob, that there is within every person what has been called the Christ, the spiritual man, the divine Self, the infinite Ego, the son of God, and although each of these ancient mystics coined new words and new terms to express this Withinness, they are all descriptive of the same experience.

Four thousand years before the birth of the Master Christ Jesus, there were teachers of spiritual vision revealing to their followers man's true identity and instructing them how to live by an internal Grace, rather than by external might and power. Those who were at all receptive were drawn to these teachings and undoubtedly some of them made the transition from the man of earth to the man who has his being in Christ. There perhaps were not too many because mankind as a whole has remained in complete ignorance of the spiritual way of life. This ignorance can be likened to a group of people, born and brought up on an island with no knowledge of, or contact with, the outside world and therefore living as if their particular island were the circumference of the entire world with nothing going on except what was taking place in that small and isolated sphere.

In much this same way the three-dimensional man, the man of earth, lives in a world circumscribed by his own limited concept of himself and his world, believing that that is all the world there is and that in order to survive it is necessary to lie, cheat, and to use all the tricks of the trade even up to, and including, warfare. To him, might is a right and normal way, and anything else is a sign of weakness. This is the life lived by the man who is in ignorance of the truth that there is another realm of consciousness which he could enter and there find a more glorious life, one not lived by might or by power, a world in which he could live at peace with his neighbors, with his competitors, and with all other races and religions on the face of the earth.

Just as the people on the isolated island could not move out into a world they did not know existed, or the American Indians of five hundred years ago could not move to Europe because they were not aware that there was such a place, so it has never been possible at any time in the past several thousands of years to tell man that he is living in the prison of his own mind, hedged in by his own limitations. How could man visualize such a thing! How could he believe something so far beyond his wildest imagination!

There have been individuals, however, who first of all had some kind of an inner conviction that there is something beyond and greater than this state of limitation, this state of mental imprisonment, and glimpsed that there is a fourth-dimensional or spiritual realm about which they knew nothing. They merely had the feeling within themselves that there must be something more to life than being born, acquiring a family, making a livelihood, and dying; there must be something better, something beyond all this.

The few who experienced this inner stirring were those who began the search. But where and how could they begin to search for the unknown? In those days, there were no books in which it could be found, no schools, and no public libraries. How, then, could man begin his search and where would he begin it? We can only speculate as to what he did, but that he had to begin within himself we can be almost certain: there was no other place to turn. So probably he began asking himself questions, pondering circumstances that surrounded him, thinking about the meaning of them, and trying to see beyond the appearance.

Miracle of miracles, one day something wonderful might happen, and he would meet another man in whom he felt some sense of kinship and attraction, and soon these two men would be talking to each other, and then it would come to light that they were both trying to fathom the same mystery and break through the veil of illusion.

It might be that one man would say, "You know, I have heard of a man over in the next village who seems to know something, a very strange man. Let us go and find him." And off they would go to find this strange character in a neighboring community. At first they may not have been able to get a word out of him, but their persistence finally might force their new-found acquaintance to recognize them as set apart and on the Path, and then he might begin to reveal to them the little secrets that he had discovered. He might tell them of a temple miles away that other men of like mind were using as a meeting place.

In a temple, in a cave, or far back in the hills, they might come upon some group of men who had found spiritual truth, and they would then join this group. As time went on, these groups multiplied until there were some who had received the full light of spiritual understanding. Experience soon taught them that there was no use going out into the highways and byways to tell this to other persons because most persons live inside their own minds, limited by their own ignorance, and are unable to visualize anything beyond their present mode of life, and therefore they cannot accept any new teaching.

In the light of the gross ignorance of humankind, is it not quite a miracle that Jesus found even as many as a dozen disciples whom he could ask to leave their nets and follow him? The man of earth, living in his shell of ignorance, could have responded only with "How can I earn a living without nets to catch fish, or without a farm to till? And you are telling me to leave all that! How can I do it?"

But evidently those who were drawn to the Master had enough inner intuition to understand that even if they did not know where he was leading them, at least they had the discernment to know that the Master knew, and they could trust him.

Today, as then, if we tell the world that it is not necessary to live in a dog-eat-dog world, but that there is another way, the question comes back, "Well, what is it?" And there is no answer. The materialist has no way of comprehending what is meant by living by Grace, or how to live "not by might, nor by power" but by the Spirit of God. This is a language that is as foreign to him as Sanskrit, and so today, as then, the spiritual message reaches only those men on earth who for some reason or other have had their eyes opened to a Something beyond themselves and their world of strife and struggle —not because anyone has told them or because they have read about it, but because of their inner feeling. These are the people who eventually are led to a spiritual teaching. These are the ones who already have eyes that can see and ears that can hear. These beginners on the spiritual path are the neophytes, who even while living on this human plane of mind and body are expanding their vision and catching glimpses of another state of consciousness. They have begun the search.

With some, the search for ultimate reality is a very long search and a roundabout way with many, many false steps. But in the end, none of this is important. The only thing that is important is that the search be begun and then that the seekers maintain within themselves a sufficient drive so that even if they have to take the long way around and meet with stumblings and barriers, with discouragements and problems, they do not give up, but always maintain within themselves the hope and the conviction that there is a way to reach this realm of the Real. With that inner conviction, step after step will unfold, until eventually they find themselves home in God. That was ensured right from the beginning of their journey on the spiritual path.

The reason they could not take the step directly or quickly is that the goal is something that as human beings they cannot conceive. They do not know how to go directly to it, and therefore they follow any little path that opens to them that promises it might take them there, and very often find themselves going down a blind alley or a dead-end street, having to retrace their steps and start all over again. If they could but know positively what the goal is, they might reach it more directly and quickly.

The things of God are such foolishness to the man of earth that even if he were told what the truth is, it would appear so ridiculous to him that he could not accept it, and for this reason alone he would be led into all kinds of bypaths, trying to find ways that seemed more sensible and reasonable to him. To the "man, whose breath is in his nostrils," the spiritual path is absolutely impractical and unreasonable.

To this man of earth, everything in the world is accomplished through external activities, and so when he begins to seek for truth, he tends to continue to search in the external, seeking in holy mountains or in holy temples, thinking to find it here or there, even though the Master stated very clearly that the kingdom of God is neither "Lo here! or, Lo there! for, behold, the kingdom of God is within you." That is plain language, but human beings cannot accept or believe it, and the reason they do not believe it is that they cannot understand it. It is so foreign to their thinking that it does not register with them as being plausible or even as a possibility.

After a person has been on the spiritual path for a sufficiently long period of time, however, eventually a revelation comes to him from within his own being, or he is led to a teacher who can reveal truth, and probably by the time he has found this teacher, he has reached a readiness which enables him to assimilate the truth that is to be imparted to him.

Human beings are the unillumined; they are born and brought up in ignorance of their true identity, in ignorance of that indwelling Something, and uninstructed by the divine Master. This is the human race as we know it; these are the people we read about in the newspapers: those in prison, in the prison of lack, sin, and disease, in the prison of political and ecclesiastical slavery, and scholastic ignorance —these are the unillumined, the earthbound.

From the beginning of all revelation it has been pointed out that this need not be, that at any time we can turn within and begin our ascent out of the tomb of our darkness, out of the prison into the light, out of ignorance into understanding. The unillumined can become the illumined. The man living in darkness can become the light of the world. The man living in sin, disease, and poverty can become the son of God, and thereby an heir of God, joint-heir to all of heaven.

Knowing this marks the beginning of our spiritual journey, the ultimate end and purpose of which is illumination. In mystical literature this illumination is referred to as initiation, or attaining that mind that was also in Christ Jesus. What difference does it make how this is expressed? The meaning is clear, and when our footsteps have been directed to a spiritual path, inevitably we shall arrive.

The ancients who discovered that within themselves was a Something recognized that whatever it was they had touched was not out floating around in the air, nor did they have reason to believe that it was up in the sky. They sensed that there was a Something indwelling—a Something with a capital "S," Something that had a voice, Something that could impart, Something that could reveal, and so they learned to be attentive. They learned the nature of the ear that can hear. They communed within themselves, and when the answer came, they knew that from some deep pool within themselves, some depth of Withinness, pearls of wisdom were being given.

So it was, then, that some one or more among these ancients declared, and later wrote, that there is an indwelling Presence, that there is a Christ, or son of God, within, but they were wise enough to realize that this was really only another dimension of themselves. It was not some other person occupying them: it was some deeper, richer Self, and gradually they learned to commune with this inner, divine, spiritual Self. They learned to receive instruction, and the instruction that they received became the basis of the religious teachings of the great mystery and wisdom schools of India, Tibet, Egypt, and later of Greece, Rome, and the Holy Lands.

Long, long centuries before Jesus, it was revealed that there is this inner Self which is our true Self, and which is the Mediator between man and God. The connecting link between us and our Source is this divine Center within us, the Christ of which Paul speaks, the Father that dwelleth in us of which Jesus speaks. This is the Mediator by means of which we reach the ultimate and absolute Source of our being from whence we derive our experience on earth, our function, task, and duty, our life, immortality, harmony, and our preparation for the next phase of life, that which is to come when we have been graduated from this earthly experience.

No one can commune with his Mediator, with his Christ-Self, except by engaging in periods of introspection and inner communion. If we keep ourselves so unreasonably busy in the outer world, however, that we do not have frequent periods of turning within, we miss the ultimate experience of receiving the word of God out of the mouth of God.

The purpose of a mystical teaching is to reveal the son of God within. It is not to instill in us the worship of another deity in the person of the founder of a new religion. True, every spiritual teacher must evoke gratitude and appreciation because of his life of dedication, but not worship. The real mission of the teacher and his teaching is to turn us back within ourselves until we, too, like the teacher, receive impartations. When this begins in our experience, the earth melts, the problems disappear; the discordant experiences of earth are resolved and dissolved—not by any wisdom that we have, not by what we have learned in books, but by the thunder of that silence which is within us.

We need not hear an audible voice—we may, but it is not necessary. We need not see any visions—we may, but it is not important. What is necessary and important is that we enter the sanctuary, this temple of God that we are and in which the presence of God dwells. When we recognize this and go within, we then begin to commune with that Presence. Very soon we shall see fruitage in our life, and things will begin to happen for which we know we were not humanly responsible. Something has gone before us to make the way straight; Something has gone before us to prepare mansions for us; Something walks beside us to protect us from the discords and inharmonies of earthly living.

Only when we begin to understand that there is an inner kingdom, only when we can agree that there is a realm of knowledge unknown to "the natural man," only then can we begin our search. We must arrive at the point where we are able to perceive what the Master meant when he said, "My kingdom is not of this world. . . . Put up again thy sword into his place: for all they that take the sword shall perish with the sword."

The mystical way, the infinite way, is not the way of the sword; it is not the way of might or force: it is the way of stillness. Sooner or later we must see that within us there is an inner realm. It will answer every question. It will teach us in the only place where we can be taught—within. The still small voice will instruct us in whatever our particular gift, talent, or field may be, whether in spiritual or mathematical wisdom, art, literature, science, or music.

So great a genius as Einstein was aware that there is a point in mathematics where the most brilliant mathematician comes to an end of reasoning and thinking and steps off into the intuitive. And so, if we wish to be limited by what everyone else has said about mathematics, or what everyone else has written about music, we will be, but we need not be.

All the art, science, mathematics, and religion have come out of the Soul of man through his turning within and bringing forth glories that have never before been known on earth, and there are still greater things yet to be revealed. How far we are from tapping the inner resources of our being! This makes it clear why it is necessary in our age to attain the ability to meditate, to cogitate, and to commune with our inner Self.

It is not too difficult to learn to do this after we come into the awareness that there is a Presence that dwells within us. That was God's gift to us in the beginning, and without this gift of God, man would be an animal. The fact, therefore, that we have risen this far above the animal stage proves that we have something within us that has been developed to a higher degree. We are only at the beginning, however, and just as the spider unfolds its web from within its own being, so we must unfold grace, divine wisdom, and divine power from within our own being.

The unillumined, unaware that they can have recourse to an inner infinite Soure, have to endure all the limitations of this world. The illumined, who have touched the infinite Divinity at the center of their being, are never limited to time, space, place, or amount. There is no limitation when we realize that the whole kingdom of God is locked up within us. It does not have to be attained; we do not have to go to God for it: we have to loose it from within ourselves.

God, in the beginning, planted Himself in us and breathed into us His breath of life. He did not breathe into us human life: He breathed into us His life. God did not give us a limited soul, but the Soul of God—infinite, eternal, and immortal—if we but go to that Center.

When we have opened this Source within ourselves, we shall find the Master there. We are never the Master: we are always the servant. But once we are illumined, the Master within us is expressing, functioning, and performing.

"Greater is he that is in you, than he that is in the world." Who is this He? The Master, the Spirit of God in us, the son of God that is raised up by virtue of our acknowledgment and humility—not humility in the human sense of permitting ourselves to be imposed upon or having to endure abuse, but humility in the sense of realizing that whatever it is we are, it is because of the Master flowing out through us. Without that, we would be nothing, less than nothing. The Spirit of God has lifted us above the animal man into a people who can live not only according to the Ten Commandments, but who can go far beyond them into the Sermon on the Mount, and beyond the Sermon on the Mount into a life by Grace in that interior kingdom.

CHAPTER IV

THE JOURNEY WITHIN

The person who is one with God is merely the transparency through which God is living Its life: he does not have a life of his own, a mind of his own, or even a body of his own. His body is the temple of God, and his mind is the instrument of God, the mind which was also in Christ Jesus. That mind can be attained only in silence, not with words or with thoughts, although words and thoughts may be used as a preliminary step in what we know as meditation, which plays a vitally important part in the development of our spiritual life.

Without the practice of meditation, a spiritual teaching, whether pursued under the guidance of a personal teacher or through the study of books, descends to a purely mental exercise. Spiritual unfoldment cannot come that way. It is meditation that makes a teaching come alive, because meditation is the connecting link between our outer life and our inner Self, which is God.

It is true that in the first stage of our spiritual life the only way we can fill our consciousness with truth is through the mind. That is why in The Infinite Way we do not seek to stop the operation of the mind; we never tell anyone to stop thinking, to make any effort to stop thought, or to try to destroy the thinking mind because the mind is the gateway through which truth finds entrance to our consciousness. The mind is the instrument through which we can become aware of the spiritual wisdom of the ages—Scripture and spiritual literature and teachings. It is through the mind that we discipline the body and that we seek to discipline our thoughts; it is the mind that keeps itself stayed on God; it is with the mind that we think spiritual thoughts; it is with the mind that we ponder the deep things of the Spirit.

This pondering, these thoughts and words, we call contemplative meditation. The words may be spoken or they may be thought, but they are only a step leading to meditation itself. Since it is almost impossible for most of us to keep thoughts from swirling about in the mind and since it is difficult to bring about a complete cessation of thought, the practice of contemplative meditation helps us reach a state of consciousness in which we find ourselves ultimately in a complete silence. A weight goes off the shoulders, and perhaps for ten, twenty, or thirty seconds we are so still that not a single thought intrudes. That stillness at best, however, is a very brief period, but regardless of how brief it is, in those few seconds we have attained our contact with God, and that is all that is necessary for that moment. Then we resume our conscious thinking and are ready to go about our business.

When we sit down to meditate, we must seek to hear only the word of God, desire only the feeling of God's presence, only the re-establishment of ourselves with our inner Source, and nothing beyond that. Then, when we feel the assurance of the Presence, our meditation is complete: the Word becomes flesh, and the Spirit felt within us becomes tangible as individual experience.

It is when we think we know what things we have need of that we are making our greatest mistake because we are measuring our needs in terms of our previous or present experience, and are looking upon life as a continuation of our past, the same, monotonous, dull way of existence, except with possibly the addition of a little more health or money; whereas, when the Spirit of God takes over in our consciousness, It fulfills Itself at Its own level. That fulfillment may carry us off into a new country or into a new activity—business, artistic, professional, or social—because we have no way humanly of knowing the will of God any more than we know the ways of God. But God's will can work through us if we surrender ourselves and realize:

Thy grace is my sufficiency in all things. I take no thought for the form in which that Grace should appear; I take no thought as to how Thy will should work in me, or Thy ways. I seek only Thy grace.

I am content to relax in the assurance that Thou art omniscience, all-knowing intelligence, divine, infinite, all-love, and I can trust myself more to the infinite Intelligence that governs this universe than I can to my own judgment as to what I need, or what I would like to do, or how I would like to live. Certainly, I can trust myself more to the care of divine Love than I can to my own finite sense of love which is not even as a grain of sand in comparison with the nature of that Love which is God.

With each meditation there must be this surrender of ourselves to the Spirit within, together with a realization that God's grace is our sufficiency and that we are in meditation for the express purpose of receiving the comfort of His presence. Nothing greater can come to us than the still small voice of assurance because then we know that all of Infinity is pouring Itself out for us, all of Omnipotence, and in that there can be no power apart from God.

Once we know the nature of God, even in a measure, doubt and fear seldom enter our consciousness because to know the nature of God means to realize Omnipresence: God, here where we are now—hereness, nowness. Knowing that, we relax in it, and we have nothing more to do than to *let* there be light: let there be light in our life, let there be love, let there be health, strength, and abundance, just *let*. We do not try to make it so because, understanding the nature of God, we know that it is God's will to provide all good.

My customary method of entering contemplative meditation is to open my ears for a second for a subject to be given me, and if it does not come quickly, then I take the word *God*. In my first meditation early in the morning before I am out of bed, I attempt to align myself with the presence and power of God so that my day will be God-governed, and not man-governed: a day of spiritual fulfillment, not one filled with accidents, limitations, mistakes, and human judgment. And so the contemplative part of the meditation might follow some such pattern as this :

"This is the day which the Lord hath made." God made the sun to shine today, giving us its light and warmth; God has provided the rain and the snow in their due seasons; God has regulated the incoming and outgoing of the tides. God has provided periods for sowing and for reaping, for activity and for rest. God governs this world with infinite wisdom, intelligence, and patience.

This day I am God-governed. God is the intelligence directing the activity of my day, the still small voice protecting and sustaining me.

This is my prayer—that I be God-governed, that I never forget to seek God every moment of the day. I pray that I may never forget to thank God for my daily bread, never forget to realize God as the Source of all, and that I am never unmindful of the limitless abundance of supply which God expresses through me to all those who come within range of my consciousness.

God's grace is with me throughout this day, and His presence goes before me and walks beside me. In this Presence there is harmony and fulfillment because where the Spirit of the Lord is, there is freedom from any and every limitation.

Then, having established myself in this meditation of words and thoughts, I can now enter the true meditation or communion in which I invite God, " 'Speak, Lord; for thy servant heareth. . . . Thy will be done'—not mine." After a short period of listening, of inner communion, stillness, quietness, and peace, the awareness of the Presence is with me. And now I am free to go about my day's work.

The stress of the day, however, and the mesmerism of the world's animosity, jealousy, and intrigue have a tendency to enter my consciousness as well as yours, and with these come disturbing moments, so there must be another period of contemplative meditation, and this time it may take a different form.

"My peace I give unto you" is the promise of the Master, "not as the world giveth"—not the peace that comes from a pocketful of

money or from a bankful of bonds, not the peace that comes from just a healthy body—but "My peace," spiritual peace, the peace that passes understanding. That peace is all I seek; that is all I desire. I do not ask for silver or gold, nor for the good or the peace of this world. I ask only that this "My peace" be upon me.

Then I wait for those few minutes of inner communion, and again I have prayed the prayer of a righteous man because I have sought nothing but that which is the divine right of everyone: God's grace and God's peace, not only for me, but for all those who may be led into the realm of my consciousness.

Contemplative meditation, practiced faithfully, leads to a moment of silence in which all words and thoughts are stilled, a silence so deep that we become a transparency for the still small voice to speak to us. The contemplation of God's grace, of God as the One and Only, and the contemplation of scriptural passages which give the assurance of the divine Presence lead to an inner stillness, and then the second phase of meditation enters our experience. That is when something comes to us, not something that we have consciously thought, but something that was thought through us. These thoughts come out of the void, from the depth of the Infinite Invisible, out of that spiritual consciousness which we are.

At other times a message may come to us, and if not an actual message, a sensing that all is well, just a feeling of peace. Sometimes it is a feeling of warmth, gratitude, or of love—not *to* anybody, or *for* anybody, or for any *thing*. It is a feeling complete in itself with no object. If we are faithful in our work, this continues to occur more and more frequently until the day comes when we abide so much in the Word that we are more or less in It all the time, and need only a moment of stillness to bring forth some particular message to meet the need of the moment. In this stage we have risen above the thinking mind, and it is no longer our master: it is now our instrument. As long as we are on earth, however, we are going to need our thinking mind, and we should thank God for having given us one, but as we go higher and higher in consciousness, this thinking mind will play a lesser and lesser part in our spiritual life.

In this stage of our spiritual instruction, the impartation of truth comes from within like an invisible Something pouring Itself out. We merely tune in, and It imparts Itself to us. This is where two enter the scene: I, myself, in meditation or contemplation come face to face with the Presence within me, with that Something other than myself. This may take the form of an inner glow, or at other times of a voice within which seems actually to speak.

Sometimes we are not sure whether it really was a voice that we heard or only an impression that we received. But whatever the form, it is in this stage that we are in communion with God. An activity takes place that goes back and forth, almost as if it were from me to God and from God to me—a gentle flow backward and forward, in and out. Then I know that the Spirit is with me. "The Spirit of the Lord God is upon me. . . . Where the Spirit of the Lord is, there is liberty." It is an actual experience of release.

The third stage, that of conscious union with God, is the ultimate, and in this stage the personal or separate selfhood disappears. It is as if one were not aware of himself as a person, but as if only God Itself were there. It must have been in moments like this that the Master spoke from the standpoint of the word I[1]: "I will never leave thee, nor forsake thee." That was not a man speaking: that was God speaking, and at such times the man Jesus was temporarily absent from the body. Later that same man said, "If I go not away, the Comforter will not come unto you." That was God speaking when Jesus was absent from himself and only the Spirit of the Lord was present.

There is a Presence that is as real as we are real to one another, and once It is felt and experienced, there is a relaxing from personal effort. When this Presence is realized, we shall find that It takes form as new organs and functions of the body, as our home, family, supply, and as our human relationships, even as a parking space.

"I can of mine own self do nothing" is the man Jesus speaking, but then as the Presence is realized, "I have meat to eat ye know not of." Later comes the third stage, when God speaks as individual being: "I am the way, the truth, and the life." This is the Word made flesh, God incarnate walking this earth, and that ultimately is the destiny of every individual.

[1] The word "I," italicized, refers to God.

There is an overturning and an overturning and an overturning in individual consciousness "until he come whose right it is." That He is God. There will be an overturning in our consciousness, and it will appear to us as a warfare between the flesh and the Spirit, a warfare between disease and health, between lack and abundance, and finally between the two I's: the I that we are as a person and the *I* that is God. And oh, the human being "dies" so hard! He wants to perpetuate himself; he wants to be something, to do something, to know something. Thus, the warfare goes on until finally that human being is shaken so thoroughly that he awakens to the fact that of himself he is nothing, but that the *I* which is God is all.

Then meditation takes on its final phase. When, in this nothingness of the individual, the Father speaks—takes over, heals, redeems, and instructs—then the Father lives that life.

Eventually, every one of us will come to Paul's state of consciousness in the realization, " 'I live; yet not I, but Christ,' the son of God, the very Spirit and presence of God, lives my life." Then, and only then, are we a state of humility that has in it not a single trace of virtue, but only the realization of the truth that we are nothing, that we can do nothing and be nothing of ourselves.

It is true that this may bring with it a sense of emptiness, but strangely enough with that sense of emptiness, there comes a sense of completeness and perfection. Yet this is not in any personal sense; it is not that egotistic sense that claims "I am spiritual," "I am perfect," or "I am whole." It is more a sense of having no qualities of our own and yet feeling this transcendental Presence and watching It live our life.

Once we are united with our Source, we discover that our life is really the life of the Life-stream, the life of the Source of life which is now flowing as our life. We are being fed by the Stream, by the Waters falling from the clouds above, by a Source greater than ourselves which is now flowing as our life.

Knowing this truth is a freeing activity. No longer do we feel cut off and alone, nor dependent only on ourselves: we are united with the Life-stream, no longer limited to our own wisdom, strength, or longevity, to our education, our social or economic status. Now we have access to Infinity: infinite Wisdom, infinite Love, infinite Life, the infinite Source of all good. No longer are we limited to our immediate surroundings, to an island or a continent, and not even limited to a whole planet. There is no limitation except that which man places upon himself by believing that what he sees of this world is all there is to it, or that what he sees in the mirror is all there is to him. What he is aware of with his senses is a part of him, but certainly not the whole of his being, just as his little finger is a part of his hand, but not the whole of it.

When we attain this contact with our Source, we have also made contact with the Source of every person's life and are now one with all spiritual life. The same life that flows in one of us is flowing in all of us because there is only one Life-stream, only one Source of life, one creative Force in life. Whether that spiritual life appears as a human being, as animal, vegetable, or mineral form, we are now one with it through the act of meditation which has united us with the Stream within us, and we are one with the Stream which was in Christ Jesus.

The mind which was in Christ Jesus is your mind and my mind, and when we have broken through this human exterior of mind and, through meditation, have contacted the Source, we are then one with the spiritual mind of the universe, which is the mind of the Buddha, of Jesus, of Lao-tse, and the mind of every spiritual saint and seer. We have become one with it when we have become one with the Source of our own life.

The Spirit that is flowing through us is now consciously flowing through all those who are attuning themselves to that One—those who may be praying in orthodox churches or those who may be praying a paganistic prayer. We are a blessing unto all of them because, regardless of their form of worship and while they may not know it, they are turning to Something beyond the human, and in turning to that Something, they are turning to the Christ, and all who reach out to the Spirit in any way are blessed.

Often people in the last stages of illness who may not be religious or may not even have thought of themselves in spiritual terms reach out to God in their extremity and receive healing. Doctors report that many times patients have had sudden healings without any known reason, but this was perhaps because within themselves there was a reaching out toward God, and they probably tuned in and made contact with someone in the act of meditation, and thus their prayer was answered. As long as we succeed in making contact with our Source, anybody, anywhere in the world, who is turning to Something greater than himself, tuning in to God on any level—a false or a right concept of God—may benefit from our meditation.

When we are filled with the Spirit, then everyone who is attuned receives that Grace, each in accord with his need at that moment. One receives God's grace in a physical or mental healing, another in a moral or financial healing, and still another in greater joy in his household. The degree of dedication of our individual lives and the purity of our consciousness and motives have an effect on the lives of all who come in contact with us. Our individual conscious oneness with God becomes a blessing unto all those who are receptive. Every time God is released into this world through us, It has the opportunity of going out into the world and neutralizing some of the carnal influences in government, the courts, business, and industry, even in the arts and professions.

Every time that we meditate—and we meditate only for the attainment of this conscious awareness, this "peace, be still"—we are at that same moment lessening the evil and selfish influences in the world. The degree to which evil seems to be lessened may be of minute proportions—it probably is—but once the Spirit is loosed, there are no limits to Its far-reaching effects because there is no such thing as a little of Spirit or a little power in this Spirit.

The Spirit Itself in infinite, and It is just as infinite through one as It is through a million. This is proved in the lives of the great mystics: the Spirit of God in Jesus Christ became the release unto a whole Christian world; the Spirit in Gautama the Buddha became the light and the illumination to all of India, China, and Japan for a long period of time. We cannot measure the effect of the Spirit, even when the Spirit finds entrance to this world through, or as, the consciousness of one individual.

The ultimate of spiritual living is to live so completely in attunement with the Source, God in the midst of us, that the influence of God which is flowing through us will flow out and be a law of good unto all who come within range of our consciousness, thereby lifting them up and increasing their desire for the spiritual.[2]

[2] For a complete exposition of the subject of meditation, see the author's *The Art of Meditation* (New York: Harper & Row, 1956; London: George Allen and Unwin, 1957).

CHAPTER V

SOWING AND REAPING

Most people of the world believe that the evils they experience have come upon them because of their sins of omission or commission. Essentially this is true. But because they also believe that God has inflicted these evils upon them as a punishment, they have been cheated of the opportunity of avoiding them in the future. As long as they believe that God, for any reason whatsoever, would sink a ship, let an airplane fall, or permit children or adults to be mangled, lost, drowned, or suffer disease, they cheat themselves of the opportunity of learning why these ills have come upon them, and what they can do to prevent them from touching their households.

The sun, the moon, and the stars were certainly not given by God to the people of the earth as a reward for anything, nor were the silver and the gold, the platinum and the diamonds, the rubies and the sapphires in the bowels of the earth, nor the pearls and the immeasurable riches in the sea. All these are but the natural order of creation appearing in wondrous ways, but never given as a reward from God, nor withheld as a punishment. The real nature of God is to express Himself, to express His qualities, character, and nature as a harmonious universe.

If we could but see this world without people, we might better be able to understand that it is a perfect creation of God, functioning harmoniously and operating continuously. Whatever problems arise, arise not from the world as such but from man himself. Acknowledging, then, that God is the creator of this universe, the maintainer and sustainer of it, and that God governs this universe perfectly, without any help, advice, or urging from man, we stop holding God responsible for our ills and turn within and ask ourselves, "What about error? What about evil? Whence come these, and how can we rid ourselves of them?"

One of the first steps for anyone on the spiritual path is to learn that on the human level of life there is such a thing as karmic law, the law of as-ye-sow-so-shall-ye-reap, a law that we set in motion, individually and collectively. Every thought we think and every act we perform set in motion a law of action and reaction. If we sow to the flesh, we reap corruption. The law within us knows what we are doing, and it rewards us accordingly. Scripture credits God with that, but it is not really God: it is karmic law.

If all our charity, benevolence, and philanthropy were done anonymously, if any and every bit of good we do were done without letting a single soul on earth know that we were the instruments for it, our reward would be tremendous. There is no God in heaven looking down, patting us on the back, and saying, "Oh, my dear son, that is so wonderful of you. I will reward you." No, nobody need know anything about what we have done: the law itself, the law that we have set in motion, knows and will operate to reward us openly.

On the other hand, we can do as much evil as we feel inclined to do, and even though it be completely secret and no one ever learns about it, that same law will react upon us, and eventually we will be punished.

Whatever law we set in operation today will return to us tomorrow, next year, ten or a thousand years from now. In other words, we are creating our tomorrows today, even unto the next century, and the next and the next. This has nothing to do with God: this has to do with you; it has to do with me; it has to do with our individual selfhood.

But because there is only one Self, that which we do to another we are really doing unto ourselves.[1] I am you, and what I do to you I do to myself, whether for good or for evil. The good that I do to you has a way of returning to me; the evil that I do to you also has a way of returning to me because there is but one Self. It is as if I took money out of my right-hand pocket and put it into my left-hand pocket. Regardless of where I send my dollar—or my love—it ends up in my own pocket. When we know that, it changes our whole concept of giving and sharing from one of division to one of multiplication.

There is only one Selfhood; there is only one Being; and everything that I do to you, I do to my Self; and everything that I do to my enemies, I do to my Self. That is why it is important for me to take time out every day to forgive all those who have aught against me, to forgive any enemy of my nation, my race, or my religion—not because I am a good man, but because I am wise: I am forgiving my Self. There is only one Self; there is only one divine Being, and anything that I do to harm your life has its reaction on mine. Anything that I do to another must return to me. I may think that it is hidden, but it is not hidden in the one place where ultimately the score is settled, and that is within me.

If we close our eyes so that we are in darkness and then think, "I seem to be in here all alone, and nobody but me is going to know about anything I think or do," we soon discover that right there with us is our Self. There is not a thing that we can think or do that is not known to our Self, nor that our Self does not return to us. It is as simple as that! We may think that our motives and deeds are hidden, but the "Father which seeth in secret himself shall reward thee openly." The divine Law that sees in secret rewards openly.

We could not give away even a nickel without our Self knowing it and reflecting it back into our experience immediately. On the other hand, we could not take five cents from anyone without our Self knowing it and immediately beginning to make restitution through the operation of karmic law, because there is a law of as-ye-sow-so-shall-ye-reap that eventually makes us pay for our wrongdoing, and rewards us for our good deeds. It is not God doing it: it is the law that operates

[1] See "Love Thy Neighbor," in the author's *Practicing the Presence* (New York: Harper & Row, 1958; London: L. N. Fowler and Co. Ltd., 1956).

within us. That which the Son does, the Father is aware of, because the Father and the Son are one.

In this whole world there is only one Self, and that which constitutes my Self constitutes your Self and the Self of every person, in spite of the fact that each one expresses his identity in an individual way. There may be a thousand oranges on an orange tree, but there is only one Life. So, too, there are millions of people on earth, but there is only one Life, there is only one Self on earth, and that One is God, Spirit: your Self and my Self.

Because of this oneness, then, what we do to another, we are actually doing to ourselves. If we do good to another, we set in motion the law which returns that good unto us: we are casting good bread on the water, and it is good bread that returns to us—but always because it is an activity of the Self. Whatever of evil we set in motion, even though it may temporarily harm someone, the greatest harm eventually is the harm done to us because it is we who have set in motion the evil.

As long as the world is in ignorance of truth, it may be possible for a person to do evil and bring harm to others temporarily, and probably even postpone the harm that returns to and befalls him. The evil that we do may not return to us today or tomorrow, a year or even five years from now, and often by the time it does return, we have forgotten the event that set it in motion. But the *law* never forgets: the law is inexorable.

In another century, or less time than that, this may not be true. By that time, man may be enlightened enough to know that any evil set in motion does not touch the one toward whom it is directed but returns instantly to the sender. No one then will be able to do evil because if he does, it will strike right back at him. It will never touch those toward whom it is aimed because they will know that no weapon that is formed against them will prosper. In the conscious realization of their divinity, evil cannot operate in their experience.

In any given moment we can begin to prove this if we set aside a daily period in which to realize that God is our Self, that Spirit is the life and essence of our being, and that no evil can come nigh our dwelling place because God is our dwelling place. To know that there is but one Selfhood and that that One is God is to set ourselves free.

We may not demonstrate this in its completeness because the world's mesmerism still touches every individual, and as long as we are on earth we will have some problems to meet. Yet, it is possible to be free of eighty or ninety per cent of our problems if we realize that God constitutes individual Selfhood: my Selfhood, your Selfhood, and the Selfhood even of those with whom we do not agree, of those who may be said to be our enemies, or our nation's or mankind's enemies.

To know this truth of God's identity as individual Selfhood means that we recognize that whatever of good we are setting in motion, we are setting in motion unto ourselves; whatever of evil we are setting in motion, we are also setting in motion unto ourselves. This begins to set us free from any capacity to do evil, even though for awhile it is not easy to become completely free of this temptation. Nevertheless, from the very instant in which we realize that there is but one Self, we begin to lessen the world's belief that you and I are distinct from one another, and that we can do good or evil to one another. Each one of us is a law into himself.

This carries us a step further to where we can realize that it is not God who is giving us our blessings, and it is not God who is visiting upon us our evils: it is we ourselves, and not necessarily because we are doing evil consciously. Often we bring more trouble upon ourselves through our ignorance of this principle than by any evil that we do. Even humanly speaking, there are very few really evil people in the world—very few. Perhaps ninety-nine per cent or more of all the evil in the world is committed through an ignorance of truth, and even the evil for which we ourselves are or have been responsible has not been so much because of an evil nature as because of an ignorance of spiritual truth. Had we been taught the principle of sowing and reaping early enough, our lives would unquestionably have been different. But it is not too late! Our lives will be different the moment we consciously accept the fact that there is but one Self, and that what we are doing to another we are doing unto ourselves.

An understanding of karmic law enables us to begin to release God. Within our own thought we hold God responsible for good and evil; we fear God because we fear punishment. Many times we worship

God in the hope of a reward, a gift, or something or other from Him. In fact, most of the prayers today are not prayers to God but prayers to karmic law to violate itself. Many persons believe they can do evil and then pray to God to give them good. That cannot be: good cannot result from evil; evil returns as evil.

To place our faith and confidence in friends, political influence, or in any form of human dependence is to sow to the flesh, and we will reap corruption because someone will betray or fail us at the most inopportune moment. If we place our hope in that which man has created, whether made of silver and gold or of stone, whether a crucifix, a star, or any other symbol of religious belief, sooner or later we will be disappointed.

If our dependence is on persons and things, in the end that is what we must reap. All this dependence on human ways and means is of no avail and must inevitably lead to the frustration and disappointment which are too often the lot of mankind.

To live the mystical life is to live in a normal, natural way, fulfilling our function in life, whether in the home, school, office, or factory, yet within ourselves realizing:

God is my good. God is the health of my countenance, my safety and my security, my high tower, my rock, my foundation.

God is my abiding place, my home. I live and move and have my being in the secret place of the most High, hidden from the world. My body may be seen, but not the I of my being because I live in an inner awareness of God. My body is out here walking and working in the world, but I am not. I am living in the temple that is within me, the temple that is my consciousness.

In any and every place or situation in life, I remember that I am invisible, I am hid in the divine Consciousness. Wherever I am, in the air or on the sea, I remember that underneath are the Everlasting Arms.

If called upon to share with others, I can do so without feeling that I am taking something of my own to give away, thereby leaving myself with less, because all that I have is of God. If called upon for extra work, I can do it without feeling that I am using up my strength because all the strength of the Father is my strength.

I do not have to fear the passing of years because "before Abraham was," I existed in the bosom of the Father, and that is where I exist now.

Only my body is visible, but not I: "I and my Father are one," and we are invisible; we live in each other—the Father in me, and I in the Father, inseparable and indivisible.

When we tabernacle in this way with God, we set in motion good karma; we set in motion the karmic law of knowing the truth, and the truth comes back to us. The reverse is true whenever we waste time in hating, fearing, or loving unduly. This does not mean that there will never be a momentary normal reaction to certain evil conditions, or a natural rejoicing over good human conditions, but it means not taking either one too seriously, not letting it eat into us, but remembering:

God in the midst of me is the only power. I shall not fear what mortal man or mortal conditions can do to me.

This is knowing the truth that makes us free. It has nothing to do with God; it has to do with us; it has to do with our knowing the truth. The more spiritual our consciousness becomes, the more harmonious our outer life becomes because we have set the karmic law of good into operation.

When we stop believing that God is going to reward or punish us, we will leave God alone to function: we will not try to advise or tell Him what to do, when to do it, or how to do it. This will be honoring God by giving him credit for knowing His own business and being willing to perform it.

What we accept in our mind as being real and as having power is what determines the kind of sowing we are doing. The more power we give to persons or to things, the more we are sowing to the flesh, and the more corruption we reap. The more attention we give to abiding in the Word, the more we dwell on the truth that there is a Spirit of God in us which teaches, feeds, supports, maintains, and transports us, the more we are letting the Christ, Truth, abide in us, and the more we are abiding in It.

As we continue a practice of this kind, we are throwing the weight on the right side of the scale; whereas before, the majority of our thoughts and deeds were bound up in human and materialistic values and power. At first we may be giving only two, three, or four per cent of our thought and time to entertaining spiritual truth, but gradually as we continue the practice of the Presence, more weight goes over on to the spiritual side, and very soon twenty or twenty-five per cent of the time there is some spiritual truth or some spiritual conviction occupying first place in our mind.

So it is that we go forward until the day comes when the weight is so completely on the spiritual side that more than fifty per cent of our waking hours and some of our sleeping hours, too, are occupied with spiritual activities. The activity of the law never stops: karmic law operates for good while we are asleep, or it may work for evil: it can produce healing in us while we are asleep, or we can wake up feeling ill; we can be so uplifted in our sleep that we wake up whistling or singing, or we can wake up in the doldrums.

To go to bed at night with the final few minutes before sleep filled with God is, in itself, enough to give us a restful night and a peaceful morning. Always, we are thinking something: we are either knowing the truth or not knowing the truth; we are either thinking spiritual thoughts or carnal thoughts. Always, we are either placing our faith, hope, and trust in the Infinite Invisible that is within our very own being or in something covered with silver and gold, or of a fleshly nature. In one way or another, we are setting in motion the law that in the end either rewards or punishes us.

That is why the Master, even when he forgave and held the sinner in no condemnation, could say afterward, "Sin no more, lest a worse thing come unto thee." Why? He was not the one to say whether or not a person should be punished. It is what the person thinks; it is what he does that determines that—not what the Christ does. When we appeal to the Christ, the Christ can set us free in that instant— but not tomorrow. It is up to us to go and sin no more, or sin less, until such time as we are fully and completely in the Spirit.

Where there is receptivity to the Christ, there is spiritual regeneration, and it makes no difference whether a person has been good or bad, rich or poor, saint or sinner. What counts is the degree of receptivity there is within him to the spiritual message because, in the last analysis, it all comes down to the individual. True, the activity of the consciousness of a spiritually endowed person can bring infinite, divine harmonies into our experience, can bring release and freedom to us, and can become a law unto us if we are willing to open our consciousness to it. Some benefit may come to us through another, but unless we carry on from that point, unless we ourselves respond and open our consciousness to let the Christ abide in us, it is only temporary.

Abiding in the Spirit, we set in motion the law of good karma. On the other hand, living with our thoughts constantly dwelling on our human affairs is setting in motion the karmic law of good and of evil with the possibility of a preponderance of error, discord, or inharmony because we are sowing only to the flesh.

To sow to the Spirit does not mean becoming ascetics; it does not mean giving up our work, our profession, our home, or our family. It has nothing to do with what we do externally: it has to do with what is going on in our consciousness while our mind and body are performing their functions on the outer plane. What is going on in consciousness determines whether we are sowing to the flesh or whether we are sowing to the Spirit, and whether we are setting in motion the karmic law of good or the karmic law of evil.

We do not always reap what we sow immediately or quickly. "The mills of the gods grind slowly, yet they grind exceeding fine." It is true that sometimes a person may live for many years in a measure of spiritual realization before the overturning comes, and He comes whose right it is. Then there are also those persons who indulge in every manner of evil and seem to be able to do it for a long period of years before their karma begins to operate. Therefore, we should not be too discouraged if we do not see the fruitage of our spiritual activity instantaneously because we have generations of humanhood and humanness to cast out of our system. On the other hand, let us never despair if the evildoer seems to flourish. We have no way of knowing what goes on in his mind, in his soul, or in his body. It may be a worse picture than we think it is, and even if it is not, the karmic law adjusts all these things in its own time and in its own way.

To seek to return evil for evil is to set in motion karmic law of a negative nature. Instead, let us, as we are taught, return good for evil—not for the other person's sake! For our own sake! For ours because we have some knowledge of how the law operates and how we set karmic law in action. When we see this, we then realize, "Well, that means that I have a lot of debts to pay for my previous sins of omission and commission." But right here is where we come to the most encouraging aspect of karmic law: "though your sins be as scarlet, they shall be as white as snow." When? Now, in this minute! We do not have to confess outwardly; in fact, it is not wise to do that, but confess within ourselves: "This was not right"; "I know better than that"; "I am done with that." Whenever we make a confession within ourselves, we have annihilated the evil results of karmic law.

In the very second of her repentance, the woman taken in adultery became a follower of the Christ, with no punishment, no period of waiting. It was *now*: "Neither do I condemn thee: go, and sin no more." The thief on the cross was not condemned to a period of purgatory, or to any suffering: "Today shalt thou be with me in paradise." Why? Because he turned to the Master and asked for help. The karmic law does not have to be worked out generation after generation unless we choose it so. In other words, if we decide to cling to our humanhood, we can be assured that the karmic law is continuing to operate, but any moment we choose to do so we can come out from among them and be separate and apart. Then the past is past—done away with.

In my work with all those sick physically, mentally, financially, or morally, I have observed that, regardless of what their past may have been or what particular sins of omission or commission they may have committed, when they seriously turned to a spiritual teaching, the penalty was erased. They may not have become angels overnight. Who does! But that is not the point, even though it is possible to accomplish that angelic state in a quick or short period of time by "forgetting those things which are behind," and by setting good karmic law in operation through sowing to the Spirit.

Our conscious oneness with God constitutes our oneness with every spiritual being and idea.[2] That means that we are one, and as we love

[2] This theme is developed in the author's *Conscious Union with God* (New York: The Julian Press, 1962; London: L. N. Fowler and Co. Ltd., 1960).

our neighbor as ourselves and act toward the other person somewhat in the same way that we would like to be acted toward, in that degree are we setting spiritual law in operation.

The responsibility of a spiritual student is great. No one else has quite the same responsibility as do those of us on the mystical path, because we cannot rely on the hope of most Christians that Jesus' dying on the Cross will save us from all the penalties for our sins, or that our minister, the confessional, the mass, or church attendance will take away our burden. We cannot lean on any system or person.

Knowing the truth, following spiritual principles, sowing to the Spirit instead of the flesh—only this will bring our regeneration, resurrection, renewal, and finally, our ascension above all materiality. In that exalted state of consciousness even the karmic law of good ceases to operate in our experience, because in the recognition that we are never the actor or the doer, but that only God is acting and doing through us, we have stopped sowing. Karmic law is then forever nullified.

CHAPTER VI

GOD, THE CONSCIOUSNESS OF THE INDIVIDUAL

Many persons think that they understand the mystery of life because they can trace the growth and development of themselves and their children from a tiny seed at the time of conception to birth, and then from birth to full maturity. But that is not the mystery of life: that is the *effect* of the mystery of life. The mystery lies in what produced the seed and in what brought this seed into expression. No matter how scientists may theorize as to the origin of life, eventually they arrive at a point that defies explanation because beyond the appearance of everything visible is an Infinitude, a Something that we call Consciousness or Life, and this Infinity is expressing Itself as all form, as the world and everything in it.

Everything that is visible first had to have an invisible Something to send it into form, and that invisible Something is Consciousness which sends Itself into expression as a seed and all that comes forth from the seed. Were it not for Consciousness, there would be nothing expressed as form. Regardless of how beautiful a thing may seem to be, how wonderful or how abundant, we must look behind it and realize that it could not exist but for the Consciousness that formed it.

A few years ago, a very severe winter was forecast for the Eastern and Middle Western parts of the United States, a prediction based on the fact that the animals were growing much thicker fur than usual, and that they were also storing up more than the customary amount of food for their use during the coming winter. But can an animal decide how much fur it is going to grow? Does an animal know that it is growing fur any more than we know that we are growing hair? Then, what is the underlying cause of the growth of fur on an animal, and why does the fur grow thicker in some years and thinner in others? What causes an animal to store up more food one year than another?

Very recently, another prediction was made to the effect that the forthcoming winter would be extremely mild because practically no fat was being found on the meat of the bears and the deer. Do these animals know whether or not they are producing fat?

To those on the spiritual path, the answer is obvious: every animal has a consciousness, and that animal's consciousness determines the thickness of its fur, the accumulation of fat, and the amount of food that it will store. It even provides coloring that blends in with its native habitat as a protection.

Every bird has a consciousness. Does a bird know east, west, north, or south? Yet the birds fly north in season and south in season, and they are not supplied with maps. Only we need those when we travel, not the birds. They know whither they are going, and why, and when. What is there about a bird that knows this? Is it its brain, heart, feet, or wings, or is it the bird-consciousness that carries the bird north and south? Is there not a consciousness that acts without conscious volition?

Does this not explain and give meaning to the scriptural passage, "I can of mine own self do nothing. . . . The Father that dwelleth in me, he doeth the works." There is something about us greater than what we appear to be. Eventually, we will discover that that something is our consciousness. It is with us up in an airplane; it is with us in a submarine; it is with us on the ocean; it is with us on the earth. Whither can we flee from our consciousness? If we make our bed in hell, our consciousness is there to lift us out of it.

If once we perceive that God is our individual consciousness and understand how this consciousness leads us in the way that we must go, then for the first time we can honestly say, "Oh, how love I the Lord, my God! Oh, how love I this God of creation."

Only when we have discerned that God, the Infinite Invisible, functions as our individual consciousness can we understand the true meaning of the scriptural passages: "I will never leave thee, nor forsake thee. . . . Lo, I am with you alway, even unto the end of the world." What can be with us throughout all time except our consciousness? The Master called this consciousness "the Father within," and he said, "I and my Father are one." Certainly, we and our consciousness are one! How can we be separate or apart from our consciousness?

Do you realize that a human body cannot stand by itself? Remove consciousness from the body, and it collapses and falls down. Only the omnipresence of your consciousness can make your body stand upright. And what about your digestive organs? Can they digest or assimilate food? Can you not see that if consciousness were not functioning in your body, the stomach and digestive organs would be just so much dead matter, without the power to move? What then causes the operation of the organs and functions of the body? Is it a God up in the sky, or is it the same consciousness that grows fur for the animals and governs the birds in their flight—consciousness, their consciousness, your consciousness?

This consciousness is all-knowing, and it molds your body in conformity with its needs. For those people who have lived for generations in tropical and subtropical climates, it has developed in them a deeper, darker skin pigmentation, probably as a protection against the intense heat of the sun; whereas for those living in the temperate zones, such protection is not necessary and, therefore, the color of the skin of the people living there is usually lighter. Here again consciousness has formed itself in consonance with where it is expressing itself. It is not an unknown God doing this: it is the consciousness of the individual meeting his every need.

"Your heavenly Father knoweth that ye have need of all these things. . . . It is your Father's good pleasure to give you the kingdom." Who is this Father? It is not any Father within your body: it is your very own consciousness. Your consciousness knows what things you have need of; it provided you with your body, and exactly the form of body you need for your present experience.

From the moment of birth, however, you were taught to look to others for what you needed; you were warned about the devil over here, and the God up in heaven over there, and you began to be separated from your consciousness. Soon you were so completely divorced from your consciousness that you went through life without ever drawing on it. Then you began blaming those who did not give you what you wanted or needed, when all the time your very own consciousness was the source, the substance, and the activity of your every experience.

If you mount up to heaven, you take your consciousness with you; if you make your bed in hell, it is with you; and no matter what problems or troubles arise, turning to your consciousness can bring release. The deepest kind of a prayer might be a smile to yourself as you think back on the animals that grow heavy fur in anticipation of a hard winter and of the birds flying north and south in due season: "If their consciousness can provide in advance for a cold winter, my consciousness can provide for an eternity. If the birds have a consciousness that leads them north and south, I also have a consciousness that leads me north, south, east, or west, and that fills my storehouses and barns, with twelve baskets full left over."

Consciousness has a way of providing the animals with heavy fur in winter and light fur in summer, and this God which is our consciousness has a way of providing for us in whatever climate we may be, whatever weather or in whatever stratum of the air we may be living. This consciousness forms and molds itself in accord with our need.

Once you understand that God is infinite, divine, spiritual, perfect consciousness, yet individual, you have come close to knowing God. How can you not love that God—perhaps not now, this minute, but after a year in which you have found that that God has gone before you to prepare the way for you, that that God has walked beside you as a protection, behind you as a rear guard? After a year of relaxing in this infinite, divine Consciousness and finding the miracle of the mystery of life, closer than breathing, how would it be possible not to love the Lord thy God?

You only have to remember those birds up in the sky and those animals out in the woods, and you cannot help but smile when you realize that their very own consciousness provided so wisely and amply for them without the birds and the animals having to say, "Father, how about a heavier overcoat," or "How about taking me out for a vacation this winter?" Do you not see that consciousness functions without taking conscious thought—without taking thought for your life, what you shall eat, or what you shall drink, or wherewithal you shall be clothed, or whether you are going to pass from sight at thirty, sixty, or ninety?

When you can bring God closer to yourself than your skin, when you can realize that the consciousness of the animals and the birds meets their needs in advance, you begin to understand that you, too, have a consciousness. Then you can relax, satisfied that yours now is not a blind faith in an unknown God.

Watch the difference in your approach to life when you know God aright, and then read the Gospels and understand life as presented by the Master. I may be wrong, but I can almost detect a twinkle in Jesus' eyes and see the look on his face when he is talking to the multitudes: "Why are you fearing? Why do you come to me for loaves and fishes? Did I not show you the mystery yesterday? Is there some power out there that is going to eat you up, or stop you? Come on, get up on your feet!"

Is God the consciousness of the animals, birds, and bees, and not of us? Does God clothe the flowers in their beauty and give them their form, outline, and perfume, and not us? Do they all have a God that does such wonders for them, and not for us? No, it is only that we have "prayed amiss."

In my mind's eye I can see Gautama before he became the Buddha. I can see him walking through all those forests in India, going from teacher to teacher, and being told that if he would sit in the lotus position, stand on his head, lie down on a bed of nails, abstain from eating meat, or cease praying to God for anything, he would surely find God. The poor man is bewildered: he is honest; he is sincere. He does it all, but he does not find God. Then when he decides to eat and be comfortable, he sits down under the Bodhi tree and there, alone with God, he meets Him face to face and receives his illumination.

He had been seeking God in practices, exercises, diets, and fasting, and God is not to be found in any of these. God is to be found only within. It is not easy to shut out the world and enter the inner sanctuary of your being, but if you have to do this and stay away from the world for a year, or seven years, it is worth it because when you find God you will find life eternal. Then you will never die. You may pass from view, but you will never die, nor will you ever again be anxious; and no matter what the human appearance or circumstance may be—wars, persecutions, disasters—you will still keep going on, knowing that this is the mesmerism of the outer senses. God does not desert you, and if you will just stand still, the storm will pass, and you will be out in the clear again.

The captain of a ship has to go through storms, but as he abides by the principles of seamanship, he will sail out through the storm. No storm can last forever. So with us. There are storms in this human life—some of our own—but often we take on the storms of our families or of our students who are unable to find their peace. Every teacher must accept the burdens of his students and patients. He cannot avoid it. He has to sit up nights sometimes; he may have to go weeks and weeks with problems of this one, that one, or the other. He is always taking on the burdens of those whom he is trying to lift across the wilderness, but that also makes life interesting, because there, too, no matter how severe the storms, no matter how difficult or deep, he proves for himself and for others that the way out is to know God aright.

To know Him aright is life eternal, but we do not know God aright until we know Him as the infinite, divine Consciousness that formed the sun, the moon, the stars, and the planets, that informs, governs, supports, sustains, leads, and directs us to our ultimate destiny, which is the realization of our true identity as that Consciousness. I do not think we could be brought any closer to God without bumping into Him.

Down through the years there have always been a few men who have realized that the goal of life could be achieved if only they could find God, but for the most part they have thought of God as something separate and apart from themselves and they, therefore, have gone out searching for Him where He cannot be found.

Success in this search is possible only when it is understood that *Consciousness* is the substance of all form and the activity, not only of all life, but even of the body, this very body with which we walk and eat and sleep.

If there were not an invisible Consciousness forcing Itself into expression as form, there could not be a tree or even a leaf on a tree. But the one Life is expressing Itself in infinite form as hundreds of different species of trees, plants, flowers, grasses, and leaves. Life must be pushing Itself into expression *as* these forms, but must not Life have been present before Its forms were able to come into being or manifestation?

The issues of life are invisible in Consciousness, and as a greater understanding of this truth is gained Consciousness will then come forth in greater measure in our experience. We are that infinite Consciousness, but we are not showing forth that Infinity at this stage of our experience. We are showing forth only the degree of Consciousness which we can realize at this moment, but because we are evolving states of consciousness, that should be a far greater degree than it was twenty or thirty years ago. In fact, one of the purposes of living on this plane is to provide our individual consciousness with the opportunity of evolving, evolving *through* and *as* us, as we open ourselves to Infinity.

The kingdom of God is within our consciousness, and when we turn within in meditation to this infinite Consciousness to let It flow, we will show forth more of the Infinity which we are and always have been, and next year a greater degree, and the year after, a still greater degree. In other words, we are expressing as much of infinite Consciousness as we can at the moment comprehend.

Let us begin with the realization that we are not form: we are consciousness, and by our devotion to meditation, we bring forth a greater degree and deeper awareness of God-consciousness. Consciousness forever expresses Itself as individual forms of intelligence. Whether it takes the form of a musician composing an oratorio, a poet writing an epic poem, an artist giving a Mona Lisa to the world, a sculptor carving out a David, or an engineer designing a bridge, it is the one Intelligence that thrusts Itself out into life as form, as multitudinous expressions of Its own infinite gifts.

When we realize that we are God-consciousness expressing Itself as individual form and variety, we do not feel so great a responsibility to perpetuate our little selves, or even to be overconcerned about our creature comforts. The Consciousness that existed before this particular individual experience had individual form is responsible for maintaining and sustaining Itself *as* us, as our business, profession, ability, and as our integrity. The government is upon Its shoulders: the responsibility for living is not ours. Our only responsibility is to live up to our present highest sense of right.

We cannot be other than we are at any given moment, any more than a sunflower can be an orchid, or a blade of grass a rose. And if a sunflower or a blade of grass should struggle to be something other than it is—if it could—it would destroy itself. Many students on the mystical path continually berate themselves because they are not more spiritual and they want to know how to become more spiritual. They cannot be! If only each one of us could relax and realize, "I am what I am, and I cannot be other than I am. That which created Itself as this form perpetuates it unto eternity."

That does not mean that we can grasp form and hold on to it. Just as we cannot keep a child a six-year-old forever, so we cannot perpetuate our own form on this earth. We all outgrow our bodies: our infant bodies, childhood bodies, adolescent bodies. Life is a continuous process of outgrowing and outgrowing.

Life cannot be seen with the physical eyes. Life Itself is invisible: we see only the forms which Life assumes. Life pushes Itself into expression as beautiful flowers and leaves, but we know that in time they all drop away. The Life does not—just the leaf or the flower does. The Life goes on forever and ever, always appearing as new forms.

We are Life—Consciousness. We are not that which is visible: we are invisible Being appearing as form, but neither that form nor that personality is our real being. Our being is Consciousness individualized, the great infinite Consciousness which is manifesting Itself as so many forms and varieties of beauty and harmony.

Living thus with the Invisible produces a miracle-change in our life. We train ourselves not to eat or drink at any time without consciously pausing for a second to realize that whatever it is that we are going to eat or drink comes out of the Invisible. God appearing as our individual consciousness is its source. Always, we turn our thought to God as the invisible Source, and then watch how in a few days or weeks things begin to take place in our life that never happened before.

With everything that comes into our experience, we dwell for a second on the invisible nature of its source, realizing that it has its foundation in the consciousness which we are. That infinite divine Consciousness which sent us into expression brings all good into our life, or it would not be here, because nothing that is not a part of our consciousness can appear to us. Everything that appears or is expressed by us first has to be in our consciousness, or we could not be aware of it.

This can be proved by any person who, after walking down a busy thoroughfare, stops to take stock of what he has seen on the street, and then upon retracing his steps observes how many things did not register with him at all. Why? Because they were not a part of his consciousness. The point is that one person walks down a street and sees every jewelry store he passes, and almost nothing else, while another one sees every dress shop, and almost nothing else.

Everything that appears in our life must first be a part of our consciousness. Therefore, when we recognize that each and every form— the very table that is set before us, the dividends that come in, the salary, allowance, interest, or whatever it is—is a product of consciousness, then the whole nature of our life begins to change. Instead of living a material life in and of things, we live a spiritual life in and of Cause, and then the things appear in our experience as added things, and by that time we no longer hate, fear, or love them: we merely enjoy them as they come and go, but no longer have an attachment to them. There is no way to break undue attachment, except through dwelling constantly in the fact that there is an invisible Cause or Source of all that appears.

And what is that Invisible but consciousness? And whose consciousness but ours since it is our consciousness that is drawing to us our experiences? When we realize God as the Substance and Fabric of our consciousness, we then begin to draw forth from it only good, but if we draw from human consciousness, there is always the possibility of drawing good or evil.

Consciousness is the essence and the substance of all that is. This, however, would be as meaningless as saying that God is the substance of all form or that God is the essence of our being, unless we understand that we are talking about individual consciousness—not *a* consciousness, nor *the* Consciousness, but *our* consciousness.

With that as a basis, our only concern is our own state of consciousness because that is what determines our individual experience. Every person benefits or suffers from his own acts, and this squarely puts it up to the individual to determine the nature of his own experience. Scripture of all times has brought out the truth that the individual is responsible for his experience.

When we understand this, we shall understand the biblical passage, "Cast thy bread upon the waters." Why should we cast our bread upon the waters? Because this is the bread that must come back to us. We cannot expect to enjoy the bread that someone else has cast upon the waters, and whether or not we expect to, we shall not be able to do it. The Master accepted this truth when he taught that as ye sow so shall ye reap, which correctly interpreted means that whatever our experience is, is an emanation of our consciousness. God—Infinity, Eternality, Immortality—is our consciousness in its purest state. We are not a self separate and apart from God: we are God expressed as individual being. That is what we are when we are the Adam and Eve in the Garden of Eden.[1]

Only when the belief of two powers enters our consciousness do we find ourselves cast out of the Garden of Eden, and then we live as human beings who have to earn their living by the sweat of their brow. We are human beings who live lives, sometimes good, sometimes evil, sometimes healthy, sometimes sick, sometimes rich, sometimes poor, and for most people the negative aspect usually predominates in their lives. All these things happen to us because we now have developed, through this belief of good and evil, handed down to us through the ages, a consciousness, a mind, and a life of our own, and we refer to it as *my* life or *your* life, as *my* mind or *your* mind. And because of this identification we find that we have a life to lose or a mind to lose.

[1] See "Who Told You?" in the author's *The Thunder of Silence* (New York: Harper & Row, 1961; London: George Allen and Unwin, 1961).

The search for truth has always and ever been a search for a way to return to God-consciousness. All human experience is the Prodigal's experience. The Prodigal had a certain amount of his father's substance with which he started out, but each day that he lived he used up some of it, and in the end he had none left. So it is in human experience. We start out in life with some measure of God-life, but because we believe our life is separate and apart from that God-life, we call it our life and begin to use it up. By the time we reach threescore years and ten, or twenty, we have used it all up and with it our strength and mental capacities.

Living the spiritual life means finding a way to return to the Father's house and there be robed with the royal robes of sonship and have placed upon our hand the jeweled ring of spiritual authority. On the spiritual path, we are seeking to "die" to our human life, a life made up of both good and evil, and be reborn in our original Essence, divine Consciousness, or God-life.

Fulfillment begins to appear with the recognition that God constitutes our consciousness and that that consciousness is infinite: it embodies our life and our being unto infinity and eternity; and therefore, our good will unfold from within us, and the human ways through which this is to appear will open.

We are Consciousness: Consciousness is our identity; Consciousness is the infinity of our being; Consciousness is the source of our being; Consciousness is the creative principle; and it is our state of consciousness that has manifested itself as our particular form and experience.

The most important factor in our lives and in our progress on the spiritual path is Consciousness—our individual consciousness.

CHAPTER VII

THE SACRED WORD

I AM THAT I AM: EXODUS 3:14

I am the bread of life: he that cometh to me shall never hunger; and he that believeth on me shall never thirst. JOHN 6:35

Before Abraham was, I am. JOHN 8:58

I am the light of the world. JOHN 9:5

I am the way, the truth, and the life: no man cometh unto the Father, but by me. JOHN 14:6

I am the resurrection, and the life: he that believeth in me, though he were dead, yet shall he live. JOHN 11:25

I will never leave thee, nor forsake thee. HEBREWS 13:5

Lo, I am with you alway, even unto the end of the world.
MATTHEW 28:20

In an attempt to fathom the mystery of God, to explain what can never be explained, and to encompass what can never be encompassed, man has used words. But words can never explain God. There can never be a word that is God. Not even the word God is God, nor the words Mind, Soul, Spirit, or Truth, for all these are effects objective to the person voicing them.

There are no synonyms for God in absolute truth. Those that we use are really only attributes descriptive of God. Soul is an attribute of the purity of God; Spirit describes God's incorporeality; love, mind, principle, and law are facets of God-being; but none of these is really God.

When we are done with all these words, we are no closer to God than we were before: we have not found God. And so, we go on to another word, and another word, and another word. Finally, we realize that we cannot find God in a word, in any word out here. Ultimately, we come back to the one word which holds the secret of the ages—*I*. *I* is neither objective nor subjective, and that *I* is the *I* that I am, the Knower. It is the Knower and the known, that which knows and that which is known; and *I* am both: *I* am He.

If all the words that we use as synonyms for God really were God, the room in which we are sitting and repeating those words would be aflame with illumination, and there would be no disease or discord in it. But all we are doing when we repeat these words is declaring or affirming them, and since nothing happens, they therefore cannot be God. There is no word that we can think of that is not the effect of the thinker, and the thinker must be greater than any word he can think, voice, declare, or write.

Regardless of what word we utter—even the word God—there is an *I* that utters it, and an it to be uttered. After all the words have come and gone, and we cannot see or hear them any more, I still remain. I must be greater than any thought I can entertain, or any concept I can hold or form, greater than any belief or theory that I can formulate or accept.

Any word for God, except one word, would still leave an It and a me. The only word that obliterates everything but itself is the word *I*. *I* is the ultimate word behind which we cannot go because *I* is the thinker, the be-er, the doer, the consciousness, the cause. There is no word that really expresses God except the word *I*. If any other word is used, there is still an *I* declaring it, and certainly the *I* that declared it, thought it up, invented, or discovered it would be greater than any of the words.

What was it but the understanding of the word *I* that made Moses the leader and the saviour of the Hebrew people? This word was so sacred that its use was reserved only for the high priests, and they were never allowed to voice it except on one day a year, when they were hidden in the Holy of Holies, in the inner sanctuary of the temple, and nobody was allowed to be there to hear it.

Moses guarded this word carefully because he knew that human beings tend to use the word *I* falsely. They use it to identify themselves as Jim, Bill, or Mary. If they were told that *I* is God, they would translate that to mean that Jim is God, Mary is God, or Bill is God; and we would have human beings going about flapping their wings and sacrilegiously mouthing, "I am God."

For that reason the word *I* was held as a sacred, secret word, the knowledge of which set the priests apart, and it was that knowledge which constituted their priesthood—this understanding of their true identity. With this understanding they could minister to the needs of those who came to them, because anyone who knows the *I* can immediately give up all concern for his own welfare, can feed the multitudes, supply, support, and heal them.

King Solomon, too, had learned this secret and, during the building of his great temple, he promised that when it was finished all those who had worked on the building would be given the password that would enable them to travel in far places and always command a master's wages. No one was permitted to know this password until he had gone through every stage of his craft, from that of the lowest apprentice up to that of a master.

Symbolically, this means that ignorant, illiterate, uncultured, and unspiritual human beings are the apprentices, the lowest grade in spiritual evolution, and in that state they could not be given this password because it would do them no good, but if they worked up through the various stages of humanhood until they arrived at a place of discernment, of masterhood, they would be given the word because they would then be able to understand it.

And what was that password? *I AM.* Those who know *I AM* will never have to look to "man, whose breath is in his nostrils" for anything. Anyone who realizes *I AM* can travel any place in the world, with or without scrip. Everything needed will be provided for him out of Withinness. He does not have to depend on charity, on the good will of anybody, or on influence. He carries with him everything that he will ever need.

The *I AM* known to Moses, Solomon, and Isaiah was the secret teaching of Christ Jesus: "I have meat to eat that ye know not of.

... I am the bread of life. ... I am the way, the truth, and the life. ... I am the resurrection, and the life. ... I and my Father are one." Yet the "Father ... is greater than all." In other words, the invisible part of us is greater than the visible, and *I* is greater than we are because we are fed by the *I* that we already are. *I* is not another word invented by the mind of man; It is not another power, presence, or character created in time or space: It is the *I* that we are that feeds us, whether in the form of material for books, lectures, food on the table, clothing, housing, or transportation. It all comes from the *I*.

The ultimate of the correct letter of truth is when we go beyond using a word like God to where we are left with nothing but *I*, or *I AM*. And that is enough.

I is God: there are not two. When this reveals itself to us, something warm, joyous, and sacred has taken place within us. This is the "pearl of great price." Would we throw such a treasure out for the lovers of baubles to trample on or to put in a ten-cent mounting and wear? If the *I* of us is God, what is there external or internal to us that can thwart God's will, destroy God's life, or destroy God's mind or body?

Is there a God up in the sky? Is there a God sitting on a cloud? Is there a God floating in the air? Is there a God walking around on earth? I know not any; I have never seen or heard of any. The only God that has ever revealed Itself is the one that has come through the still small voice which is uttered within me. But there is nothing within me but me; I am the only being that I am, and if I hear a still small voice, it must come from within the depths of my Self. It cannot be what is called a human self; it must come from that Self of me which I recognize to be divine. If "I and my Father are one," I must be that one; and therefore, unless I know that *I* in the midst of me am He, I do not know God.

I AM—not the bold, brazen "I"-man that wants to walk up and down the street saying, "I am God," but the *I*-man that sacredly and secretly has received this inner assurance:

Be still, be still: I am God. You be still! Do you not know that I

*in the midst of you am God? I will never leave you. I am come that
you might have life, and that you might have it more abundantly.*

*You be still! I am in the midst of you. I am your being, I am your
bread, your meat, your wine, your water. Let that mind of yours be
still; let those fears be still! There are no powers external to you; there
is no God in words or thoughts. I am God!*

This is the "pearl," "the pearl" that must be hidden so that it is
not trampled upon, but it is a "pearl" that must be shared. It can
be shared, however, only with those who can receive it sacredly and
be trusted with it, because when it is given to the unprepared human
mind, that mind wants to use it to conquer the world: "Oh, I am
God, now I want a million. Ah! I want ten million, a hundred million. Why not? I am God!"

But to the Soul that is prepared, It whispers: "Oh, *I* am God: *I*
do not need anything, *I* do not want anything. *I* have all that *I*
need, *I* have all that *I* want, and the world's baubles are of no interest to me." We cannot be that *I* that is God and still be interested
in name, fame, or fortune. These will come to us, but by that time,
we will not value them.

As long as there is an "I" seeking God, we have not come home.
Only when we realize that *I* is God are we at home in Him, at peace,
for when we know that *I* and the Father are one, we have nothing to
be unpeaceful about, nothing to fear and no one to fear, nothing to
hate, nothing to resent. Neither life nor death can separate us from
the love of God.

In sharing this "pearl" it may be that a few who learn of it will
misuse it and thereby destroy themselves. They will not destroy us;
they will not destroy the world: they will destroy themselves. Nevertheless, in spite of such persons, this truth must be revealed in order
that those able to accept it can be completely free—spiritually free
in the realization of the great wisdom that Moses veiled from his
people and that the Master was crucified for revealing: "I AM THAT
I AM. . . . I and my Father are one."

If divine Grace has given us the wisdom to accept this—and

nothing can give it to us but divine Grace—let us accept it sacredly and keep it secret, not mouthing it or letting anyone know that we know it.

If we tell a person not developed or trained in spiritual wisdom that God is I, in his unillumined state, he will think that we are deifying a human being. This is not true at all. The human being has to "die" in order that the I which is his true identity may be revealed in all Its purity, completeness, and fullness. That I which is God is the I of you, but it is also the I of me, for there is only one I, one Ego. There is only one divine Life which I am and which you are.

The Infinite Way teaches that a person must never say "I am God" because it is not true. No human being is God. If a human being were God, then every word that he spoke would heal the sick, raise the dead, and open the eyes of the blind, but it does not. Why? Because a human being is not God. But when he goes back into the Kingdom of his own being in peace and in quiet, and hears the Voice speak to him, "Fear not; I am here," that is God within him uttering His voice, and the earth, the error, melts.

We are the instruments, the witnesses to God's word, and that Word is I. But we must not speak I: we must hear I. These things are so sacred and so secret that they should never be voiced by anyone: they are true only if they well up within and are heard in the inner sanctuary of our being.

When we are in prayer and feel that stirring which means that God is on the field, a healing or an improvement takes place because nothing can ever stand in the way of that I—nothing. We could voice It from now until doomsday, and nothing would happen, but if It voices Itself through us, then It becomes the Word made flesh.

The only thing that heals is the word of God, and even though it may use the old familiar language, it always comes through as fresh inspiration because it has come up out of the depths of the Soul. This teaching does not claim that you and I are God: this teaching reveals the I within you and within me, not by virtue of our speaking It, but by our hearing It. This revelation does not *make* us one with the Father: it establishes within us the realization that before Abraham was, I and the Father were one. That I is the presence and the power, and It is omnipresent and omnipotent.

I is the embodiment of everything necessary for our unfoldment, so that if we should leave our home with nothing, we could walk wherever we chose—around the world if that is to our purpose—and reach our destination, as long as we did not look outside ourselves, hoping someone would help us or give us a ticket or a dollar. Anything is possible as long as we hold to I AM.

When we know that I is here, I is there, and I is everywhere, we can use any one, or all, of the many synonyms there are for God—Life, Truth, Love, Soul, or Principle. It makes no difference because we are merely using terms describing attributes of God. No one can ever define God for us, however, because I is indefinable. We do not know what we are: we are a mystery even to ourselves. There is an I within us that has never been known to anybody.

If, in sacredness and secrecy, we keep locked up inside our own being the word I, that which we are entertaining secretly will reward us openly, and all those who are brought into our presence will feel a divine impulse. It is as if a voice inside of us were speaking and saying, "I in the midst of thee am God, and all that I have is thine." Then we rest on the promise that the Infinite Invisible within is the very Source of our life, that which created us in the beginning. God created us—not human parents, but God. We are spiritually created and spiritually formed, even though to human sense we entertain a physical sense of that spiritual creation.

If we will learn to withdraw our gaze from this world and realize that we are not dependent on anything in the external world, we shall begin to understand that I in the midst of us is mighty:

I need not put my faith in "princes"; I need not trust "man, whose breath is in his nostrils," but neither need I fear what man can do to me because I carry within me the great Saviour, the great Principle, the I of my own being, the I which created and maintains me, the I that is the very bread of life: my meat, my wine, my water, my salvation, and my resurrection.

If this temple of my body is destroyed, in three days something called I will raise it up again. Even if I were unconscious, even if I were dead, I in the midst of me am alive, and that I will resurrect even the body should there be any occasion for that.

What is it that restores the lost years of the locusts? *I.* What is it that resurrects our body, business, home, strength, health, and vitality? *I.* There is only one divine Presence and Power, and It is all embodied in that which, sacredly and secretly, is called *I.*

The Master had great difficulty in imparting this idea to the Hebrews who had observed ceremonies, rituals, and holy days, but who had been given little or no spiritual enlightenment. All their instruction had been in the realm of the mind and in the observance of outward rites, and that is not sufficient. Spiritual teaching must enter the heart; it must be in the Soul: it must be felt rather than reasoned or thought; it must be intuitively understood. Only then can we take the word *I* into the sacred and secret place of the most High and dwell there with It. If we dwell in the secret place of the most High and abide with that *I,* let the *I* abide in us, let that *I* flood our consciousness, It will impart Itself to us and say: "Know ye not that *I* am God? 'Be still, and know that *I* am God'; *I* in the midst of thee am mighty. *I* will never leave you, nor forsake you."

Are we looking to some God other than the *I* for our health? If we are, we are missing the way. The Tree of Life is truly planted in the midst of our consciousness, and it is all embodied in that little word *I.* "It is I; be not afraid. . . . I will never leave thee." Let us keep this Word in the center of our being, in our consciousness, keep this Word in our heart. Let us not parade or flaunt It, for if we do, we will lose It. The more silently and the more sacredly we hold It, the greater will be our demonstration of It.

No one can boast in the Lord; no one has the right to act as if this secret were his personal possession. It is a secret, but it is not your secret and it is not mine: it is the secret of the mystics of all ages. It was known to Lao-tse of China; it was known to Gautama the Buddha; it is the central theme of the teaching of Shankara; and it is the central theme of the teaching of Jesus Christ as revealed in the Gospel of John. It is the central theme of the life of every mystic.

The word *I* is the secret of the mystic's unfoldment! Even before there was a concept of God in the mind of man, *I*, God, existed. Before there were any human beings on earth, *I* existed as the creative Principle of all that is. It is difficult for a person to accept this idea unless there is an answering response within, a something which says, "Yes, that is what I have always believed, but could not voice. That is what I have always known; that is what I feel."

I is the sacred word. It is a soft and gentle Presence, yet withal, a powerful Presence. If we have a sense of rightness about this sacred Word, then we can begin to hold It within ourselves and to live out from the center of our being. Then it is that we can walk up and down this earth as a blessing to all who come our way.

When a person has attained a realization of God, his very presence is a benediction to others; and if he is charged with the care of some consecrated place such as a church, temple, synagogue, or truth-center, the atmosphere of his consciousness so permeates it that even entering it is a blessing. Any place of worship where there is a minister, rabbi, priest, or any person who is truly dedicated to the spiritual way of life is holy ground, so holy that we have only to walk into it to find healing. The stones themselves must cry out with spiritual tongues, "The presence of God is here."

It is not the temple that consecrates a man: it is the man who consecrates the temple. It need not be a temple, a church, or a synagogue. What it is, is of little importance. It can be a room in our home, or a chair, but if we are consecrated to God and if we fill ourselves with the conviction of the omnipresence of God, the very atmosphere around us is charged with spiritual power, and those who walk into that place feel its healing influence.

Wherever there is this recognition of the presence and the Spirit of God, the power of God is flowing, maintaining our mental, moral, financial, and physical freedom, and then whenever a need appears, we create what seems like a vacuum within us, a listening attitude, and in that second, the right word comes to us, the word of God which is quick and sharp and powerful, and which does the work of healing, reforming, and sustaining.

There is only one *I* permeating every person, constituting all individual life, whether human, animal, vegetable, or mineral. That one *I* is the Soul of all being, the creative principle, the activity, the cause, the life, and even the body itself. It is both cause and effect. It is *I* which is the sacredness of our being, the Consciousness of our being. That it is that governs us. *I* in the midst of us is mighty.

Take off your shoes in the presence of that word *I* because you are speaking the holy name of God.

CHAPTER VIII

THE MYSTICAL *I*

The search for God must be conducted within, but this does not mean within our body because no amount of mental or physical probing has ever revealed the kingdom of God in any person's body. Therefore, we can quickly put aside any idea of searching for it in the spinal cord, stomach, heart, or even in the brain. *The Kingdom is to be found within—within us.*

This leads us to the questions: Who are we? What are we? Where are we? Most of us already know that we are not confined to our body, and once we know that, we have taken a tremendous leap forward on the spiritual path, because if we are convinced that we are not in the body, it should not take very long or involve overmuch reasoning to establish the truth that being out of the body and invisible, we must be incorporeal and spiritual, something other than body. So, when we seek the kingdom of God within, we are not seeking for it inside the body, not even in the mind: we are seeking within ourselves.

To understand the nature of life as consciousness reveals how it is possible for the kingdom of God to be within us, within our consciousness, within that part of us which knows, but within no particular part of our body. Consciousness alone constitutes the Self.

When we have realized ourselves as consciousness and can look at our body in a mirror and thank God that we are not there, thank God that we have a body, but that we are not in the body—we are invisible—we shall begin to understand the Master's great teachings which are the "open sesame" to progress on the spiritual path.

"Call no man your father upon the earth: for one is your Father, which is in heaven." How can the son of that Father be other than spiritual being, spiritual entity and identity, incorporeal and invisible being? How can that son of God be seen walking the earth? The truth is that our real Self is never seen by anybody: it is completely invisible. True, our body is visible, but we are not. We are hid with the Father.

The spiritual identity of our being is Melchizedek, the man who was never born, can never die, and is always invisible.

I am Melchizedek. I am He that was never born and will never die, Self-maintained and Self-sustained. I am the offspring of God, God Itself springing forth into manifestation and expression, God Itself appearing as individual being with individual identity.

Nobody has ever seen Melchizedek—not with his eyes. Nobody has ever seen you; nobody has ever seen me. You and I can see the forms as which we appear, but we cannot see the reality because that is invisible. We merely see a form, so big or so small, and who knows ten years from now what size it will be, or where it will be, and it makes no difference because it will not be the *I* of you or the *I* of me.

So we look in the mirror with a new kind of vision: Now I know that *I* am not inside of this form: *I* am that which governs this form; *I* am that which moves around in, and is identified by, this form, but *I* am not this form. *I* am in the bosom of the Father, and the Father is in me: we are both in heaven, both spiritual. God the Father and God the Son are one, and that One remains our eternal spiritual identity, that part of us which was never born and can never die.

"Neither death, nor life . . . shall be able to separate us from the love of God." There is a Self which is inseparable from the love and the life of God, and when we discover that Self, we find the God with which we are one: the one Life, one Love, one Substance, one Being.

The materialist cannot perceive this: the materialist looks in the mirror and says, "There am I," but on the spiritual path we search ourselves from head to foot and from foot back to head, and arrive at the conclusion, "There am I not."

If we are honest, we will have to admit that nobody knows us except ourselves, and perhaps more than ninety-nine per cent of us do not understand or know even ourselves. There is an area of our being that is not known—not to mother, husband, or wife. It is a secret place in us, the real, true individuality of us that nobody can quite perceive or understand, and that we keep hidden from the world.

That part of us is the I, that I which is individual identity, that I which must have existed before conception, before there was a form as which to manifest, just as that I will continue to exist after I relinquish this form. This does not mean that I will be without form: it means that the form of that I will probably be of a different nature and texture. It is merely this particular concept of form that will be outgrown and will disappear. But I, I continue forever.

Does this mean reincarnation? In many cases it does because if we are born into this particular plane once, there is no reason why we could not be born into it a dozen times if there is a valid reason for repeating the experience. The questions that must be answered by each one of us are: Why did I choose to come here? Why was I sent here? The answer depends on our point of view. Were we sent into expression here? Did we choose to come into expression, or did we just come? That you can only determine for yourself.

If, in the light of my experience, I say to you what I am convinced is true, that we are sent here for a specific purpose and that that purpose is being worked out, there is no way that I can convey it to you so that you will believe it. It is up to you to arrive at that conviction within yourself, so that you can receive enlightenment on it.

My own conviction of the truth of this is the result of my particular life-experience, and even now as I try to compare my former life here on this plane with the one I am now living, the questions arise:

How could this happen? What could make such a thing happen? How could one live two such completely different lives and be two such completely different persons in the same lifetime? Then I go back inside and ask: Is this really true? Am I not now the person that I always was, but unable to show outwardly what was inside because I did not know how to reach it? Is not this what I have always longed for? Is not this what I have always visioned, but could not break through?

I can recall the day when, as a very young boy, my mother said to me, "I know what's wrong with you, Joel. You're looking for God."

"Mom, how can you say that? I don't even know if there is a God."

"Oh, but I know. You're looking for God."

Certainly I was, and this life today is just the fruition. I came into this world looking for God, but no one would believe that judging by my first thirty-eight years. That hunger was all locked up inside of me. I would not have dared to tell that to anybody, although when I was nineteen, I could tell my mother, "I've discovered you're right. There is a God, but I can't find Him. No matter with whom I talk, they don't seem to know Him."

And she said, "Well, please don't stop, and when you've found Him, come and tell me"—and I hope I'm telling her.

That is one way I know that *I* am the same *I* that I was when I came into this world, the *I* that was born at a level that was seeking God-realization, and It had to break through the shell and find Itself.

This, I cannot prove to you. You will have to take my word for it, or doubt it until you have an experience of your own that shows you that this *I* of which you have been aware since you were born really existed before you came forth into this experience. By divine Grace I have been shown other lives which I have lived, so I know that I was here before and I also know some of the experiences that I have had.

Every one of us in some time past, in some earlier form of evolution, was the animal man, then the mental man, and later was prepared to come into this particular state, evolving into some measure of spiritual man. All this takes time although it is really not a matter of time: it is a matter of evolution which in our experience appears as time.

This is because eating of the tree of the knowledge of good and evil in what is known as the Garden-of-Eden experience has resulted in the false state of consciousness which we call humanhood, and in this state of humanhood we not only need one another, but we need things, we need money, we need this, we need that. All human experience is a going out and a getting of things.

There is the man who is the purely animal man who goes after what he wants with hammer and tongs, using the sheer physical force of his body or the might of temporal weapons. Then there is the man who goes after things with his mind, and although most persons are honest and try to earn what they want, when these things do not come easily, they sometimes develop tricks to get what they want legally, but not too ethically, and if that does not work, they may go outside the law and steal or even kill to get what they want. On a larger scale, man resorts to a legal form of murder that is called war.

Eventually, perhaps after many lifetimes, that man who has depended upon physical and mental force begins to rise to the status of spiritual man, and that is the story of unfolding consciousness.

Whether you or I will be born again depends on this question: Will there be a reason for it? There was a reason for my being born this last time. It was because I had not made God-contact; the I had not broken through, and it took this experience to break the shell. What further lessons have to be learned that can be learned only in the context of a life-experience and whether there will be a need for me to be born again will depend on whether there is a need for the particular service I have to offer on earth. If there is, I will reincarnate.

So with you. It is your unfolding consciousness that has brought you into this particular phase of experience sufficiently developed to open yourself to a spiritual approach to life. You have lived on the animal plane; you have lived on the mental plane; and now you are approaching the spiritual plane. Let us not forget that during all this time, there is still a little of the animal left in each one of us and a little of the mental also, but by now most of us are committed to the spiritual way.

Each one has formed for himself a body, a home in which he is brought up, and an activity in which to function, all of which serve the purpose of developing consciousness to the point of recognition or realization. Every experience of our childhood, the good as well as the bad, and every experience in our business or home life have been necessary to bring us to this unfoldment. We have always been functioning at the particular level necessary for our spiritual development because the purpose of our being here is to unfold spiritually, moving from experience to experience until the *I* that we are stands forth in all Its purity and fullness.

I is neither male nor female: *I* is *I*. *I* is neither bond nor free. *I* is the universal, supreme, divine, true identity of all of us, regardless of what form it may have assumed in this incarnation.

We must learn to live with this *I* in the midst of us, learn to look to It for all inspiration. If we need an idea for a book or for a painting, for business or for law, regardless of what it is, the *I* encompasses it. And this *I* is within us. Then if it is necessary to find a book, a teacher, a publisher—whatever it is—when we turn within, the *I* will appear outwardly as the form necessary to our unfoldment at any moment.

We never discard our form—our concept of form, yes. We discarded one such concept when we were three years of age, one when we were thirteen years, another at twenty-one, and still another when we were in the forties. So we keep on discarding these concepts of form, yet the *I* goes on forever, and the *I* always has form; *I* is always embodied *as* form. *I* can never lose Its form any more than I can lose my identity.

My true identity was never born, and it will never die. It was present when I was conceived in my mother's womb, and it will be present and looking on when I pass from this scene, when my body seems to remain here as *I* progress onward. That *I* is the *I* of me which was born, that *I* is the *I* of me which was a child, that *I* is the *I* of me in my maturity, and *I* is the *I* of me in my ongoing. *I* is immaculately conceived, Self-created, Self-maintained, Self-sustained, infinite, individual, eternal, and immortal.

That is my true identity, and that is the *I* that is looking out through my eyes. That is the *I* of me that now is a teacher and a healer, but that same *I* was with me when I was a salesman selling merchandise. That *I* is the same *I* that was there when I was in school. This same *I* kept watching these different stages of my unfoldment, but It could not function any faster than Joel could catch up with It. It is the *I* of me; it is the *I* of you; it is the *I* of our friend and the *I* of our foe.

All those who put their hand to the plow must determine never to turn back—never. Lot's wife turned away; she looked back, away from God, and was lost. The way is straight and narrow, and few there be that enter, but those few are those who attain. And when they attain, what is it they have attained? The awareness that *I* in the midst of them is mighty, the realization that *I* has been with them since before Abraham, and that *I* will never leave them, nor forsake them.

I in the midst of me feeds me, clothes and houses me. I in the midst of me has never been limited. I in the midst of me has provided me with everything necessary, for I is not dependent on "man, whose breath is in his nostrils."

I in the midst of me need not advertise Itself; I in the midst of me dwells secretly, sacredly, silently, abiding in God, and together we two, who are one, walk this earth.

I in the midst of me is the spiritual son of God, the Christ, Melchizedek—He who was never born, who will never die, and who is and always will be invisible.

I am the invisible Presence within me. I am the invisible Presence which goes before me to make the way clear; I am the invisible Presence which walks beside me as protection. I am the invisible Presence which follows after me as a rear guard.

I am the life of my friends, and I am the life of my foes: we are one, yet each, individual in expression—one in essence, infinite, but individual in form and modes of expression.

I am the author in one, the composer in another. I am the healer in one, the minister in another. I am the painter in one, the poet in another. I am the inspiration unto my life and the inspiration to everyone who seeks inspiration. I can close my eyes at any time of the day or night and turn to this Infinite Invisible, to the I within me, and receive new illumination, new light, new health, new strength.

Inwardly and silently, say the word *I* softly, gently—*I,* meaning your Self, your true identity. Close your eyes to all outer appearances, and inside the inner sanctuary, alone with God, listen to the voice of God as It speaks to you:

I say to you: Son, cease from depending upon man. I am here in the midst of you—this I that you have declared.

Listen to Me.[1] Look unto Me, the I of your being, and be saved. Do not look to effects, do not look to persons, do not look to fame, fortune, or position.

Look unto Me, for I in the midst of you am your bread, your staff of life. You need not earn your bread by the sweat of your brow. Work, but enjoy it. Work, and love it, but never feel dependent on it for your living, for I am living you: I am your living.

I am your Being. I have placed Myself as the Tree of Life in the midst of the garden which is your Self. I in the midst of you am mighty.

Even your body is the temple of the living God which I am. Your body, your mind, your soul: these are all dedicated to Me, and I have ordained them. I have given to you your mind and your body. I am the substance of your body. I am that which beats your heart. I am that which governs every organ and function of your body. I did not make your body and then leave it to control itself. I made it in My image and likeness, of My substance. I knew you before you were conceived in the womb. I formed your very body in the womb. I have never left it, nor forsaken it.

Many times you have left Me. Many times you have made false gods: gods of gold and silver, gods of pills, powders, and plasters, and looked to them for health and joy. You have looked outside for pleasures, satisfaction, for peace, and yet I am the wine of inspiration. Seek Me while I may be found, and be at peace.

---

[1] The word "Me," capitalized, refers to God.

Does the creature talk back to the Creator? Does the clay talk to the potter? No! I am the potter, I am the creator, and all creation hearkens unto Me. The heavens declare My glory. The earth showeth forth My handiwork. Do you know that I have given you dominion over everything on earth, everything in the sky, everything in the waters and beneath the earth?

I am the way: live by way of Me. Do not live by way of the world. Do not live by way of form—even so powerful a form as a hydrogen bomb. I am your high tower, and I am your fortress. Hide in Me, hide in the understanding that there is only one power, and I am that. Look unto Me and be saved—not by might, not by power.

Put up your sword! Those who live by the physical or the mental sword will die. Live by My Spirit—not by might, not by power, but by My Spirit.

Dwell in Me; let Me dwell in you. If you dwell in Me, and if you let Me dwell in you, if you live in the recognition that I in the midst of you am your true identity, your eternal life, I will draw unto you whatever is necessary for your harmonious unfoldment, be it person, place, or thing.

Go into the inner sanctuary of your being and be quiet. Do not pray in public. Do not tell man what you need. Do not tell man what you would like to be. Do not tell man what you would like to do.

Live in Me! Let Me live in you, and let Me be the invisible Presence that goes before you to prepare the way for you. Let Me go before you, silently, sacredly, secretly.

Do not be impatient if it takes a little time for you to reach home. You have already become involved with people and entangled in situations that you cannot leave suddenly. You will have to be led away from these without injury to the life, the well-being, or the comfort of others. You cannot have your life and well-being at the expense of others. That is not the law. "Love thy neighbor as thyself" is the law. That, you can do, if you look unto Me, if you understand that I in the midst of you am Self-sustained.

Do not be impatient if you have to take some long way around. I will bring you by a way you know not of. It will not always appear to you as a short cut; it will not always be without a few bleeding footsteps or even a cross, but nevertheless I am leading you through this world of illusion back to your Father's house which I am.

I have meat—be assured of that. "I have meat to eat that ye know not of." Do not let your mind get weary wondering how you are going to get a home, companionship, supply, or health. Be assured that I have meat. I already have meat, and wine, and water. Rest here, and let it come to you.

Do not try to attract supply—not mentally, not physically. Just do your work each day, the work that is given you to do. Do it in the best way you know how, but do not do it for a living: do it for love. Let the living be the added thing. I, your Father which art in heaven, I, who am in the midst of you, I know your need before you do. It is my good pleasure to give you the kingdom if you abide in Me and let My word abide in you.

Live in Me, live in the realization that this I in the midst of you is God, this I in the midst of you is ordained of God, for God is both the Father and the Son, God is both the giver and the gift.

Trust this I at the center of your being. Trust It with your secret desires, but do not let your secret desires be aimed at persons, places, or things. Your secret desires must be for rest in Me, peace in Me, satisfaction in Me, joy in Me.

Tabernacle with Me, for I in the midst of you am your life. I am That which prospers you. I am That which draws unto you all that is necessary for your spiritual development and unfoldment.

If there be forty years of wilderness before you reach the Promised Land, be patient, be patient. You have made this wilderness through which you must be led. If there is the experience of the cross, accept it. You have brought it upon yourself, and it is just another way out of the wilderness. Whether you make your bed in hell or in heaven, I in the midst of you will never leave you, nor forsake you. Even if you are the thief dangling on the cross, I will take you with me this very day into paradise.

Do not fear effects, do not fear outer conditions. I, the I of your being, I am that part of you which was never born. I brought you into this experience; I will carry you through it; and I will carry you on into the next experience, even unto the end of the world.

Have I been so long with you, and you have not known Me? Have I been so long with you, and you have not recognized that I am Melchizedek, I am the Christ, I am the spiritual Son? When you have gone far enough you will understand that I am God the Father as well as God the Son. And then you will understand oneness.

You will understand that because I am infinite, there are no evil powers. The evil pictures that you see and hear and touch and taste and smell are made of the fabric of nothingness, the fabric of hypnotism, the fabric of suggestion. Do not fear them. They have no entity; they have no identity; they have no real being. Only understand them to be of the fabric of mental illusion—nothingness— for I in the midst of you am the only power and the only presence.

"Love the Lord thy God with all thy heart, and thy neighbor as thyself." I am He, and I in the midst of you am the I in the midst of your neighbor. Inasmuch as you have done it unto the least of these neighbors, you have done it unto Me, for I am he, even as I am you. Inasmuch as you have not done it unto the least of these, you have not done it unto Me. Anything that you have withheld from anyone, you have withheld from yourself, for I am your Self, and I am your neighbor's Self. I, God at the center of your being, am He; I, God, am your neighbor.

I am Melchizedek. Everything that has form must pay tithe and honor to Me. I am Melchizedek, the unborn, the undying. I am the Spirit of God in you. I am your true identity. I am the very Soul of your being, the very life of your being.

"Awake thou that sleepest." Awake, and when you awaken, you will see Me as I am, and you will be satisfied with this likeness!

On the spiritual path, we make a transition from living under the law to living under Grace, and consciously remember that we are not under the law. This means every kind of law: medical law—infection, contagion, and heredity; theological law—punishment for sins of the past or of the present, or sins of the parents or of the grandparents. We no longer live under the laws of matter; we no longer live under the laws of mind; we no longer live under the laws of theology: we live under Grace.

Thy grace is my sufficiency in all things—Thy grace, not money, not my heart, liver, or lungs. Thy grace is my sufficiency in all things —in health, in supply, in companionship, in freedom, in joy, in peace, in dominion.

Thy grace! I no longer live under the law. I do not live by taking thought for supply, for God's thoughts are far greater than my thoughts. I live by every thought that proceeds out of the mind of God, by every Word, which is Grace. I live my life listening to that still small voice.

I am the child of God, heir of God, joint-heir to all the heavenly riches. I have been given dominion over this body. I am free. I have found my freedom in the realization of my true identity as I. As the child of God, I am free, and I no longer live under the law of limitation, but under Grace.

As human beings we are in the tomb where the Christ lies buried, and all that the world sees is this living corpse in which we are entombed. Within us, in this tomb of human selfhood, is the Christ, and in certain moments of our lives, such as can happen to us this moment, an experience takes place, and then a few hours later when we look in the mirror, we suddenly find that our eyes have been opened:

I have been limited by a finite body and a bank account, circumscribed by their dimensions. Even my wealth was a tomb in which I have been buried, but now I am not in these: I am risen. I am no longer buried in the tomb of a body, nor am I any longer subject to its limitations.

This form is now a vehicle unto me, just like my automobile. And this money—this also is a tool, an instrument, and a medium of exchange, something that has been given to me to use.

I am no longer in the tomb of finite belief: I have risen. I am no longer entombed in a body or a checkbook. Now I am outside of these: they are my servants, the tools given me for my everyday life.

Do not fear to step out on the waters of Spirit. Remember, you can only fail, and there is no disgrace in failing. There is only disgrace in not trying. Everybody stumbles a little bit as he goes forward. Even Jesus Christ was subject to temptations up to the last moment. Do not be ashamed of the temptations that assail you. It needs must be that we stumble and fall, that we be subject unto temptation, for each of these strengthens us in our ongoing until we reach the Mount of Transfiguration, and there having "died," we are reborn of the Spirit, and those of our disciples who have risen sufficiently behold us as we are, in our pure spiritual perfection, even the perfection of the body.

Through Grace we attain a point of transition, and then our friends and relatives say, "You have changed. Something wonderful has come into your life."

CHAPTER IX

AN INTERVAL IN ETERNITY

Life has frequently been depicted as a circle, representing eternity, without beginning and without end. If we visualize life in that way and realize that our immediate human span of life is confined within a segment of that circle and that all the other segments of the circle are yet to be encompassed, we can see that within the confines of that circle, there is a past as well as a future.

One mystic described this life as "a parenthesis in eternity." *This* life! Observing life objectively and using the circle as symbolic of all life, it is obvious that we have come from the past into a parenthesis in the circle, and when this parenthesis is removed—the one marking birth and the other marking death—we will be on our way into another parenthesis, or what is called the future.

This should help us to understand that our present life on earth is only an interval in eternity. We have come from somewhere and we are going somewhere, but because life is an unending circle, we are again going to come from a somewhere, and we are again going to go to a somewhere, and this will go on, and on, and on. Will it ever end? Who knows?

The ancients tell us that when we are perfected, that is, when we live this life as God lives life, in that degree of purity, we will not enter the parenthesis again: we will just live in the circle, outside, beyond, and above all human experience.

Even though the unillumined and uninitiated may claim that all this is only speculative, I can tell you that there are those who have completed their cycle of life on earth, and therefore would not have to return to this-world experience. Nevertheless, they do reincarnate, in some cases voluntarily and in others under instructions from those who likewise have been graduated and who perhaps act as spiritual influences behind this earth-plane.

That there is an evolutionary life process going on in this human picture, surely few can deny. That human consciousness is unfolding on a progressively upward spiral is born out by the fact that years ago when nations had conflicts of interest, they seldom sat down to discuss their problems, but settled them by going to war. The very horrors of the wars that have been fought in the twentieth century, however, have forced such an evolution in consciousness that nations are now trying to work out their problems without warfare, even though here and there, there is still a desire to return to the old way. On the whole, the trend is away from war, perhaps because the realization is dawning that war as it would be fought in this nuclear age would completely annihilate the human species.

In other areas as well, a significant change has been taking place in consciousness. Those of us whose memory goes back far enough can recall that during the strikes in the ready-to-wear industry of New York, in the coal mines of Pennsylvania, and in the automobile industry of Detroit, it was not an unheard of occurrence for management and labor to engage in what at times amounted almost to a shooting war. There is little of that today, and more and more of arbitration and mediation, all of which represents an evolution in consciousness. In legal disputes, too, there is a greater attempt today to settle lawsuits outside of court rather than to force every case into court.

If such a tremendous evolution has taken place in the past fifty years, how much greater has been the evolution over the past thousand years! Cannibalism is now practically extinct; tribal wars which often resulted in the defeated men and women being pressed into slavery have been almost completely wiped out.

Thinking of the progress and changes that have been made must cause one to speculate as to how and why such an evolution has taken place, inasmuch as every generation eventually leaves the human scene, and a new one follows. Is each new generation better than the one of twenty, thirty, forty, fifty, or two hundred years ago? Are these men and women better, or could they conceivably be the same men and women who learned lessons in their previous experiences and are now profiting from them?

Is not everything that we learn in this lifetime transmitted to the next generation? Will not the new generation take up where we leave off? Will it not accept unquestioningly the mechanical and material progress made by preceding generations?

Today we do not use whale-oil lamps, we do not study by candle-light, we do not have to go out and hunt or fish for our food. And why? Because we were not born at the same state of development as our ancestors. Had we been compelled to begin where our great-grandparents began, we would have had to go through the same process of life as they, but we are the beneficiaries of an evolutionary state of consciousness. We have come into this world more highly civilized than our predecessors, but that would have been impossible if they and we, too, had been born from a standing start.

How can anyone fail to recognize that there is an evolutionary process of consciousness going on constantly? This means that regardless of what conditions of evil we may behold they are transitory and temporary. The next generation will have less of them, and the following generation still less of them, and so on, and on, and on.

This does not mean that individuals in every succeeding generation will avoid problems characteristic of its particular time or resulting from catastrophic upheavals like world wars and economic disasters which often bring on waves of juvenile delinquency, alcoholism, drug addiction, and crime. With maturity and an exposure to a better and higher way of life, many problems harassing the world today will disappear.

Is it not possible that those engaged in crime may have carried some of this over from a previous still lower state of consciousness in a former life, just as very young children who give evidence of great musical skill or of an artistic or religious nature must have lived before, been on the Path, returned, and brought with them a developed state of consciousness? Is it possible to believe that they could have learned all these things from birth to three or four years of age? Is a mathematical skill or an inventive turn of mind inherited, or is it the embodied development that was attained in a former life?

Probably nature has wisely decreed that we carry with us into this present experience no memory of specific hardships endured, or the sordid aspects of former lives, but that we carry only the attained, developed consciousness, whether it be of music, literature, art, science, or spiritual wisdom, and probably not even a memory of the particular form it took.

If we could see this life as a parenthesis in eternity, we would realize that each one comes into this parenthesis to advance himself beyond what he was before, and therefore, there must be a going on from this experience in order to evolve into the next.

There is no denying that in the consciousness of most people there is a natural reluctance to leave the human scene, a reluctance to pass on, make the transition, or whatever we may choose to call the change. There is also a reluctance and resistance to having our friends and relatives leave this experience. Strangely enough, there is no resistance to birth which ushers in most of mankind's troubles. Then, why should there be a resistance to death, which in most cases is an end to many of our problems? True, we have formed the habit of being with certain people and have become attached to them, and when they are gone, a void is left which causes grief.

But even from a common-sense standpoint, how dull and monotonous life would eventually become if we had nothing to do but go to sleep at night, wake up in the morning, and unendingly go through a round of doing the same things that we have been doing for sixty, seventy, or eighty years! There has to be a break in that. What would happen to men who today retire at sixty-five and sometimes are frantic by the time they are seventy or seventy-five, if they were to go on forever and ever living that same kind of useless, monotonous existence? There must be an escape from this kind of "vegetating."

The beginning, then, of overcoming this dread and fear of death is to realize that our human span here is but a preparation for another experience, and we should bid Godspeed to those who have finished this cycle and are ready for the next. This very overcoming of the fear and dread of death would prepare us for a more harmonious experience on earth and undoubtedly prolong our life, because many of the passings are unnecessary and are brought on by the very clutching to ourselves of a material sense of life which often works in reverse and hastens us out of this experience.

To understand, however, that we cannot be moved outside of our cycle, that we are part of an eternal destiny, and that as we were moved into this parenthesis, so we will be moved on out of it—but only in accord with the unfolding of consciousness and not by being pushed out of it—would expand consciousness and contribute to a more satisfying human experience.

When we realize that we are a part of a circle, we no longer fear what mortal conditions can do to us because we are under a divine destiny, and nobody, no thing, and no condition can push us out of this body until our time has come. Our time does not necessarily mean the commonly accepted human span of years: it means the time required to reach the individual development of consciousness that is possible to each one of us on this plane, a development which cannot expand any further until it has made the transition into another experience.

Instead of pitying those who have reached advanced years and are not functioning vitally and actively, let us realize that they, too, are a part of a cycle, not acted upon by the human belief of threescore years and ten or by the belief of deteriorating matter, but that they are a part of this circle of eternity. With that realization, one of two things happens: they either revive and lose ten, twenty, or thirty years from off their shoulders, or if they have arrived at the fulfillment of time, they will be released into their ultimate attainment. Whichever it may be, they will no longer be victims of fear or dread, or of the loneliness of those who hold them here because they want their companionship.

From the standpoint of our spiritual development, it is important for us to learn that when we came from that unknown somewhere, we brought with us an attained state of consciousness, and that while we are here, we are expanding that consciousness. The period in which we live on this earth is like a school. If we go through life wasting our time and not availing ourselves of the opportunities for spiritual unfoldment provided here, when we leave this plane we will have to return and go through the entire experience again, just as children who do not learn the lessons of one grade in school must repeat the grade in order to be ready for the next one. If we go out on a down cycle and come in on another down cycle, it will just keep on, and on, and on, until eventually every knee bends to God, to the spiritual life. So, if we have to come back a thousand times—experience a thousand or more parentheses—it is because we have brought it on ourselves.

This is a hard saying, and it is especially hard for those who are afraid to face up to themselves, who are reluctant to admit that they have brought all their problems on themselves. "Whatsoever a man soweth, that shall he also reap. For he that soweth to his flesh shall of the flesh reap corruption"—not only in this world, but in the worlds to come.

As we visualize the circle and move around it, it is apparent that everything we do at any given point of the circle determines what and who we are at the next point of that circle. We either stay a mortal material being and keep on going around and around, repeating the same life-experience and reaping the same karma over and over and over, or we are an expanding consciousness, and with every time around we are a bigger, better, more spiritual consciousness with greater dominion.

As we sow in this lifetime, so will we reap in the next. Many persons have thought of the doctrine of karma and reincarnation as being primarily an Oriental teaching, and while it is true that it did originate in the Far East, this doctrine has been accepted and acknowledged the world over by mystics, poets, and philosophers to whose attention it has been brought and who have seen the rightness of it. Many of these very people, however, are unaware of the Christian teaching of repentance and do not understand that the Christ-teaching, unlike the Oriental teaching of karma, does not doom a person to his karma until it has been exhausted, but rather wipes out the past in the moment of real repentance. With the recognition of the Christ, with repentance and with turning, karma is instantly erased.

The approach of The Infinite Way to the concept of karma and reincarnation, however, is different from that of other teachings which embrace this doctrine. The Orientals teach that every bit of sowing creates a corresponding karmic debt which must be paid off in this lifetime or in subsequent lifetimes, and that regardless of any change of consciousness in us, we must pay to the uttermost farthing, whereas The Infinite Way teaches that irrespective of what sin of karma has been stored up, in any second of repentance, in a breath, we are as pure and white as snow. In a moment of real repentance, in an awakening which brings the realization that sin is no part of us and has no right to be, in that second, karma is wiped out, and we are on the spiritual cycle.

From there on, the sowing not only results in reaping while we are still here, but it results in an ever-greater reaping as we go on. Every bit of metaphysical or spiritual wisdom that we have attained in this lifetime is of value to us on this plane as well as hereafter, so that we cannot separate karma from reincarnation, any more than we can separate karma from our next year. Our next year is being built this year. The degree of spiritual consciousness we can attain this year will be evidenced in our outer life next year. An expanding and evolutionary consciousness will continue to operate forever—inside the parenthesis and beyond.

This must be true if there is any reason to life or any purpose in living. Were the millions of people of India, China, and Russia born to know nothing but the suffering and horror of their lives for the past hundreds of years? Are they only living out the destiny of the karma they have built up in preceding lives, or are they struggling for freedom from hunger, exploitation, and oppression because they are the very ones who will return to enjoy the better conditions they are helping to create?

Are the efforts that parents make to educate their children, even though it may involve such a life of sacrifice that they themselves are never free from backbreaking labor or household drudgery, made only for their children, or are they building their own karma? Their children may not even benefit by their sacrifices, and it would make no difference if they did not because no one can build another's karma, not even that of his own children. Each one builds his own, and whatever form this present life takes, even if it is a complete cycle of sacrifice upon sacrifice, struggle upon struggle, it is for the development of his own consciousness and will come back to him in the form of education, freedom, and opportunity—whatever it is that he has given to others.

There again is a wider application of the truth that the bread we cast upon the waters will return to us. Some persons complain that they have gone through their whole lifetime without having any bread return. No, they have only gone through this parenthesis. This present parenthesis eventually is rubbed out; and then when the next parenthesis comes into being, there is a higher experience, which is the evolutionary fruitage of the one before.

It really is a form of ignorance and egotism to say that we have laid down our lives for our country or for our children. We never did; we never did! We have been building our own karma, and it would be impossible to sow to the Spirit and not reap life everlasting, to sow to freedom and not reap freedom, to sow to love and not reap love, to sow to friendship and not reap friendship. Even if every friend on earth betrayed us, that is only inside this parenthesis.

There is no need to feel sad or discouraged, therefore, about those closest to us who have never touched the spiritual path because this condition exists only within the limits of the parenthesis. Everyone is free while he is here, and he is just as free to find his way when he is no longer here. He has not wasted his life: he has merely wasted a parenthesis. He will still have his awakening, and the fruition and the fullness, because undoubtedly each one of us has lived the same stupid life that the majority of mankind lives—the life of the walking dead, the Soulless life—and probably lived it dozens of times.

Just as in this particular experience we are beginning to awaken, so as we witness those who are living this experience or passing from it still unawakened, we can look at them with the realization that it really does not matter. This parenthesis is only a period of threescore years and ten, twenty, or thirty, but they have all of eternity in which to awaken, and will.

If we are not building for eternity, of what benefit is sacrifice? Why not live today because tomorrow we die? Why not enjoy it while we are here? No, that we cannot do because we would be reaping a negative and selfish karma, an ingrown self. If that is what we sow, that is what we shall have to reap.

Many persons have never been exposed to the as-ye-sow-so-shall-ye-reap teaching, nor to the teaching that the bread they cast on the waters returns to them. These ideas have not been taught because they are not popular subjects. Few persons want to be faced with the truth that they are manufacturing their experience of next year right now, and furthermore that at this moment they are manufacturing what their life will be ten years from now. It takes only one step of the imagination to see that karma really means that we are building not only for the next ten or twenty years: we are building for eternity.

The only persons who are willing to face that are those who can turn their backs on the past and determine to sow to the Spirit, determine to have an end to this human bickering, greed, jealousy, and fear, to stop worrying whether they pass on at thirty or at a hundred and thirty, and to be willing to live each day as if they were building tomorrow, and consciously to realize when they think or do wrong that it has to be undone and cannot be left to accumulate.

It takes spiritual courage to face the teaching contained in the Bible because when its true meaning is understood, it compels us to live in the *now*, repent, and to begin sowing the right kind of seeds.

Our life-expression within the parenthesis need not be limited to threescore years and ten or twenty, but on the other hand, it would not make any difference if it ended at twoscore years or less because it is not the number of years that develops us: it is the intensity of the experience that expands consciousness. There may be those who complete this earth-cycle within the parenthesis at thirty, forty, or fifty, and there may be others who will go on to seventy, eighty, ninety, or a hundred; but whether early or late, the life-span can be completed in health if it is done in the understanding of life as expanding consciousness, not as finite time.

It is possible and highly desirable to reach a place of recognizing that our present state of consciousness embodies the spiritual progress of every life-experience we have had since the very beginning—not that there ever was a beginning to the circle or to what we call co-existence with God. Every time that we meditate, we can realize that our consciousness embodies the fruitage of our spiritual development for a million years. It embodies every bit of spiritual development and attainment that we have been accumulating throughout all time, and it is present here and now as the degree of maturity that we have attained. If it were actually the full maturity itself, we would no longer incarnate except either voluntarily or under orders to perform a specific mission.

In each parenthesis within the circle, we draw to ourselves the atmosphere and environment in which we can best unfold: the particular parents who can give us the lessons we need whether they be harsh or gentle ones, and the companionship needed for our development. If we look back on our life now, many of us can recognize that we would not be where we are except for some of the experiences that we have gone through, even some that we would like to have avoided.

But whether we have or have not the courage to admit it, to face up to ourselves, the truth is that we have drawn unto ourselves our own state of consciousness, and so, too, as we enter the Path, we are drawn into a spiritual atmosphere and companionship which have no relationship whatsoever to racial, national, geographic, or religious roots.

Let us carry this a step further and realize that as we pass from this experience and leave this plane of consciousness, we will be drawn into the very atmosphere necessary to learn the lessons important to our unfoldment, whether intellectual, emotional, or spiritual.

If we are on the spiritual path, are we not then going to be drawn into an atmosphere of service where we will be companioning with those of our spiritual household? If that does not include husband or wife, parents, brothers, or sisters, it is because they are not a part of our life. As long as we are on this earth-plane we do not disown husband, wife, mother, father, sisters, or brothers. We have a human obligation to them which we fulfill, but aside from that, we follow the Master's teaching, "Who is my mother? and who are my brethren?" recognizing our companions on the spiritual way as mother and brethren.

There are persons who are greatly concerned for fear that they will not rejoin their mother or father, their sister or brother, or their husband or wife. They will rejoin them if that is their state of consciousness; and, if that is what represents heaven to them, that will be their heaven, even though it really is hell. But to them it will be heaven—to be tied.

The moment that we are spiritually endowed, however, and have attained the correct sense of who our mother and brother really are, then we find ourselves tabernacling with those of our spiritual household. We fulfill ourselves spiritually among the spiritual lights who have gone before us, and we are drawn higher, and higher, and higher, and then we do not have to fulfill ourselves humanly, even if we return to earth.

The higher our spiritual development here, the higher we attain there and the more quickly we attain even greater spiritual heights because we are now free of the fetters of fear, ambition, lust, greed, and hate. So our unfoldment is increasingly progressive after we have been drawn into a spiritual atmosphere, just as our spiritual growth is so much greater because we have been drawn to one another here. If each one of us were trying to work out his spiritual salvation alone, he would not make the progress that can be made in a united spiritual atmosphere.

As we leave this plane and are drawn to those who have attained spiritual wisdom, our development continues. Then, even if we do reincarnate on earth, we will be fulfilling ourselves in a sphere more closely akin to a spiritual activity. Those who have not gone far enough spiritually will fulfill themselves culturally, educationally, artistically, or musically, but if they are developed spiritually, there will be a spiritual function for them to perform, even before they incarnate, because there are influences working behind the scenes that animate those who are on the spiritual path here.

Nobody who is in a position of leadership in a spiritual activity here is dependent entirely on his own state of consciousness. He has attracted to himself a spiritual atmosphere, a spiritual support and guidance, because on the spiritual level there are no such barriers as heaven and earth, as over there and over here: they are one. Once we are in some measure spiritually attuned, we are in the consciousness of all those who are so attuned, whether they are here or there. In other words, we are in and of the household of God.

The household of God is composed not only of people who are here on earth, or of those who have passed: the household of God encompasses the universe. The household of God is embodied in our consciousness, and we are embodied in the consciousness of the household of God.

Those who love God are brought into one household, one family, one companionship, into a sharing with one another; and just as we are sharing with those coming into the Light, so somebody with an even higher consciousness is sharing with us.

CHAPTER X

REALITY AND ILLUSION

To recognize that we live in two worlds, the world created by the five physical senses and the world of Consciousness, is to bring ourselves closer and closer to illumination.

In the first chapter of Genesis, God made man in His own image and likeness, without any help from anyone. This pure spiritual birth, this immaculate conception, is God manifesting and expressing Himself and His qualities, Consciousness revealing Itself as form. This is pure, unadulterated, spiritual creation, the immaculate conception of man and the universe, God, the infinite Life expressing Itself individually without any material forms, processes, or systems.

In the second chapter of Genesis, God not only creates but He miscreates, and because of His mistakes, He has to do it over and over again. First, He "formed man of the dust of the ground," then, He brought woman forth from man's rib, and finally He decided to bring man and woman together for the purpose of creation. Is it reasonable to believe that the infinite Intelligence of this universe needed to make two attempts at creation? This man of earth, "the natural man" who is not under the law of God, "neither indeed can be," is not a man at all: he is a mythical creation of the human mind, of the five physical senses.

To make clear how this mind creates, let us examine how it has created a man-made God. Close your eyes for a moment, and take the word *God* into your consciousness. Do you believe that this is God, or is this not a projection of your mind? Has this God any power? Is there really such a Presence, or is this just a self-created image of your own thinking?

Let us go further afield and let us attempt to decide what God is. Instantly to our thought comes an answer, but the answer is not truth, and the answer is not God because the answer is a projection of our background. Anyone who has been an orthodox Christian almost immediately thinks of Jesus Christ. If one's background is Hebrew, he probably thinks of a dear old Gentleman up on a cloud with a long beard, looking down and wondering whom He is going to smite or reward next; if one's background is metaphysical, he probably thinks of God as Mind, Principle, or Law.

Regardless of what comes to our thought when the question "What is God?" is presented, is it not clear that it is a picture projected into our thought, usually by someone we recognize and accept as an authority. Perhaps the truest words ever spoken in reference to God are: "If you can name It, It is not That." If we can think God, It could not possibly be That because how can we encompass an infinite God in our thought processes? The harder we pray to this God that we have in our mind, the more barren will we become. All we have is a man-made projection of God, an image in thought. We cannot pray to that—yes, we can, but we know what kind of an answer we will get.

Now let us dig a little deeper into this subject. Suppose you ask yourself: "Who am I? What am I? What am I like?" Would any answer you gave to those questions be correct? Would not you or your dearest friend answer those questions in one way and a person who does not like you answer them in another? Could they come to any agreement on the kind of person you are? Whatever opinion they may have, they are merely projecting their own thought about you, their own prejudice or concept, or an opinion based on something that someone has told them. They do not know the real you: they entertain beliefs and concepts, many of them good, but all of them subject to change tomorrow.

The very ones who pledged their undying allegiance to the Master were the ones who ran away while he was being crucified. Some of those who were sitting at his feet adoring him when he healed them of their ills were among the loudest shouters of "Crucify him, crucify him." They never knew him. They had a picture in their mind, an image in thought, but it never revealed the Master in the fullness of his spiritual identity.

If we would know anyone, we have to discard everything that we now believe, everything we have heard, and everyone's opinion about him. We have to clear out and rid ourselves of all our concepts of him. We first have to acknowledge that all we know about him is some concept that has become crystallized in our mind. To know a person, we would have to empty our mind of all opinions, concepts, theories, and beliefs, and train ourselves to shut out every opinion we have ever heard or formed because these opinions have been formed only as the result of some personal experience which pleased or displeased us.

If we could erase from our thought everything that we have heard or read about a person—everything, every opinion that we ourselves have formed—and say, "Father, wipe all this away. I am willing to start all over. Show me this man as he is. Show me his name and his nature. Reveal him to me," we would find that by turning within with a listening ear, the truth would be revealed to us. In this way we would know him aright. The *I* of him would be born in us immaculately.

Are you beginning to see how much we all have accepted about God and about one another without any real knowledge? Those of our friends and relatives whom we like have in some way pleased us, and when they do not, very often we do not like them any more, which should prove to us that we are accepting others, not as they are, but because of the concepts we entertain.

Is this not also true in politics? One President is a hero to some, and a devil to others. Another President is a devil to one, and a hero to another, and this country has never yet had a President who was not both a devil and a hero, depending on to whom we went for our information. Could anyone be a hero and a devil at the same time? No; these opinions are not the truth about the man: they are concepts of him formed by the five physical senses.

The world that we see, hear, taste, touch, and smell is the world the Master overcame, but it is not a real world: it is a world formed by our sense impressions, by what we like or dislike at the moment. So it is that this world of the second chapter of Genesis, the world of a man created out of dust, of a woman created out of a rib, and of children created from the union of man and woman—this is not a world, this is a dream. This is the world of sense impressions, beliefs, and theories which exists only as a mental concept, just as our man-made God exists as a mental concept, and not as God.

This world of sense impressions is not under the law of God. All kinds of fanciful ideas can whirl around up here in our mind, all kinds of fanciful pictures, but they are not under the law of God, they are not an expression of divine Intelligence. We can have opinions about God, opinions about man, and we can have opinions about one another, but they are not the truth, and they do not come forth from God. The world that we can see, hear, taste, touch, and smell is not under the law of God, and yet this very world that we are living in is under the grace of God when we see through the appearance to Reality.

In this world created by the senses, this unreal world of mental images, we are deceived by appearances because in "this world," unlike in "My kingdom," we are faced always with the pairs of opposites. Everything has its opposite: up, down; health, sickness; life, death; wealth, poverty; good, evil; purity, sin; white, black; gain, loss.

There is nothing in the world of sense that does not have its opposite, and if we analyze human experience, we will see that life is just a continuous effort to change one of the pairs of opposites into the other. We are always trying to change sickness into health, lack into abundance, sin into purity, or evil into good, knowing that even if we attain it, tomorrow it can be reversed again, with a continuation of the same merry-go-round. The reason for this is clear: there is no law of God in human activity. If there were, good would be maintained and sustained. But in the kingdom of God where the law of God operates, we not only do not have all these pairs of opposites: we do not have even one of them. We do not have life any more than we have death; we do not have health any more than we have disease; we do not have abundance any more than we have lack; we do not have good any more than we have evil. None of these things exists in the kingdom of God.

The kingdom of God is a spiritual universe, and it has no qualities and it has no quantities. The kingdom of God is the realm of being, but that being is divine being—not good being because good has its opposite, evil; not live being because life has its opposite, death; but being—possessing no degrees, amounts, quantities, or qualities. "The darkness and the light are both alike to thee."

Now close your eyes again, and as you look into the darkness, if you see anything that looks good, it looks good or desirable only because it is a mental image in your thought, and its goodness is based on your concept of good. Someone else might look at that very same thing and find it valueless because nothing is good or bad but thinking makes it so: it is the concept of it that a person entertains that makes it good or bad to him.

In this world of the senses, there is good and evil, and there is the centering of attention on changing the evil into good. In "My kingdom," the spiritual kingdom, we ignore the appearances and seek to realize spiritual truth, to realize God's grace, God's presence, and God's power. The moment that we feel a conscious oneness with God, the appearance changes. To our human sense, the evil appearance now has a good appearance, the appearance of lack has an abundant appearance, the sick appearance has a well appearance, sometimes even the dead appearance has a live appearance. But we are not fooled by the changed appearance. We know that in seeking the kingdom of God within, we are merely beholding Reality appearing, the grace of God appearing. We come face to face with God; we see Him as He is, and we are satisfied with that likeness.

To understand the illusory nature of the finite world is to grasp the kernel of all mystical teaching, but if it is misunderstood, it can act as a deterrent to progress as it has in India which has one of the noblest spiritual heritages of any nation on earth.

Perhaps the greatest of all the Indian seers was Gautama the Buddha whose revelation of absolute truth was so profound that while there are other revelations equal to it, there are none which have surpassed it. Gautama had the full realization of the one Ego, the one *I* which constitutes the Consciousness of the universe, and he himself understood and proved that the appearance-world is *maya*, or illusion. Because of its fruitage, his message spread like wildfire across all of India, but his teaching of *maya* was misinterpreted. The belief that the world is an illusion led to a do-nothing attitude, a passive acceptance of the evil conditions in the world. His followers failed to see that it is not the world that is illusory. The world is real: the illusion is in the misperception of the eternal, divine, spiritual universe which is the only universe there is, and which is here and now.

Because of an illusory sense of the universe, however, the mortal scene appears as mortality with all its errors, whereas it is in reality a divine universe. This world is God's world; it is the temple of the living God; but when we see it with finite eyes and ears, what we see and hear is but the illusory picture of the reality that is there. The illusion is in the mind that is falsely seeing the world: the illusion is never out in the world. An illusion cannot be externalized. An illusion is a deceptive state of thought, and it can take place only within a person's mind, not outside it.

With our human eyesight we see a world constantly changing: a world made up of young, middle-aged, and old people, of the sick and the well, of the poor and the rich, of the unhappy and the happy. All this is an illusory picture in the human mind, but because there is only one human mind, it is an illusory picture in your mind and mine. Such a world has no externalized existence.

We are aware of the world through our senses, but what the senses cognize is illusion, an illusion not outside the mind but in it. To be able to understand and grasp this idea, therefore, is also to be able to grasp the idea that this illusion cannot be corrected in the outer picture. That is why so much prayer fails. Through prayer, people are trying to improve the illusion which, if they succeeded in doing, would still be an illusion except that it would be a good illusion instead of a bad one.

God is not in "this world," contrary to the doctrine of pantheism which teaches that this world is a manifestation of God, that God transforms Himself into the world, so that God and the world are of the same substance though the form is different. If this were true and if the world really were a manifestation of God and made of the substance of God, it would be eternal, and there would be no changing process going on: no aging, no dying, and no decaying of either animate or inanimate objects. There would be no seasons if this world were of the substance of God because it would then be of the substance of eternality and changelessness. God changes not: God is the same yesterday, today, and forever; God is from everlasting to everlasting; and if this world were made of God-substance, it would be as immortal and as eternal as God, but it is not. It is changing moment by moment, dying every minute and every day.

The erroneous assumption in the teaching of pantheism and of much of modern metaphysics is that man is spiritual, that his physical body is spiritual, that trees and flowers are spiritual. This is true of the reality of these, but it is not true of the physical manifestation as it is appearing to us through the senses. If the world were spiritual, we could eat our food and have it too, we could drive automobiles that would never wear out, and we could have trees that would grow forever.

But the substance of the forms we behold is not of that substance which is God, and once we perceive that, we shall understand the true meaning of the word "illusion," which is that our perception of what we behold constitutes the illusion. It is not that there is an externalized illusion: it is only that what we behold is not the real substance of which it is made: it is of the substance of mind, the substance of *universal* mind.

Theism goes to the opposite extreme. Theism regards God and the world as two distinct substances, each having its own independent existence as a creation of God, yet not made of the same substance as God. How impossible it would be for God, the creative Principle, to create anything unlike Itself, anything different in nature and character from Itself, anything other than Consciousness! If Consciousness is infinite, there is no other substance beyond Consciousness, and the world of God's creating must therefore be Consciousness formed.

The next question then is: What about this physical universe? The answer to that is the Master's statement: "My kingdom is not of this world." "This world" is the world of the Adamic dream; this is the world of mortal conception; this is the world of mental projection. When we recognize this and are able to close our eyes and realize the *I* in the midst of us, this body loses its sense of mortality; even the material universe loses its mortal sense and becomes what God's world really is—harmonious and perfect.

The truth is that God is Spirit, Consciousness, and therefore all that really exists is God formed, God in manifestation. The world that we cognize with the five physical senses, however, is not the world of God's creating: it is the finite sense of the world which universal mind has created. With our mind, we cannot discern the world of God's creating. We do not see God's kingdom: we see only the human, limited, finite concept, or mental image, only the physical concept of the spiritual universe. That is why it is changeable and changing, sometimes good and sometimes bad, sometimes sick and sometimes well, sometimes alive and sometimes dead, all these conditions existing only as concepts and not as reality. It takes spiritual discernment to know the things of God.

Let us not look at this visible world and call it spiritual, but on the other hand let us not look at it and call it a creation separate from God. Let us rather cleave to the Middle Path which leads to our inner spiritual center where we are the Christ of God, and where we can see that we are one with the Father.

Some of the people we see on the street, on television, and even those around us certainly do not appear to be one with the Father, and surely many of us must wonder how this can be. Of course, we know it cannot be because a person who is one with God would look different and act differently.

To call a human being the Christ is an indication that we either have been endowed with interior vision and are able to see the person as he really is, or that we are lying to him and to ourselves. No human being can look upon physicality and with his mentality detect anything Christlike. All the human mind can be aware of is a physical body, and with it probably a personality, a personality that he may or may not like, or one that he may like today and not tomorrow. Only inner discernment, inner light, only an inner vision that beholds something the eye does not see and the ear does not hear can discern the Christ in any person.

To go into a prison, look at the assortment of men and women there, and say, "You are spiritual; you are the Christ," would be ridiculous, but if we went there clad in the Spirit, the Christ is what we would see. We would never make the mistake, however, of voicing such a statement to them or to anyone in charge.

When the Master asked, "Having eyes, see ye not? and having ears, hear ye not?" he was referring to an inner vision, an inner hearing, which we call spiritual discernment or Christ-consciousness. Only the Christ can recognize the Christ, and when we understand this, we will never look at a human form and declare, "You are well! You are healthy! You are young! You are spiritual." We would never do that, but if we could look through the appearance to the Christ of God, the Christ ever-present, although not apparent to our human eyesight, we would be able to break the mesmerism that looks at the body with the mind and believes the evidence of what it sees, hears, tastes, touches, and smells; and in breaking the mesmerism, we would be able, through our inner discernment, to behold the spiritual nature even of a dying or a sinful person.

This is the difference between The Infinite Way and such teachings as pantheism and theism, and that is what makes it possible for healing work to be carried on in this teaching. In our spiritual work we are not deluding ourselves with the idea that this physicality that is wasting away with sin, disease, and death is spiritual, nor are we trying to spiritualize it and make it perfect: we are looking through the appearance with inner discernment and there beholding the invisible, spiritual child of God who was never born and will never die, eternal right here on earth.

Miracles can be performed by the person who does not try to heal disease and who understands that he is but the instrument of God, that God constitutes individual being, and that any appearance to the contrary is illusory, a picture in the mind, without spiritual substance, spiritual cause, spiritual law, and without spiritual entity or identity—*maya*, illusion.

On the spiritual path, we do not try to change the external world; we do not try to change our friends and relatives—their temperaments, their dispositions, or their health—but we recognize that the very omnipresence, omnipotence, and omniscience of God within our own being make it impossible for sin, disease, death, lack, and limitation to exist as externalized reality. These can exist only in the mortal dream which consists of the belief in two powers. As that belief in two powers is surrendered, so is the dream punctured.

Living in the fourth-dimensional consciousness, we seek nothing from the dream. To seek supply, companionship, a home, or employment is to seek an improved dream, an improved illusion. It is seeking our own concept of good which, after we get it, may not prove to be the thing we wanted. We seek nothing of this world: we seek only the realization of our oneness with God.

Whatever is to come forth into expression must come forth from deep within, even though it still comes in ways that appear to be external. When we see fruit on the trees, we are seeing the fruitage of an invisible life, an invisible activity, an invisible unfoldment appearing visibly. As we lead the spiritual life, looking to no man, seeking nothing in the outer plane, but living in continual rapport with the Life-stream, our experience will unfold as the fruit appears on the tree, as an externalization of an inward Grace.

When enlightenment has been attained, the temporal picture is recognized for what it is: *maya* or illusion. Then when we are faced with evil people, evil or erroneous conditions, we will not fight them or try to get God to do something to them or for them: we will relax, knowing that this is the illusion or hypnotism of the five senses. When we awaken from beholding this mortal dream as if it were reality, we will see one another as we are, and then we will love our neighbor as ourselves because we will discover that our neighbor is our Self.

All this is apparent to us, not through knowledge, not because we have learned a little more truth, but because we have developed a deeper inner spiritual awareness and are able now to perceive the Christ. The object of The Infinite Way is to develop spiritual consciousness, not primarily to produce health out of sickness or wealth out of lack. Those are the added things, and those who catch even a grain of spiritual perception are showing forth health, prosperity, and happiness, and thus they are living more useful lives.

But this is not the goal. The goal is attaining the spiritual vision, so that we can behold God's universe and can commune with Him, walk and talk with Him, live with Him, and learn to live with one another, not merely humanly because our most joyous human companionships are much more worthwhile when we have attained a measure of spiritual companionship.

Spiritual companionship is achieved, not because we are studying the same books, not because we belong to the same church, not because we owe allegiance to the same flag. None of these things ensures harmonious companionship. Only through our being united in a spiritual bond, owing to our having attained some measure of spiritual light, do we find companionship with people of any country or of any religious conviction. There are no barriers once we have perceived the nature of true being. Being has no nationality, no race, and no religion. The reality of our being is God; the nature of our being is Christ; and when we are able to discern that Being through inner spiritual vision, we have a relationship that is eternal, eternal on earth and eternal forever afterward.

Looking at life through the materialist's eyes, we would have to grant that God has never overcome evil and that He never will overcome evil, but if we look out at life through spiritual discernment, we are convinced that God is infinite and that there never has been an evil power, a negative power, or a mortal power. That heightened vision heals sickness, changes sin to purity, insanity to sanity, and death to life.

The attaining of some measure of this spiritual vision is enough. It is an awareness that reveals that God is Spirit, that all that really is must be spiritual, and that all the power there is, all the law there is, and all the life there is must be spiritual. There will never be any confirmation of this through our eyes because Spirit cannot be seen with the eyes. The eyes must be closed to the objects of sense so that we can inwardly behold God's creation.

The development of spiritual consciousness is the greatest attainment there is. Only in the degree of this attained consciousness are we able to see the spiritual forms of God's creating. This has nothing to do with the development of the mind or with any intellectual powers; it is not attaining the feeling of knowing more than we knew before: it is a matter of attaining a depth of inner awareness, an awareness that expresses itself not so much in words as in feelings.

CHAPTER XI

THE NATURE OF SPIRITUAL POWER

The development of spiritual consciousness is possible when we learn that there is only one power. If we can rise in spiritual vision to the apprehension of the one truth that God is, that God is infinite and omnipotent, and therefore nothing else or nobody else is power, that is enough. This is spiritual discernment.

To the world, there are great powers and little powers, but he who is anchored in spiritual consciousness knows that no weapon that is formed against him shall prosper. If we accepted that literally, we would believe that there is a deadly weapon that could prosper except that God in some way is going to save us from it. To the uninitiated, that passage would indicate, "I have an enemy who has a deadly atomic bomb, and I know what it can do to me, but fortunately God says that no weapon that is formed against me shall prosper, and therefore I am now immune, and this deadly weapon can no longer harm me."

But the weapon does do harm when it is let loose in the world. And this is because people do not understand the real meaning of no weapon having power over them. The truth is that no deadly weapon has power because Life is God; and God has never made anything to destroy His own immortality and eternality. God is our life: we are eternal and immortal.

If we look out at this life through our mind, we are subject to every manner of deadly weapon: germs, bullets, bombs, and so many other things we need not rehearse them. Even an automobile on the road can be a very deadly weapon, and, above all, the calendar is so deadly that all we have to do is to keep looking at it for threescore years and ten, and then any day we are due for extinction. But the deadliest weapon of all is the mind of man that believes in two powers, and therefore accepts a mind of its own in which evil is a power. Neither bullet-proof vests nor bomb-proof shelters can save us from that weapon. Only in the understanding that we are life eternal, that God is our life, that we are immortal and spiritual, and that in the entire kingdom of God there are no deadly weapons—physical, mental, or otherwise—can we find safety and security.

With practice and meditation, we shall come to see that it is literally true that there is no weapon that has power because there is only one power, and that is the immortal life and the divine truth which we already are. There is no life for us to attain; there is no truth for us to attain: there is only the recognition of the truth that we are the truth, that we are life eternal, and the realization that the infinite nature of God makes it impossible for any deadly weapon to exist.

When this becomes realized consciousness, we can face the bomb, the bullet, the lion, or the weather: "I have lived in fear of you, but the truth is that you exist merely as a belief in two powers. The only existence you have is in the mind of man, and you cannot get outside of that mind to do anything to anybody. All you can do is to destroy those who entertain that same belief in two powers." These powers that appear to be destructive are so only to the individual who insists that there is a "this," a "that," or an "it"; but it is he himself who has formed the weapon, and all that weapon is, is a belief entertained in his own mind.

Once we accept the principle that because God never made a deadly weapon, no weapon that is formed against us shall prosper, then the bomb will explode in the midst of the very person holding it in his hand. He is the person with the belief in two powers, and he must reap the results of his belief.

That is why wrong mental practice, mental malpractice, whether it is done individually, collectively, or by universal belief, has no power whatsoever except on the malpractitioner himself. The malpractitioner accepts two powers, and he is, therefore, a victim of his own belief. Harm can come to us if we agree with him that there are two powers, and seek refuge behind a wall or in a statement of truth; but if we know that we are life eternal and that nothing can destroy the immortality of life or create a power destructive to the life of God, we are no longer the victims of the belief in two powers. The malpractitioner believes in two powers, but as he sends out his belief in two powers, it touches our understanding of one power, and all it can do is to boomerang because those who accept the belief in two powers go down under their belief.

If there is a person left in this enlightened age who is still engaging in malpractice—trying to destroy the life which is God, or trying to prove that there is a power other than God-power—it is an object lesson to watch what happens to him when his malpractice hits up against a person who has perceived the truth that God is individual life. If we believe that there is an evil power from which our understanding of God will protect us or if we believe that we have an "in" with God that will save us from some evil, we are lost: we have accepted two powers, and according to our belief so is it unto us.

The spiritual path demands complete purity, and by purity is meant an absolute conviction that God is the only power there is: there are no other powers. Omnipotence, which means All-power, is spiritual; and if Omnipotence is spiritual, then neither material nor mental powers can be power. To perceive that is to prevent not only the individual, the group, or the universal belief from functioning in our experience, but also to begin to destroy it for the whole world.

Realizing that no weapon formed against us has power develops in us the mind that was in Christ Jesus which knows that there are no powers, physical or mental. The only power that exists is the power of God, which is spiritual. Only a person who has that conviction has some measure of the Christ-mind, and even a tiny measure, a grain of that consciousness, can do wonders.

Even after Jesus had revealed the nature of spiritual power to his disciples, they were unable to catch the full import of it sufficiently to carry on his teaching to any great extent. And how many have there been since the time of the Master who have discovered this teaching in the Bible? The reason few, if any, have found it is because spiritual teaching is something that cannot be grasped by those living primarily in the material and mental realm. As a matter of fact, no one will ever learn the secret of spiritual power with his mind.

Spiritual power is not a facet of the mind. There is no amount of knowledge that anyone can attain that is spiritual power because knowledge alone cannot move mountains, heal disease, raise the dead, or forgive the sinner.

Spiritual power can be brought into expression only through the attainment of the fourth-dimensional consciousness, a higher awareness than that which is possessed by the human mind. It makes no difference what truth we study, or what truth we believe we know, there is no spiritual power in it. There is no known truth that will ever function spiritually.

If we were asked to give spiritual help to someone who needed physical healing, mental stability, or moral regeneration, our only possibility of success would be in proportion to our ability to be still, to refrain from *using* spiritual power, and *let* spiritual power flow through us. If we attempted to heal anyone spiritually or to try to exercise a spiritual influence, we would set up a barrier that would prevent our success.

Did Jesus make any conscious attempt to heal the woman who broke through the throng and touched the hem of his robe? She was healed, but he could not have consciously brought forth that healing because he did not know she was there, and if he had seen her, he would not have known whether she was sick or well. He was merely standing there being himself, abiding in the consciousness that the Father within was doing the work, and letting the Father have His way and His will, not trying to channel it, or to make any attempt to use spiritual power.

Spiritual power cannot be used, and yet it can manifest itself as our life and being. We can come into an awareness and an understanding of its nature, and thereby that power operates as Grace in our life, but we cannot pray it into doing that for us. We cannot bribe God into doing anything for us: we cannot promise to be good; we cannot even be good, and expect God to do something for us. What God is doing, God is doing, and no man can influence God.

God-power is not to be invoked by man. God-power is not attained by attempting to influence God in our behalf. God-power is not a power over sin, disease, or death, any more than light is a power over darkness. God is the creative, maintaining, and sustaining power, and God never made sin, disease, or death. Had He done so, they could never be changed or removed. What God creates is forever, and that which God did not create was not made. Therefore, we do not need any God-power to do something that never was made in the beginning, that never had existence, and that represents only our ignorance of the truth. If God ever created a disease or a law of disease, we might as well give up all hope of overcoming it, for no one is ever going to overcome God or God's works.

God is the all-power, and that power operates in our consciousness in proportion as we know this truth. When we begin to realize God's omnipotence, omnipresence, and omniscience, we shall need no power, and we shall live "not by might, nor by power, but by my spirit." When we have learned not to resist evil, not to fight it, and not to try to get God to fight it for us, we will not have to labor for our good: we will receive it by Grace.

Our very acknowledgment of the unreal and illusory nature of the discords of this world is the spiritual power. If God is omnipotence, then what power is there in any physical, mental, moral, or financial condition? If God is all-power, can there be a power in any negative condition? Every time we become aware of some negative, material, or mental power, we must realize the truth of Omnipotence:

Spirit is the only power; spiritual law is the only power; spiritual grace is the only power.

If God is omnipresence, we must be the very presence of God. That must mean that there is no other presence, and even we, then, have no presence. Why? Because God fills all space, and that does not leave any room for us, except in the degree that we are a part of that Omnipresence. This wipes out that false selfhood, that ego-selfhood, and leaves only the divine Selfhood which we are.

If we are the presence of God, we must act like it. We never will live by Grace until we make that acknowledgment and until we know the truth that we are the presence of God, that each one of us is that place where God shines through, that place where God is fulfilling Himself individually. Every time we become aware of a presence, whether it is a person, or a condition, or anything contrary to what we know God to be, we have to know the truth: Omnipresence. We will not judge by appearances and believe what our eyes see: we will judge righteous judgment:

God is omnipresence; therefore, Spirit is the only presence—spiritual law, spiritual life, and spiritual formation—even though my eyes cannot see it.

All this remains in the realm of theory or belief until we take the next step which solves the mystery of spiritual power: we do not have God and us. God is manifested as us; God is incarnated as us; God's life is our individual life, and we have no life of our own. Only the life of God is made visible as our life. God is our mind. We have no Bill-mind, Mary-mind, or Joel-mind, no young mind or old mind, no stupid mind or intelligent mind: there is only one mind, the mind which is the instrument of God, and that mind is our mind. Without this understanding of one mind, there is two-ness; and twoness, the sense of separation from God, is the source of the world's discords. There is no separation from God.

The truth is that God, divine Life, is our life. God, immortal Soul, is our Soul. God, divine Being, is our being, and even our body is the temple of God. This is the truth that makes us free. It is not praying to God to do something; it is not seeking a God-power: it is knowing the truth, and this knowing of the truth is spiritual power. It sets us free from the continuous struggle and striving to do something, be something, or accomplish something. It sets our minds free to rest, to be still, and to know that we are one with the eternal, infinite, omnipotent, omnipresent, and omniscient God.

Omniscience—All-science, All-wisdom, All-knowledge! What is there to think of a person who is trying to tell God, Omniscience, what he needs? God is all-wisdom, and yet we in our ignorance beg God, "Send me my rent next Monday." If God has a sense of humor —and I am sure He has—He would wink and tip His halo, and reply, "Are you telling Me?"

When we stop taking thought for our little selves and live in a conscious realization of Omnipotence, we shall know that there is no power to prevent God's grace from reaching us because there is no power other than God-power. If we live in the realization of Omnipotence, there is no power creating sin, disease, death, lack, or limitation for us, no power delaying our good, no power interfering with our life by Grace.

We have been praying to a hole in the sky and expecting it to shower down blessings, but how can we need blessings if Omnipresence is true? If God is omnipresent, can there be God and any other person or thing to be sought after or desired? If we already are the presence of God, what more do we need? In God's presence is fulfillment, and we are that Presence; therefore, in us in fulfillment. There is no next Monday about it. Omnipresence means that we are one with the Father now.

We can know Omnipotence, but we must know *Omnipresence* to put the seal on it. We can know that God is infinite, all-power, all-good, all-life, all-wisdom, but then we have to conclude with "And I am the presence of that. That constitutes my being. That which I have just declared about God is the truth about me. Since I already am the presence of God, I do not have to look for any more God-power than I already embody."

Intellectually, most persons agree that there is only one power, but seldom do we find an individual who believes in one power enough to rely on it. The attainment of the spiritual or transcendental consciousness brings the conviction of this truth.

To attain that mind that was in Christ Jesus and to develop that consciousness which is the source of spiritual power, it is necessary first to adopt the principle of one power, and then after having adopted it, begin to apply it in every circumstance of life that presents itself to us, to face every situation with an understanding that there is no power except what is derived from God because there cannot be an infinite God of Spirit and material power, too.

"Choose you this day whom ye will serve": the belief that there is material force and power, or the truth that the Spirit within is the only power. If we are reading the newspaper or listening to the radio and hear threats of war or disaster, we must be alert within ourselves to realize that there is but one power, the power of the Invisible. We have to be able to meet every circumstance of life with the same answer Jesus gave to Pilate: "Thou couldest have no power at all against me, except it were given thee from above."

Why should we need to use power if there is only one power—God? What would we want to use it for, on whom, or on what? And why do we need any power to correct a *belief* in two powers? When, through practice, we have trained ourselves so that we no longer use the power of mind or try to use the power of Spirit, we are in spiritual consciousness and we have the secret of spiritual power.

Spiritual power is the power that animates each and every one of us, but it operates only when we stop trying to use God. The nature of spiritual power is *being*, and it is being spiritual power here and now, it is functioning here and now, and there is no other power functioning.

We cannot expect the Spirit of God to go out and do things of a temporal nature for us: find a house, provide an automobile, or put our competitor out of business. Spiritual power is not temporal power; it is not a power that is subject to our bidding or our will; it does not punish those who wrong us; it is not something that we can use; it will not give us a monopoly of all the dollars, nor will it make us dictators or help us pull down existing dictators.

The Christ is a spiritual power which reveals harmony, peace, abundance, and wholeness to us and transforms our affairs. This it does not do by destroying anybody or anything. God has nothing to do with temporal power. God is Spirit, and He does not remove fevers, enemies, lumps, obstacles, limitations, or restrictions. But when we worship Him in Spirit and in truth, we find that there are no such things. This can come only as we turn from praying to God to remove a fever or rheumatism to praying that God reveal Himself to us as Spirit, that God reveal the divine harmony of His spiritual nature.

Let us surrender all belief in a God of temporal power—bury that idea—and let us resurrect from the tomb within ourselves where it is hidden the truth about God as Spirit, Life, Love, and Light. Light dispels darkness, but in the dispelling of that darkness, the darkness does not go anywhere; it is not overcome or destroyed. So, too, when we realize God as Spirit, our sins and diseases will disappear, but they will not go any place: they will only be dispelled as illusions, just as the light of knowledge dispelled the illusion of the horizon for those who believed it was the edge of the world.

Human beings in their extremity seek to find a God of power. Such a God is not to be found, for God is being, and when we overcome any sense of wanting or expecting God to be a power over any person, thing, or condition, knowing that there is no other power, we will be able to abide in the Master's teaching of "resist not evil." Why should we resist that which has no power?

There is no God that has to do something: God is already *being* life, the life of all being; God is already *being* love, loving the saint and the sinner. The emphasis is on *is*: God *is* life; life already *is*; eternal life already *is*: there is but one life. Love already *is*. Let us relax and rest in the is-ness of God, right where we are, giving up the concept of God as a great power, and rejoicing that we can put up our sword and that we need not fight—not physically, not mentally. With this spiritual vision, we stand still and see the salvation of God, resting in Omnipresence, Omnipotence, and Omniscience.

CHAPTER XII

THE DISCOVERY OF THE SELF

And the Lord said unto Abram, after that Lot was separated from him, Lift up now thine eyes, and look from the place where thou art northward, and southward, and eastward, and westward:

For all the land which thou seest, to thee will I give it, and to thy seed for ever. GENESIS 13:14, 15

Was God speaking only to Abraham? Does God speak only to a certain person, in a certain place, at a certain time? Or when the voice of God speaks, does it not speak to His son, wherever that Son is? Are not you and I that Son? Is not the Father saying to us, "Look out there. As far as you can see, *I* give this land to you, because all that *I* have is thine"?

Our astronauts have seen half the world at one time. They have encompassed this whole world, and for a few fleeting moments it was theirs. They had conquered it, and yet not by themselves, but by the *I* of all the scientists that made possible this feat—by the *I* that is you and the *I* that is I. We possess all this world—all the way to the moon. True, nobody has a guaranteed title to it: it is ours in joint-ownership, as joint-heirs in God:

I have access to all the heavenly riches; I have access to all of the creative Principle of this world. I can look into infinity, claim it all, and enjoy as much of it as I need for my daily use.

In the materialistic way of life, it is a natural thing, humanly, for us to be proud of being American, Canadian, English, German, or whatever our nationality may be. But what happens to that swash-buckling materialism when we discover our Self, when we discover that we all are brothers and sisters, regardless of the flag that flies over us, the color of our skin, or the church to which we belong, and realize:

Never am I limited to a country, to a nation, or to a state. I am limited only to the kingdom of God, and there I am of the household of God, heir of God, and joint-heir with every spiritual being in this great wide world of ours, of one great family, one great spiritual brotherhood.

To rise above the limitations of personal sense does not make us any less good citizens; in fact, it makes us better citizens, but better citizens because we respect the citizenship of other persons. Real citizenship is to live in fellowship, but this cannot be experienced until the nature of our true identity is understood, and then, whether we are Jew or Greek, bond or free, we are all of one spiritual house-hold.

Nothing can establish permanent peace in the heart of an indi-vidual except the entrance into that heart of the Christ, the Spirit of God. As peace is established in the heart of the individual, ulti-mately it will be established in the world, a peace that comes, not by the knowledge of man, nor by the wisdom or power of man, but by the Spirit of God functioning as the consciousness of man.

This Spirit which God has planted in the midst of each one of us seems to be absent because of our ignorance of Its presence, but when we become aware of this invisible, transcendental Presence as our Self, in that moment does It begin to function in our experience. We then become something more than creatures sentenced to earn our living by the sweat of our brow or to bring forth children in pain and suffering. No more are we separate and apart from God.

How could the son of God have any power other than to be the son of God? Is it possible for God to lose His son, or so to lose His power that He would allow one of His sons to wander from His household? God has never lost His dominion over the spiritual kingdom, and spiritual man has never left his Father's house. Just as there is no fallen man in the sense of God's man falling into a state of mortality, so it would be equally impossible for mortality ever to rise into immortality and become a child of God.

To know our true identity destroys the mortal sense of existence which has kept us earthbound. Earthbound! Some of us can remember how our cities and towns looked before there were automobiles on the streets and airplanes buzzing overhead. How earthbound we were! How limited we were to the little plot of ground where we lived! Even our work had to be close by because of the limitations of early forms of transportation.

The first release from that limitation came with the automobile which made it possible to travel as far as twenty, thirty, or forty miles in a single day. With that, our vision increased, and our knowledge grew because we could take in greater territory, meet more people, and come into contact with broader areas of life. How different life is now when we travel easily and comfortably four, five, or six hundred miles a day in an automobile! Almost simultaneously with the increased mobility made possible by the automobile came the day of the airplane which took us completely above the earth, and made our travels and our experience almost limitless. We were no longer earthbound. We had entered a new dimension of life.

But those who have experienced the limitlessness and boundlessness of the Spirit have gone far beyond the new dimension of the automobile and the airplane into still another dimension of life—unbelievably higher and wider.

Just as men were limited in the early days by the existing means of transportation, so are we earthbound by the belief in a limited being, a limited life, and a limited mind. The process of dropping this belief is exactly the same as the process of dropping our sense of limitation in regard to travel at sea, by automobile, or by airplane. It requires rising to a higher altitude of understanding, recognizing the laws of Spirit, and letting the sense of mortality drop away.

The kingdom of God is, and always has been, perfect. What is called mortal existence not only is no part of God's kingdom, but cannot even evolve into God's kingdom. Mortal sense and mortal creation have no part in God, never have had, and cannot be returned to God. Mystical wisdom does not teach that a mortal is to become immortal, but that he must "die daily" and be reborn of the Spirit, that is, he must awaken to the awareness of his true identity, and just as he would drop any illusion, so he must drop once and for all time the belief that he is fallen man.

When we are unclothed of mortality and clothed with immortality, there is no fallen man: there is only the original, perfect man, the spiritual identity which is now, and always has been, intact, just as a child taken from a family of wealth and culture and brought up in poverty, possibly in sin, disease, and ignorance, is still the child with the same identity and potentiality with which he was originally born. He has merely been clothed upon with an illusory identity, but his name, identity, wealth, and all the other things that belonged to him at birth could be restored in any moment. This child did not fall: he is the same child he was at birth. All the experiences that he has gone through have merely been imposed upon him, but his original heritage and identity are what they were in the beginning.

Ultimately, we shall all discover that our true identity is Christ, and although we may have been brought up as Jones, Brown, or Smith, our real name—our identity and our potentiality—is Christ, the spiritual offspring of God. In the moment that this truth is revealed to us, all that has been imposed upon us by human belief will drop away, and as soon as we begin to perceive our true nature and identity, it will not take long to become accustomed to the atmosphere of Spirit which is our original abiding place.

Bit by bit, as we pursue the spiritual path, as we realize that our real heritage and identity are in God and that we are of the household of God, living in fellowship with the children of God, we begin to lose pride in our family name and heritage, and, inwardly, we may take on a new name, indicating that we have come to a place where we identify ourselves with our Source. Now when we say *I*, we understand that we are not speaking about five-foot-five or six-foot-one of flesh, about a white skin or a black one, or about Occidental or Oriental features. Now we are identifying ourselves with our Source, which is God, the creative Principle of our being.

While we were living the materialistic life, we depended on relatives, friends, parents, husband, wife, children, employer, business, investments, and, in the end, on social security. How sad that the God-created, God-maintained, and God-sustained man should have to look forward to living on some pittance handed out to him near the end of his days—especially in the light of the truth that he is an heir of God. An heir of God, and thinking in terms of pittances! We have to make a transition from the materialistic concept that believes that we must earn our living by the sweat of our brow, or be dependent on someone else who is doing it for us. We have to come out and become separate from the atheistic belief that we do not have contact with Infinity, with our Source.

Let us in this moment do away with the belief of being that fallen man who in some way or other has to struggle back to the kingdom of God, and let us realize here and now:

I and the Father are one. The Father is Spirit, and I am the offspring of that Spirit, therefore I am spiritual. I am of the household of God, under the dominion of God, "joint-heir to all the heavenly riches" by virtue of the Spirit of God that dwells in me.

God has never removed His Spirit from me, and certainly no man has the power to undo the work of God. The Spirit of God that dwelt in me in the beginning must be the Spirit of God that dwells in me now, awaiting first, recognition, then, acknowledgment, and finally, realization.

Something must sing within us that this is true, or else we are in the untenable position of having to acknowledge that God is not omnipotent, that God permitted His son to fall, that God made possible the failure of man to live, move, and have his being in God, or that God instigated the Fall. How can we ascribe such things to God? How can we believe that there is a God capable of losing a Son—even one Son out of all the billions of Sons that have been manifested as form? How could we trust such a God or have faith in the infinite capacity of God, if we also believed that a son of God could be lost out of the kingdom or that one single child of God could go astray with or without the knowledge of God? If God is all-knowing—and God is—then nobody wanders out of the kingdom of heaven without God's knowing it, not even a sparrow.

We have never left the kingdom of God: we have never left the jurisdiction and government of God; we have never come under any law but the law of God, and have never lived any life but the life of God. God-life is the life of all being, and there never has been any other.

Whether man accepted the belief of limitation in the form of being confined to the earth and not able to travel on water, or in the air, or of being able to travel only a few miles in a day, let us understand that all these limitations are not, and never were, actual limitations: they were but due to man's ignorance of the laws governing these activities. These laws have always been available to man, and at any time a knowledge and application of them would have enabled him to rise above his bondage to the earth. They became practical in his experience, however, only when he was able to open himself to receive the wisdom that is beyond the visible.

So we enter the Fourth Dimension of life in the same way, by realizing that we need not be earthbound. Being earthbound or limited to the three-dimensional world is only a sense of limitation that has been imposed upon us because of our ignorance of that transcendental consciousness which is our heritage. It was our birthright, and it is ours now because the kingdom of God cannot be restricted or limited, nor remain forever hidden. We do not have to fight our way back to God; we do not have to find God: we have only to open our consciousness in the assurance that God could never lose us. How could God lose His Self? His Self is our Self, for there is but one Self.

Your Selfhood is the unconditioned Self. So is my Selfhood. It is wholly spiritual: It is, in fact, Spirit Itself, which has no race, nationality, or religion. This Selfhood of you and of me co-exists with God, has co-existed with God in the Is-ness which God is—without beginning and without ending—and this Selfhood has known individual expression throughout all time.

You are this Selfhood, and I am this Selfhood, living as one of God's incarnations; and that Selfhood remains eternal in the heavens, untouched and unaffected by the surroundings in which we find ourselves. With birth, however, there has sprung up around the one Self a sense of human identity, and from the moment of conception this begins to be identified with its surroundings.

Selfhood Itself, the Selfhood of you and of me, is unconditioned, and therefore, in the actual realization of our previous life-experience, it becomes possible to know the unconditioned freedom of the Self, to be wholly and completely free of national, racial, and religious theories and doctrines, and all inhibitions or conditionings.

To accept intellectually the truth that we are that unconditioned Self is one thing, but to experience It in a measure is another thing, and to experience It in Its completeness is quite another. A step leading to the realization of the absolute, unconditioned Self is to experience the Self as It lived in Its previous incarnations, or at least in some of these, so that it becomes possible to live free of one's immediate surroundings, or free of the surroundings of this present incarnation.

When I have been able to see myself as an American, as a Hebrew of two thousand years ago, as an Arabian, or as a Chinese, it is a simple matter to see the trappings that have attached themselves to me in each of these incarnations, and to see that the I never came down to the level of these trappings or conditionings, but remained, as It always is, the Self. Then, and then only, did I have the ultimate experience of realizing the unconditioned, absolute Self. In this, of course, I see it is possible to have been either male or female, white or black, Occidental or Oriental, and although the Self that I am has never been any of these, yet It has drawn unto Itself all of these as the need was established for the particular experience at specific times.

This realization of our Self enables us either to surrender this present incarnation, or to remain in it, and yet not be of it or conditioned by it, but to live always as the Self. In this realization, we become the universal Self, or the Self of all others, more especially of those with whom we come in close contact.

Separate and apart from our fellow man, there is no God to worship, no God to love, and no God to serve. We are loving God only as we love our fellow man; we are worshiping God only when we are serving our fellow man.

When Jesus taught, "He that seeth me seeth him that sent me," when he referred to your Father and my Father, was he claiming to be God's only child, or was he not rather speaking about a universal relationship? Is there any God separate and apart from man? Has not God manifested and revealed Himself on earth as man, and when we look upon one another, are we not seeing the Father that created you and me and sent us forth into expression? And since you and your Father are one, in serving you, I am serving my Father; in loving you, I am loving my Father.

There is no God up in the sky, or down below in the earth or the sea. "The kingdom of God is within you." If we are to find that Kingdom, therefore, we shall have to seek inside to find it, for that is where it is; and if we wish to show our love for God, we shall have to express love to one another because that is where we will find the God to love. If we want to serve God, we had better learn to serve one another, because only in that way can we serve the Father that sent you and me into expression.

Every bit of love that we express is a love that is expressed to us. When we are expressing love impersonally to the downtrodden and abandoned people of the world, we are really expressing love to ourselves because the Self of those others is the Self of us. This is the Way: there is but one Self. I am that Self; and I am that Self even if I am appearing as you. I am that Self, even when I am appearing as the beggar or the thief. Is it not easy, then, to forgive, knowing that I am forgiving myself, that I am forgiving my own ignorance, forgiving my ignorance even when it appears as someone else?

"Love is the fulfilling of the law." Therefore, love is the Way, and this means the love that I express, for I am the Way. I must express love, forgiveness, and patience; I must pray that the light of the world be revealed even in the darkest consciousness. I must do unto others as I would have others do unto me, because the I of me is the I of the other: we are one. The Self of me is the Self of you, because there is only one Self, and this is God's Self. This is oneness; this is divine sonship. The spiritual way of life is a recognition of one-ness, sonship.

The Way brings the recognition that the *I* of me and the *I* of you are one and the same *I*. The *I AM* that I am is the *I AM* that you are, because this is the *I AM* that God is, and God is the *I AM* which is the *I AM* of you and the *I AM* of me. Therefore, the recognition of *I AM*-ness is the Way.

It is some measure of this realization that enables us to live as if I am you and you are the *I* that I am, and therefore we are one; and since all that the Father has belongs to me, all that I have also is yours. This is a state of consciousness which is a step beyond doing unto others as we would have others do unto us, because it recognizes that the Self of us in the Self of the other, and therefore, all that we are doing is always done unto the Self that we are.

There are no boundaries in the spiritual relationship, for there is only one *I AM*, and that *I AM* is universal, individually manifested and expressed as every individual, past, present, and future. *I AM* is the Way, and the more we dwell in the remembrance of our true identity, the closer we are living to the Way.

I AM-ness is oneness, divine sonship, and because of this sonship, we have a spiritual relationship of brotherhood based on the understanding of our oneness with our Source. The Way is oneness; the Way is love; the Way is the recognition of our true identity as the son of God; the Way is the recognition of the nature of God and the nature of the Son.

The goal of mysticism is the attainment of the realization of one's self as Self, so that life is a continuing experience of the Self, with a coming down to the personal sense of self only for the purpose of the immediate work to be done. The attainment of the mystical estate is, of course, the ascension out of the personal sense of life into the experience of life lived as the Universal and the Divine.

I AM is the Way. *I AM* is the life of me and the life of you. *I AM* is the immortality of me and the immortality of you. *I AM* is the divine Grace by which we live. And this is the basis of all mysticism.

PART TWO

RISING OUT
OF THE
PARENTHESIS

Attaining the Mystical Consciousness

CHAPTER XIII

THE UNILLUMINED AND THE ILLUMINED

The parenthesis in which we live consists of the degree of mental or material limitation that we come under through the universal belief in two powers. Removing the parenthesis means unseeing the human picture and becoming consciously aware of our spiritual Selfhood.

What we are really doing on the spiritual path is trying to wipe out that parenthesis by realizing that we are not living in any form of human limitation: time or space, calendars or climates. The more we attain a living realization of the spiritual nature of our being through meditation, the fainter the parenthesis becomes and the closer we are to becoming one with Infinity and Eternality.

The moment we perceive that there is but one Life and that we are living that Life, the parenthesis is being removed, at least being so rubbed out that there are only faint traces of it left. For centuries to come, there may be remnants of that parenthesis in the lives of all of us, but it will not be such a hard and fast parenthesis that it imprisons us in mortality, that is, in a material concept of life.

Every meditation that results in an inner response hastens the fading out of the parenthesis. Every experience of depth in meditation makes us less subject to the limitations of the parenthesis, less subject to the calendar, to climate, and to the changing economic conditions of the world.

One of the evils of living inside the parenthesis is that we resist change. As long as our particular parenthesis is halfway comfortable, we want to live in it. It does not even have to be a healthy or wealthy parenthesis so long as there is enough for survival and the pain is not too severe. But while human nature resists change, spiritual unfoldment compels change, breaking up the old patterns continuously. In fact, spiritual progress demands that every form be broken, no matter how good it is. No matter how comfortable life may be, Spirit will not let us rest in some degree of finiteness, even if that finiteness should be what the world calls a million dollars or its equivalent. To Spirit, that is still finiteness, and Infinity does not mean that Spirit is going to give us two million: it means that It is going to give us greater freedom, greater harmony, and increasingly less dependence on material forms and limitations.

Advancing evolving consciousness would ensure an improved state of affairs, but that improvement probably will not come, as it should come, as a natural evolution of progress, because human beings are too determined to hold on to what they have, and they will not give up their limitation for something unknown. Human nature tries to hold on to the past, to hold on to present limitations: it is unwilling to break through for something else.

If we were willing to surrender each day what we had yesterday, we would find something better tomorrow, but our very attempts to hold on to what we have takes it away from us by force. The only way in which we can remove the parenthesis harmoniously and without pain is by allowing the changes to come without living in, or trying to hold on to, the past, and by not believing that every change means failure, even though it may temporarily carry with it a lack of some of the material comforts. The spiritual universe has a different set of values from that of the material.

Even death does not remove the parenthesis and put us into the circle of eternal life. The wiping out of the parenthesis is accomplished as an activity of consciousness; it is a "dying" to our humanhood and a "birth" to our spiritual identity. That is not a physical death or birth: it is the "dying daily" and the being reborn of the Spirit of which Paul spoke. It is an act of consciousness.

The parenthesis is human life, and our purpose on this Path is to remove ourselves from the parenthesis while we are here on earth. If we do not do that here, we will still have the opportunity afterward, but the passing from this plane into another experience does not of itself remove the parenthesis and place us in eternity or give us immortality. In fact, if we leave this stage of our experience in a human sense of life, we awaken in a human sense of life in another parenthesis. The other side of the grave is still a parenthesis.

In the degree that we become more and more aware that Spirit is the only power, and that we do not have a separate life or consciousness of our own, but that God constitutes our being, does the parenthesis become lighter—fading, fading, fading. With every spiritual realization that we have and with every meditation that results in a conscious contact with God, the parenthesis is growing fainter until eventually, in the final conscious union with our Source, comes the complete elimination of the parenthesis.

The function of a religious teaching is to lead man to the awareness of his true identity and to reveal secrets of life that have, heretofore, been hidden because human obtuseness has rendered man incapable of understanding the underlying principles of existence. In his unillumined state, man does not realize that in order to prosper and be fruitful he must live in accord with spiritual laws, not in accord with his own will or personal desires. He cannot act as if there were no such laws and then expect to live harmoniously, nor can he escape the operation of spiritual law by attempting to make up his own laws as he goes along.

The great masters who brought forth the original teachings upon which modern religions are built knew that there were invisible laws governing this world, and they taught man how to bring harmony to himself through an understanding of these laws, promising, as the Master did, that those who follow in this Way would bear fruit richly. In other words, they would be working with the laws of life, instead of working in antagonism to them.

In their gross human ignorance, most persons accept the appearance that they have come into this world with nothing. Working from that basis, almost from the beginning, they try to add to themselves. Whether it is a baby trying to take some other baby's rattle away, or whether it is a nation trying to take some other nation's land or industry away from it, most persons live their lives on the assumption that they have nothing, and therefore, they must get something, work for it, plan and plot for it.

Then there are those who reach a stage in which they realize the futility of this constant striving and struggling for the things that perish, things which after they are obtained prove to be shadows. It is at this stage that some persons turn from this seeking for things in the outer realm to a seeking for them from God. That which they have not heretofore succeeded in gathering to themselves by material means, they now hope to get from God. Even though this is only a faint glimpsing of the Path, it is at least an opening wedge because it does turn some people from the expectation that they can get from the material world that which will satisfy to the belief in some invisible Source from, or through which, their good may come. Those who fail to find God an open door to health, wealth, and success are naturally led to seek further for the Way, or to seek the meaning of the Way.

It is not given to a human being of himself to decide when or whether he will enter the Path or the Way, and until the Spirit of God touches a person, he has no interest in finding it, and certainly no inclination to follow it. In the life of every person, however—and not necessarily in this particular lifetime or lifespan—at some time or other he will be touched by the Spirit. He may never know when this actually happens: all he knows is that a curiosity has developed in him, a hunger, or a thirst for something—he knows not what— that drives him forward. It is at such a moment that he enters the Path, and from that point on, it does not lie within his power to decide to what extent he will embrace it, or how far he will go.

Early in his progress, however, he learns that there really are not bad people and good people; there are not sinful people and pure people; there are not sick people and well people: there are only those who do not know the truth, and those who do: the unillumined and the illumined.

Those who are in sickness, sin, or poverty are the unillumined: they do not know their true identity, and they are therefore wandering in the wilderness, seeking for harmony, but seeking for it in the wrong direction. They are struggling for things, for fame and fortune, honestly believing that when they attain these, they will have attained their goal of happiness, peace, and contentment. But do they? Are they not usually in the same misery they were before they attained them? True, they may be enjoying their misery in more luxurious surroundings, but the misery is there nevertheless, and the reason is that regardless of the outer attainment, the inner self is still starving and thirsting.

In his state of unillumined being, each person has a life of his own to live, a life probably destined to be manifested on earth for threescore years and ten—a little less or a little more—a life subject to disease and death, a life that began and must therefore end. This constitutes the unillumined, the human race.

When a person is illumined, however, that is, when he knows the truth of his real identity, he loses all capacity for sin or poverty, and for disease as well; he loses the propensity and the potentiality for evil in his life, but only in proportion to his illumination.

The illumined do not live by laws of limitation, by the law of threescore years and ten, by the laws of good and evil. They live by the Grace and Truth the Christ reveals, not a Grace and Truth separate and apart from the son of God, but a Grace and Truth *as* the life of the son of God. The individual illumined with the understanding of the nature of God and the nature of his own being is no longer the "creature," but is now the son, the heir of God, living under Grace.

Once even the tiniest little crack of insight into the nature of God is opened, the rest comes more or less quickly, because now, instead of blind faith, there is a complete relaxing from mental strife, struggle, and effort in the realization that, since God is infinite wisdom and light, we can rest and let God illumine, instruct, and guide us.

With even a small measure of spiritual illumination must come the realization that God is not to be prayed to and that there is nothing for which we can pray. This first glimmer of light reveals an all-knowing God with a wisdom so great that it would be presumptuous on our part to advise or attempt to enlighten Him.

"The Lord is my light and my salvation." Though I walk in the spiritual darkness and ignorance of the unillumined, this light is with me whenever I open my eyes to behold it.

Even "though I walk through the valley of the shadow of death," this light of life is here with me, and in my moments of darkness, I need only turn within—not beg, beseech, implore, or sacrifice, but quietly, peacefully, and gently turn within: Father, open my ears that I may hear, open my eyes that I may see, for Thou art the light of my life.

The illumined rest in thankfulness that God is light, wisdom, and all-power; the unillumined beg God, plead with Him, and try to enlighten Him as to what they need on earth. This is one of the differences between the unillumined and the illumined.

The unillumined and the illumined are the same person living two different lives. In the absence of illumination, we are individuals with many, many problems, and with unhappy, unfulfilled, incomplete, and unfinished lives, but with our first glimpse of the spiritual life, even though we seem to remain the same person—wear the same size clothes, the same size hats and shoes, and probably even look the same in the mirror—we are not the same: we are living from a different standpoint, with a different experience, and under different conditions.

Regardless of what or who we may have been as an unillumined human being, regardless of the condition of our human sinfulness or purity, lack or wealth, in the moment of our illumination, the past is wiped out, and the new way, the new life, opens.

This way is the acknowledgment of our divine sonship. No matter what appearance touches our life in the form of sin, illness, lack, or unhappy human relationships, the way to surmount these is the way of sonship or oneness, and this way no one can walk for us: it can be walked only by us. Spiritual teachers can be our guides on the Way; they can make smooth our path today or tomorrow, but we alone can take the Way, we alone can live by the Way, we alone can walk the Way. And how is this done? Only by an activity of our consciousness, only by virtue of our consciously knowing the truth of the Way:

"I am the way." By virtue of my oneness with my Source, I am infinite, I am spiritual, and I am under spiritual law which means I am under Grace—not under the laws of matter, but under Grace.

To most of us there seems to be some form of divine Grace missing—with some more and with some less—but what we are dealing with at the present moment is not the appearance, but the way through which appearances disappear, the way through which to surmount the difficulties of the moment, the way through which we are to enter the spiritual kingdom, the way through which we are to seek first the kingdom of God and His righteousness.

Spiritual illumination comes in a moment when "ye think not," but that moment comes only as the result of days, weeks, and years of effort and dedication. Fortunate, indeed, is the student who has a teacher to guide and instruct him as he travels the Way, and to say to him, "This is the way, walk ye in it."

In the early days truth remained hidden from the people and could be found only in schools of wisdom, in monasteries, or in secret societies. The elect did not believe that the people—and when I say the people, I am speaking of people like you and me—would be interested in truth or able to understand it.

There was perhaps some measure of justification at that time for withholding truth from the masses because of the very difficulty of circulating truth-teachings widely. There were no printing presses, and inasmuch as all manuscripts had to be written by hand, there were not many of them available. Reading and writing, too, were skills which even kings had not mastered, and for this reason, if for no other, any kind of study met with almost insurmountable difficulties.

Furthermore, after struggling against great odds and working with only the most primitive of tools to provide shelter, food, and clothing for their families, it is quite understandable why, upon returning home from a day of such labor, the men would be more eager for food and sleep than for study and meditation. The women, also, with their large families and arduous duties would hardly be ready for serious study or have any interest in the deep and abiding things of life.

For these reasons, and probably many others, practically the only place where revealed truth was taught was in the mystery schools that existed thousands of years ago in Egypt and later on in Greece and in Rome. There were also such schools in India, and some of them were found as far north as Tibet. Those of a religious or philosophical turn of mind became the students in those schools or in the religious orders where truth was taught.

In order to ensure against the misuse of truth, a candidate for membership in a school of wisdom was required to pass very rigorous tests and give evidence that he was not entering the school for personal or selfish motives, or with any idea of immediate material gain, but that he was entering it in a sense of dedicating his life to the most High and proving his dedication by service to mankind.

One of the main requirements was that students remain for at least six, seven, eight, or nine years in order to receive instruction, and as they absorbed the lessons taught, they were advanced by degrees. Undoubtedly, in some of these schools, there were teachers of great spiritual wisdom, although it was the mental and the occult realm of thought that received the most attention in those days.

The early Hebrews also conducted religious schools where those with a religious bent were accepted for instruction and eventually became priests or rabbis—some lesser lights and some greater.

At the time of the Master, Judaism was divided into three major sects, the Essenes, the Sadducees, and the Pharisees. Of all these, the Essenes probably had developed the highest degree of spiritual wisdom. The practices of this sect, however, differed in so many respects from those of other groups that it was greatly persecuted and eventually became almost an underground movement. Because of this, and in my opinion, primarily because of this, the Essenes became the most highly organized and disciplined of any of the

Judaic sects. They came to a place where they lived almost entirely by rules and regulations, and the impartation of spiritual wisdom played only a minor part. In fact, for the first seven or eight years of a person's membership in that order, he was not allowed to know any of the secrets of its wisdom. Such an emphasis on discipline, rules, and regulations not only killed whatever inspiration an individual might have brought to a group, but it undoubtedly destroyed any hope he may have had of reaching his goal.

Some scholars believe that Jesus was a member of the Essenes, but parted from them because he felt that truth should be given to the people, whereas the hierarchy felt that the people were not ready for it. It was because Jesus imparted truth to the people, the truth that would have set them free, that he was crucified.

Although the Master did teach this truth, he perhaps recognized that the masses, as such, could not at their stage of consciousness understand it. Probably, he hoped that here and there among them, there would be one or two, a dozen, or a hundred who would be able to perceive the spiritual nature of truth and demonstrate it, and that as time went on these dozens here, and hundreds there, would perpetuate the message and continue to give it to succeeding generations until eventually everyone would have the truth.

Even though the masses could not receive the truth the Master taught, there were many persons who did, and because of that, for the next three hundred years, mighty works were done by those who had become followers of the Master's teaching: spiritual healing continued to be practiced; every person was given freedom of thought; and inroads were made on the dogmatism of some of the Hebrew sects which taught that only the Hebrews were worthy of being given the truth.

It must have been a great struggle for Paul to break through the traditional narrowness of the existing Judaic sects and to begin giving truth to the Gentiles. It must have been a great wrench for Peter to learn that he must call nothing unholy that God had made, and for him, too, to begin preaching to the Gentiles. But when Peter and Paul arrived at the state of consciousness where they were willing to preach to the pagans, and as they began to bear witness to the spiritual truth that there is neither Greek nor Jew, bond nor free, and that we are all one in Christ Jesus, they broke down the barriers of spiritual ignorance.

The moment a person begins to know the truth, he breaks down barriers: he is set free, whether from economic lack, bigotry, bias, nationalistic pride, or from narrow religious convictions. The truth reveals the universal nature of God's love which is bestowed alike on saint and sinner, and is not reserved for those who belong to a particular church.

This truth was in existence thousands of years before Jesus. It did not set many people free, but that may have been because only a limited number were permitted to learn about this truth. Unfortunately, it has not set many free since that time because of mental inertia which is only a polite term with which to describe downright laziness.

Let us face it: we are mentally lazy. The truth is available, but we do not *know* the truth. We *read* it. We read it and say, "Isn't it beautiful!" We hear it, and we say that it is even more beautiful, even more powerful. And then probably we go home and either wish we could make it come true or hope to find a spiritual master who will do it for us. The fact is that it is not going to be done for us by any spiritual master now, any more than it was done by spiritual masters in the days when there were more of them on earth than there are today.

Many years ago this wisdom was taught in the mystery schools, in some fraternal lodges, and in religious orders, but today there are no such schools on earth. Such as do exist on the inner plane are available only to those who have spiritualized their consciousness to the extent that they can find entrance into the spiritual orders which exist behind the scenes, that is, beyond the realm of the human mind. Those who have thus spiritualized their consciousness through knowing the truth make a transition from being the man of earth, described by Paul, to being that "man in Christ . . . whether in the body, I cannot tell; or whether out of the body, I cannot tell."

We are men of earth until we know the truth and demonstrate a sufficient degree of it so that we reach a state of consciousness which is no longer fettered by ignorance, superstition, and fear. In that state of consciousness, we are enabled to penetrate behind the realm of mind into the realm of divine Consciousness, but it takes spiritual illumination to make that possible.

These ancient schools of wisdom had neither silver nor gold to give, neither name nor fame. What they had to offer was spiritual illumination, the transcendental consciousness which would lead the aspirant into harmony, joy, peace, and glory, but not always in the way that he might outline.

In such a school, initiation, which was a significant landmark on the spiritual journey, always took the form of going from darkness to light, from material sense to spiritual consciousness, from the un-illumined state of consciousness to the illumined; and while the method of study, practice, and unfoldment might differ from place to place, and from one era to another, the goal and the result were always the same—the development of a transcendental state of consciousness.

Many different terms have been used to describe the enlightened consciousness. In Christian mysticism, this enlightenment is some-times referred to as Christ-consciousness; in India, the aspirant who has received a measure of spiritual light is said to have attained the Buddha-mind; whereas in Zen Buddhism the term used is *satori*. The terms are different, but the idea is the same.

Whenever an individual attains a very high state of consciousness or what is understood to be illumination, he is said to be enlightened. Each of the great spiritual teachers, Christ Jesus, Buddha, Shankara, received complete illumination and became the light of his particular world.

Illumination really means going from a human state of conscious-ness to a spiritual state of consciousness, the transcendental or Christ-consciousness, which is above and beyond the human. While it is not beyond possibility for any human being to attain this in some degree, it cannot be experienced by the human state of consciousness.

When a measure of light comes to a person, it brings with it new faculties and new experiences. "There are diversities of gifts." Among these is the gift of healing which some enlightened leaders have had; others have had a gift for spiritual teaching, that is, the ability to lift a student above his own humanhood into an enlightened state;

others have received by Grace an inner power of prayer which has enabled them to release many, many persons from their discords and inharmonies.

A case in point, of course, is Moses who, brought up in the social climate of the court and well educated, was just an ordinary person until that one great mountaintop experience when he came face to face with God, received his illumination, and attained transcendental consciousness to the extent that a whole new faculty developed within him. He was lifted to such heights that he was enabled to return to Egypt and, without taking up the sword, to lead the Hebrews right out from under Pharaoh. Under the direction and protection of this transcendental consciousness, he guided them out from slavery, lack, limitation, ignorance, and superstition, across the wilderness until they came into view of the Promised Land, and brought them into some measure of freedom and light, the measure of course being only that of which they were capable at the time.

So it is, then, that this man Moses, with no special or outstanding talents to set him apart from other men, became at that moment of attainment a leader and a liberator of a whole people. Throughout the history of the Hebrews, from Abraham right on up to Christ Jesus, whenever an individual was endowed with the transcendental consciousness, he, too, was given the strength and wisdom to bring a measure of freedom, light, grace, and healing to the people under his care.

Christ Jesus is perhaps the most outstanding example of an attained transcendental consciousness. Very little is known of his early life beyond the fact that he was of a family of carpenters, that he himself worked as a carpenter, that it is believed he was educated in the Essene Order, and that he was trained as a rabbi. Eventually, he went out to preach, but because he possessed gifts that the other rabbis of that day lacked—gifts that even Gamaliel, the greatest of the Hebrew teachers, did not possess—the great gifts of healing and supplying, of leadership, teaching, and of revelation, and because he often preached contrary to the teachings of the Hebrew hierarchy, he aroused its ire.

During this period, and a thousand years or more before it, man learned the hidden secrets of the spiritual life in these schools of wisdom. It should be remembered, however, that the secrets imparted were not the same in every school because when we come to the subject of truth, we find that truth is revealed on two different levels, the mental and the spiritual.

Two types of schools therefore developed side by side: those that taught the power of the mind, and the purely spiritual that revealed how to unfold spiritually and develop the transcendental consciousness. On the level of mind, great works and great feats of magic can be performed, and sometimes this deludes people into believing that they are witnessing God in action, when it is nothing more nor less than the action of the mind.

It is vitally important that every aspirant on the spiritual path should recognize and know the difference between these two approaches. Whatever exists on the material or mental plane of life can be used in two ways, for good as well as for evil. The effects of spiritual or transcendental consciousness, on the other hand, can be only good.

Seeking entrance to the spiritual path is no different today from what it has always been. It must always be, not for the purpose of personal gain, not for a selfish motive of any kind, but only for the purpose of enlightenment.

CHAPTER XIV

"AND THEY SHALL ALL BE TAUGHT OF GOD"

All work on the spiritual path is directed toward the development of a consciousness higher than that of the intellect or human mind. In the beginning, when there was no awareness of good or of evil, man lived out from the divine Consciousness, but after what is known as the Fall of Man, he took unto himself a consciousness of his own. He no longer had an awareness of the Father-consciousness: he now had a mortal consciousness, a consciousness of death, as does everyone who is under the universal belief in two powers. The purpose of work on the spiritual path is to bring about the return to this divine state of consciousness.

In some cases, the impartation of that mind which was in Christ Jesus takes place in an individual when, through some act of Grace within himself, the Master—I am not speaking now of a man: I am speaking of the Master, the divine Consciousness—touches an individual and operates in him without the help of a teacher or without the help of a teaching.

Paul, who received his illumination thirty years after the Crucifixion, had no personal teacher to help bring about the spiritual transformation which took place in him. His religious teacher, Gamaliel, was a scholar with a thorough knowledge of Hebrew theology, but probably with little spiritual awareness, and spiritual power seems to have been completely absent from him. So, this Saul of Tarsus, who had been out on the mission of persecuting and helping to kill Christians, this Saul, one of the most highly educated and trained of religious scholars, but apparently without a trace of the spiritual, received his illumination from within himself without the help of a teacher or of a teaching on the outer plane.

Paul may have received his teaching and illumination directly from the Spirit of the Christ Itself, but it may well be that because of his identification with the Judaic movement in the days of the Messiah, he attributed his illumination to the man Jesus who may have appeared to him and taught him. It may even have been that the consciousness of Jesus actually was there as the instrument of this illumination, just as in the case of John who claimed that he was taught by Jesus Christ, and this fifty years after Jesus had been crucified.

Gautama the Buddha went from teacher to teacher for at least seven years, and some say more; and while he must have absorbed something from each one, it was only after he departed from all teachers and began to draw upon the resources within himself that he had the experience of complete illumination under the Bodhi tree.

Without the aid of human teachers or teachings, these men undoubtedly all received their illumination through their own inner devotion to the search for truth, and they are all in agreement that without this illumined mind, man is spiritually nothing: with it he is spiritually everything.

There are two ways of receiving instruction leading to illumination, but always that instruction involves a progressive unfoldment and is by degrees. One way is by direct impartation from God to the consciousness of the student, the way Gautama, Jesus, John, and Paul attained it. The other way is through a teacher and his teaching, whether by direct contact or through his writings. In either case, if the instruction is truly spiritual in nature, it is God revealing Itself.

Bringing about some degree of development of that mind which was also in Christ Jesus has for centuries been the activity of teachers working with students; and these students, through learning and applying specific truths, plus the contact with the teacher's consciousness, gradually take on spiritual light and spiritual power until they finally attain the ultimate.

No one can attain spiritual illumination by choice. If that were possible, probably those with the greatest financial resources would be the first to receive it because if they were interested in finding God they could search out a spiritual teacher and arrange to have him give them all the instruction needed until they reached the goal. Spiritual illumination, however, cannot be bought with money.

No teacher ever chooses a student for any human reason: because he has money, time, or because he may be a good friend. The teacher knows the consciousness of the student and leads him on, and on, and on, watching and waiting for the signs that indicate that there is now a preparedness not only to receive the divine Grace but also the capacity to continue in It.

Unless a person is one of the few able to receive Grace without a human teacher, undoubtedly there comes a time when it is necessary for him to be in the physical presence of his teacher. It is said that when the student is ready, the teacher appears. This does not mean when the student thinks he is ready; it has no relationship whatsoever to what the student thinks. It means when the student is actually ready.

But how will the student know when he is ready? When the teacher appears and taps him on the shoulder. Until then, a student has nothing to do but abide within himself, perfect himself, accept whatever guidance is given to him of which he feels a rightness, and then pray that his day of illumination will come. This day the teacher will recognize before the student does, and usually the teacher is standing by waiting for the student to look up. There comes an experience which in human life is called love at first sight, and that is what happens when the teacher recognizes his student, and the student recognizes his teacher.

It is possible that sometimes a spiritual teacher may misjudge the readiness of the student. Certain it is that Jesus miscalculated the readiness of about twelve of his disciples, but he took those who were most nearly ready, and he did not do too badly with them. Two or three of them turned out fairly well, and that is a good percentage. We must remember that he came in contact with only a limited number of people, many of whom were ignorant, illiterate, and certainly untrained in spiritual matters. Had they all been Essenes, probably his disciples might have accomplished more than they did, but they were not.

It is difficult, almost impossible, for any teacher to say, "You are perfect. You are going to attain the full selflessness." The best that a teacher can do is to sense that a student is ready, not necessarily that he is going to fulfill himself or that he is going to attain the heights of spiritual realization, but that he shows forth all the qualities necessary for attainment, and from then on, it is up to the student whether or not he can attain.

At this point the teacher gives the student all that he has to give, and then it rests with the student to what extent he will be able to complete the journey. No teacher can complete that journey for a student: the teacher can only take the student, lift him, bring him to discernment, and, at a specific time when so instructed from within, confer the initiation. From then on the student, working with the teacher, can go forward, but whether he attains the full measure in this lifetime is something no one can foretell.

The giving and receiving of spiritual instruction is a sacred act and one which must be undertaken by both the student and the teacher with the utmost dedication and consecration. Real spiritual instruction begins only when the student is able to turn to God with such receptivity that he can hear Him speak to him, or when the student has found his teacher or his teaching and comes into the presence of that teacher or teaching with no questions, with no desire but one: Reveal truth to me.

The proper attitude of the student is one of sitting at the feet of the master, not with questions, but almost with a pleading, "Give me an understanding of God! Reveal God; reveal Truth." As the student sits in quiet expectation, confidence, and assurance, the teacher is able to let the word of God pour through his consciousness, and then it is not a teacher talking, not a man or a woman, but the very Spirit of God.

In the Orient this kind of teaching was known long, long centuries before the Christian era. In this system there is a spiritual teacher who has attained some measure of spiritual wisdom—some more and some less—and who by sitting quietly in his cave, in his mountain retreat, or by the riverbank gradually attracts those individuals who feel drawn to him. These, then, become his student body. They will sit around the teacher, come back day after day for a session, and sometimes remain for two, three, or four nights and days, or for years, sleeping outdoors if necessary, until some measure of light begins to dawn in their consciousness.

There are other teachers in India who have founded ashrams or have established small temples or places of worship where students can come to them, led there by an inner impulsion. There is no advertising, of course, nor is there ever any reaching out for students. People sometimes travel thousands of miles just to spend a week or two with a particular teacher. Some students come and remain with the teacher for many years because today, in spite of radio and television, there are people, particularly in the Orient, who know that truth cannot be imparted or absorbed over a busy weekend, and they therefore find it quite normal and natural to spend from three to seven or more years with their teacher.

When the student comes into the presence of a spiritual teacher, if he has prayed earnestly and sincerely to be led to his teacher or teaching, he will be in the presence of one who has little knowledge to give, but one who, because of his hours of meditation and attained conscious union with God, will be such a transparency that the Spirit pours through him either in words, thoughts, or in complete silence. In whatever form the instruction is given, however, if the student is receptive, he will receive the impartation. So the work is primarily meditation, with occasional impartations of truth from the teacher which the student can use in his meditations until he attains a degree of awareness of some of these truths.

If the student's mind is in a state of questioning and disputation, if he doubts or has not yet recognized his teacher, he cannot accept spiritual instruction from him. Truth can be received only when the student reaches that deep humility which is willing to admit, "I am empty; I know nothing. Fill me." Then when he comes into the presence of his teacher or finds his teacher's writings, he will be prepared to accept the teaching in humility and without argument, just as we have been prepared to accept the teaching of the Master, not because there is the authority of Christ Jesus behind it, but because something within tells us that this is the truth and we must follow in this way.

No aspirant on the spiritual path should ever be influenced to follow a spiritual teaching simply because his friends have embraced it, are enthusiastic about it, or because it appears to be successful or popular. That has nothing to do with him.

No one should ever be in a hurry to choose his teacher or his teaching. Rather should a person wait until he has such an inner conviction that he has found the right way for him that there is no turning back. Then, when it is revealed to him that this is the way for him, he will follow it even if it is a very difficult one.

When a student finds his spiritual teaching, he should thereafter give up all others, and be as true to that teaching and the teacher as he expects the teacher to be to him. A student has a right to expect from his teacher complete and utter devotion to God and also all the assistance he can give to the spiritual unfoldment of his student; but the student must give that same devotion to God, to his teacher, and to his teaching, abandoning all others and clinging only to the one.

No one should try to ride two horses in the same race. It has never been successfully accomplished. The Master warned that there are many, many persons taking upon themselves the Robe and setting themselves up as the Christ who are not "Christs" at all. There are many teachers parading under the banner of truth who have no understanding of, or relationship whatsoever to, truth. No one can tell another who these are. The student himself will have to be led of the Spirit to find out whether the teacher with whom he is working is "he that should come."

When John the Baptist questioned whether Jesus was the Promised One, Jesus' answer was, "Go and shew John again those things which ye do hear and see: The blind receive their sight, and the lame walk, the lepers are cleansed, and the deaf hear, the dead are raised up, and the poor have the gospel preached to them." That is the only proof that can be given.

Nobody can decide for another which teachers and which teachings are true or false. Each one has to stand within himself and measure whatever is offered to him against what he witnesses as demonstrable truth. By the fruitage of the teaching and by the life of the teacher, each one will have to determine which teaching is for him, but no one should attempt to work with two, three, or four teachings at the same time. The Master called upon his disciples to leave their nets—leave their past, leave everything of which they were convinced, leave everything behind them—to follow him, and he would make them fishers of men.

When a person goes to God, it must be with complete surrender and a complete yielding. At first that is not possible because everybody has some religious convictions, even if his convictions are atheistic ones. The student who turns to truth discovers that many of his former beliefs were erroneous man-made teachings or interpretations of teachings, and that he has followed them only through blind obedience and ignorance. Then when he comes to the truth, he is shocked to discover that he cannot continue to accept some of his most cherished beliefs because, to his enlightened sense, they are not true. Some of these he is able to surrender easily, but to others he will cling with unswerving tenacity.

The surrender of all that the student has held most sacred oftentimes takes place against his own inner convictions, against the faith and beliefs that have been stored up for years and years. These he finds difficult to relinquish, and so he continues to attempt to grasp the new while still clinging to the old.

The way of truth is not easy. It is not easy to be a seeker after God because in the end we have to drop all our cherished convictions and come to that new day when we make the great discovery that God is in the very midst of us.

One function of a spiritual teacher is to reveal the principles with which the student must work in order to lift himself in consciousness to an apprehension of the Divine. The Master gave his disciples just such a way when he urged them to pray for their enemies, to pray for those who despitefully used them, to pray in secret, to give alms in secret, and to forgive unto seventy times seven. Jesus' followers were expected to put these teachings into practice, and just as he pointed out certain principles, so today does a teacher of spiritual wisdom receive his own spiritual impartations and reveal them to his students. Such teachings are of no value, however, as long as they are merely impartations from the teacher to the student. They become meaningful and effective only when the student puts them into practice.

Some persons think that reasoning and logic are sufficient for the attaining of the spiritual life, but I learned long ago that no spiritual teaching can be imparted intellectually. The reading of books alone will never give the majority of seekers the real import of a truly spiritual teaching because no one can grasp a spiritual teaching from books unless he is spiritually attuned.

Only through spiritual consciousness can truth be imparted, and it is for this reason that so much time must be devoted to meditation, both on the part of the teacher and of the student. If a student has lifted himself up out of his reasoning, thinking mind into that area of consciousness where his intuitive faculties have full play, then he can comprehend and understand what the teacher is imparting. Otherwise, he is able to hear only with his ear, and in imbibing a spiritual message, hearing with the physical ear is meaningless.

After he has revealed the principles with which the student must work, the second function of the spiritual teacher is to open the consciousness of the student so that a way can be made for the student to reach the center of his own being where God can reveal Itself to him. God is no respecter of persons. God does not choose out of all mankind a Lao-tse, a Buddha, a Shankara, a Jesus, a John, and a Paul and expect all the rest of the world to sit at their feet. No, the world sits at the feet of the enlightened one to learn how he became a light and how it can go and do likewise.

If the student is faithful, a spiritual teacher can open that student's consciousness to a receptivity to the Father within, so that the actual God-experience can come to him. Some persons receive spiritual light very quickly, others more slowly, depending upon the development of the individual: what his background is, how prepared he is to give up the reasoning, thinking, arguing mind, and how willing he is to sit, as it were, at the feet of the master and receive, and receive, and receive.

While there is nothing that can either be asked or answered

through the mind that will enhance a student's spiritual understanding or powers one iota, in the beginning it is natural for students to have questions which, when answered, may in some measure correct any false impressions the student may be entertaining and help clear away some of the underbrush in his consciousness, thereby preparing him for a spiritual experience. The teacher does answer the student's questions, but the continued asking of questions means that the student has not attained that inner awareness, and his attention must be directed, not to having his questions answered, but to going deeper and deeper into consciousness until he comes up with the "pearl."

No spiritual teacher avoids answering questions that will clarify the meaning of the message, but once a student has attained the actual contact with his Source, questions seldom arise. As God unfolds in his experience, he is left without questions, without any doubt about what to do, or why. He is not concerned about understanding what sin is, or about being guided as to what he should or should not do. If he knew of how little importance these things are, he would never let them disturb his thought. His one concern would be to follow the light that is within him.

Since spiritual impartation does not come through the human mind or through the reasoning faculties, the only reason that questions have any place at all in the unfolding of spiritual consciousness is because the hodgepodge of erroneous teachings, which many have been taught from their earliest years, will continue to puzzle them until it is cleared out. The day must come, however, when the student realizes that all his questions, together with their answers, are absolutely worthless so far as his spiritual development is concerned.

Spiritual development comes about through the experience of God, not in questions or answers. Through meditation, the teacher works to elevate the consciousness of the student, and this makes the student free. It is not a matter of knowing or not knowing the answers to questions posed by the human mind: it is a matter of attaining spiritual consciousness. Real spiritual teaching begins when the attitude of the student is: "I have no more questions. All I want now is answers, and I want those from God. I want them to come through inspiration either from my teacher or directly from the Spirit of God within me."

Up to the time that such answers are received, the student must satisfy his mind by asking questions. That is the only method by which he can dispose of his queries, skepticism, and doubt, but he should rid himself of these as quickly as possible and then be done with that phase of his spiritual journey, which is only the pre-beginning stage. Even the beginning of spiritual wisdom is not attained until the questions are out of the way and the student is completely emptied and pleads, "The past is passed. I am not even interested in what I heretofore thought or believed. I do not care about answers to questions: I care only about the God-experience. Fill me; fill me with spiritual wisdom; fill me with the presence and power of God."

With that attitude, the student has entered the beginning stage—the First Degree. From then on, by the grace of God which has been given him, the teacher can impart not only spiritual wisdom, but spiritual consciousness. Sooner or later, the way opens so that the student will receive his own impartations from within. The same light that has come to every mystic can then come to him; the same truth that has revealed itself to every mystic can then reveal itself to him. Truth in its essence is the same, but it comes in different language and in different degrees to each and every person.

Truth has come to hundreds of people, but it always comes through an individual. Just as God spoke through Gautama the Buddha, Lao-tse, and Shankara, through Jesus, John, and Paul, so God can speak through the words of any God-realized person, and when the student himself has made the God-contact, truth will come through him.

The teaching that is imparted without words and without thoughts is the only absolute teaching there is. There have been students in The Infinite Way who have been able to receive such teaching, and when that happens there are long periods of complete silence in which no word is spoken, and none thought, and yet the message is conveyed to them.

There does not have to be any conversation between teacher and student because there is an area of consciousness which is really an area of impartation, so that without speech and without thought whatever communication is necessary between the student and the teacher will take place. It is not necessary to speak or to think when two people are attuned, but they cannot be attuned by having something in common humanly—only by knowing that *I AM*.

When no personal sense enters, either in imparting or receiving, that is absolute teaching. It is accomplished entirely on the spiritual plane. When the Absolute is reached and the student rises with the teacher into divine Consciousness, the human sense of truth drops away.

The spiritual teacher is not a mentalist. He never intrudes into the mind of his student, nor does he ever try to influence his student's thought even for good. The teacher's work is the purely spiritual work of making contact with God, and then letting it appear to his students as it will.

The ultimate destiny of a student has to be realized in his own consciousness. True, he may avail himself of a teacher, of a teaching, or of books. Books, of themselves, however, will not make his demonstration: they are merely tools or instruments for his use as he goes into his periods of contemplative meditation. When he is in prayer and communion in that inner sanctuary within himself, there the transition takes place, the Word is heard, and ultimately the indissoluble union is revealed.

If the teacher is in conscious union with God and the student is attuned to the teacher's consciousness, sooner or later the student will have some kind of an experience. It may be an experience in which he has an actual realization of the presence of God. If he is a Christian, it may result in his recognizing a presence that he identifies as Jesus Christ; if he is a Buddhist, he may identify it as Buddha; but it is the same Consciousness appearing as different forms. Even though It appears as a person, It will be God appearing, and what the student has done is merely to translate the appearance into what most nearly approaches his idea of a spiritual teacher.

The spiritual teacher makes conscious contact with God, and then if the student is sufficiently attuned, that conscious union may on occasion appear to his student as a mystical experience in which he will behold some form of Reality that he will translate in accordance with his own state of consciousness.

Through the God-contact of the teacher, the student receives the God-experience and his illumination, but no teacher can do this for, or to, a person by willing it, desiring it, or trying to make it come about through any mental means. This will only thwart it and can lead to danger.

Truth imparts itself through the teacher-consciousness, and when the student is receptive, that teaching is received, but because the instruction is not received in the mind, but in the Soul, the student would not be able to pass a rigid examination on it. The only way to know whether or not he has received it is that the light is shining in his face, and the fruits of the Spirit are appearing in his experience.

Within the consciousness of each one of us there is a something. It is impossible to reveal the true nature of it, except to explain that to me it seems as if it were a tightly closed bud, almost like a fresh new rosebud. As students come to me, I can sometimes feel that something in them, that tight little bud in their consciousness, and I know it is their spiritual nature, the Christ or the divinity of them.

In Oriental teaching this is symbolized by the lotus. As the lotus opens, it represents a greater degree of spiritual illumination, and this can be observed in all Oriental art where figures representing attained spiritual consciousness are depicted as either sitting or standing in the middle of the open lotus. Spiritually interpreted, that means that they are rooted and grounded and established in the divine Consciousness.

Often I see this little bud in the consciousness of an individual, and as the relationship of student and teacher continues, I can watch as it opens and unfolds until it is a full-blown flower.

Some of us may not humanly have a spiritual teacher or even know of one, but inasmuch as no spiritually illumined person has ever passed from Consciousness, all the great spiritual lights of the past are still functioning, and they are just as available to you and to me as is a teacher living on this plane right now. There are many persons who have contacted a teacher within their consciousness without ever having had a teacher on the outer plane. This does not mean that they have achieved their spiritual light of themselves. No one can do that. The light is awakened in them by someone who is the light, whether or not they contact him in the human experience or are even aware of his existence.

Should it be necessary for us to find a teacher or even to contact some teacher on the inner plane who could be an instrument for bringing this wisdom to us, he will appear. When we are in meditation, we are tuning in to the *I* that we are, the Source, and receiving whatever is necessary from that Infinity. It may be that right from the pure Source Itself wisdom comes, unfoldment and revelation. Sometimes it leads us to a book in which we find what we have been seeking, but that is only because we are not yet fully attuned to receiving it directly from the Source. There are other times when the great spiritual lights of past ages serve as teachers to us. God never brings the activity of the spiritually illumined to an end, and that spiritual illumination is available now and is operating on earth, inspiring, teaching, and helping all those who are turning to God.

For example, today I am a teacher revealing truth, but if tomorrow I should do what we call "die" and my physical presence should leave this world, that would not remove me. My *I* would still be here. What is done with my body would make very little difference because the *I* of me would still be here and could still teach if only those reaching out for that teaching can realize that there is no death and that we are separated from physical sight but not from actual communion.

If we truly believe in deathlessness, we know that Lao-tse, Gautama, Jesus, and John are still functioning, but because we cannot be aware of anything outside our consciousness, the only place they can function is in our consciousness: they cannot be up in heaven and they cannot be out in space. It is perfectly possible, therefore, for any great teacher to be our teacher until such time as we have complete access to the Source and Fount Itself without mediation.

Many persons receive impartations in this way without even knowing that they have a teacher because all teachers do not announce or reveal themselves: they merely work through the consciousness of the individual in a completely impersonal sense. Whether we are touching the *I* Itself or whether there is mediation is of no importance. If the impartations are coming *through* a teacher, they are coming *from* the Source—not *from* the teacher, only *through* the teacher. No teacher could be a teacher if he were not one with the Source.

There is an invisible bond connecting us with every spiritual being, person, activity, thought, and thing in the entire world. Through the realization of that, we are instantaneously at-one with the spiritual consciousness of those who have lived throughout all time. We are instantaneously at-one with the spiritual consciousness of everyone functioning on earth, and of all those who have not yet been born.

Everyone exists here and now. But where is here? Are we talking about a room or about consciousness? The *I* of us is not, and never can be, in a room. The room in which our body is, is in our consciousness. That is what makes us aware of it. So, if we are attuned to the inspired masters of all ages, we have them with us at this moment in our consciousness.

On this point hinges a tremendous revelation: we are never alone. Just as we attract to ourselves the companionship we deserve at any given moment, so in our invisible life there is companionship. As Jesus could tabernacle with Moses and Elias whom he looked upon as great teachers and spiritual seers, so do we today have those who are our companions on the spiritual path. You have yours, and I have mine—if so be we awaken to the realization that none of these has died, that our own is with us, and our own teacher is within us. Your teacher may be a man or a woman living in this particular parenthesis, or your teacher may be an invisible Presence and Power. Such is the mystical life.

This communion is always with a divine state of consciousness, not with a human consciousness existing on another plane. Regardless of how many generations have elapsed, the possibility of contact exists because merely possessing a different form would not change the situation. We are not limited to a body; we exist not as a physicality, but as the *I* that we are, that *I* which we know ourselves to be.

If I wish to commune with you, I have to close my eyes, shut out the appearance, and go deep down within my consciousness. There I find the *I* that you really are—the Soul, the divine child of God, the *I* that lives in the bosom of the Father and has never left the Father.

We do not have to go any further than to turn to the *I* within to receive impartations of truth and of wisdom from the Source because that *I* is one with the Source. In the very chair where we are sitting are both the Father and the Son—God the Father, and God the Son. We have only to turn within, and the *I* which is the Father begins to reveal Itself, Its truth, Its wisdom.

Then if these impartations do not come in the form of words or thoughts, it makes no difference: they will still appear as effect. We may have no awareness that anything has taken place, but as long as we have gone within and made ourselves a state of receptivity, we can be assured that something is going to happen in the visible.

Let us never forget that we do not have to go out searching for masters, or turning round and round in our mind trying to find them. What we have to do is to seek the kingdom of God, to desire God-consciousness and God-awareness, and if this is to come to us through the God-inspired, they will find us. It may not even be necessary that we know the identity of those who are destined to guide us. There are many inspired and illumined men and women on earth who are totally unaware of that identity or of the individual source of their inspiration and strength. Others are consciously aware of specific identities, but I have never known of one who had this awareness who sought it. It was the grace of God that brought it to him.

If we seek illumination from any being less than God, we certainly can be led astray into idolatry. But if we seek it of God, and it comes through an instrument of God, through one illumined of God, there is no idolatry in that, and there is no personalizing of it. If we understand that masters are merely those individuals who, by their spiritual preparedness, have been illumined of God, we will not worship them: we will appreciate them and be grateful to them for being instruments through which God appears to us. If we see them as something separate and apart from God, however, we may make the mistake of worshiping them as masters, and that can lead to trouble, just as if we were to worship human teachers on this plane instead of understanding what their function is and what makes them teachers. Teachers are not teachers because of themselves: they are teachers because of a preparation that has been going on over many lifetimes and has made of them transparencies through which God, Truth, can be revealed to human consciousness.

When we understand teachers in that light, we will be grateful to them for the life they lead, but we will never go so far afield as to worship them; and when they pass from our personal experience, we will not feel that truth has been taken from us. Rather will we understand that from then on, truth will come either directly to us from within our own being, or if we have not yet reached that stage, another teacher or master will find us.

So whether our particular teacher is on this plane or another, we can understand him correctly only if we understand that he comes to us as an instrument through which God, Truth, can reach us. Then if perchance we become aware of someone acting as an instrument from another plane and if through that contact the fruitage is good, we need not fear it, but welcome it. If, on the other hand, we find ourselves touching a realm on another plane made up of good and evil, we can know that we have touched only the human plane, whether here or there.

The real teacher knows that I was before Abraham, and that I will be with him until the end of the world. That we are unable to see this teacher or this I with our human eyes makes no difference because I is not a physicality: I is Spirit; I is consciousness; I is life eternal, and if we can understand that, then where the I of the teacher is physically will never concern us, for that I will always be where we are, unto the end of the world, unto the end of time. I will be where we are, but inasmuch as the I of the teacher is the I of us, we can have that individualized I with us wherever we are by knowing that the I of our being is where the I of the teacher is: we are inseparable and we are indivisible.

At a certain moment, when all the necessary requirements have been fulfilled, the light of the teacher's consciousness illumines the student, and then the student comes into the full awareness of his true identity and has a transcendental experience. When that takes place, the student is as free and independent as the teacher, and is in the full and complete realization of his true identity and of the identity of every man, woman, and child in the world.

Through this developed spiritual eye, we see the heart of an individual and the heart of nature: the heart of a leaf, of a flower, and even the heart of a stone. There is no such thing as dead matter. Everything there is lives and breathes, and everything there is has a soul. There are souls in stones, and there are souls in trees, but these souls are the one Soul interpreted at different levels. Seen materially, a stone is a stone. Seen mentally, a stone can be a weapon. Seen spiritually, a stone is really a little spark of God—a jewel, a gem—and strangely enough, it is incorporeal: it has form, structure, color, and beauty, but it does not have density. So with a tree: a tree has form, light, beauty, color, grace, but it has no density when perceived through the transcendental consciousness.

No man of himself can bestow the Holy Ghost upon another, but as an instrument of God, the teacher becomes the transparency through which God reaches human consciousness, elevates and purifies it, lifts it from the stony soil into the barren, and from the barren into the fertile.

CHAPTER XV

SELF-SURRENDER

Students setting out on the spiritual adventure often labor under the misapprehension that they are going to mount up on to Cloud Nine, Ten, or Eleven and not come down to earth at all except perhaps to help a few of their neighbors. But it does not work out that way, although at first there may be for them an "adding to" kind of experience.

The spiritual path is a way of sacrifice; it is a giving up, a surrender. If we can picture the Master saying to his disciples, "Leave your nets," or the disciples, the apostles, and the two hundred going about carrying the Christ-message far and wide, yet taking no thought for their life, depending upon neither purse nor scrip, suffering persecution and later on death itself, we can begin to realize that the way of the Christ is not a way of getting, but of givingness: it is a way of surrender.

Usually the metaphysical student does not come to a truth-teaching to surrender or to give up anything. His primary thought is on what he will get out of it, and while there should be no criticism or condemnation of those who are on that level of consciousness, it must be recognized that getting has nothing whatsoever to do with a spiritual teaching.

It is true, however, that the first year or two of study does result in a considerable amount of getting for most students. Their personal lives begin to be adjusted; harmonies come into their experience: greater health, sometimes a greater supply, and nearly always a greater sense of peace.

A year or so later they run into a little trouble: the ego comes into the picture as students begin to realize that in order to attain spiritual grace they are called upon to surrender all human qualities, desires, and passions—not only their evil ones, but also traits labeled by the world as good. Many cherished things have to go out the window when the Spirit comes in. Many comforts have to be relinquished, and this is the period when even physical difficulties may arise.

The human body has within itself the potentiality of discord and disease, and if it is left to itself, these errors would just continue multiplying until they became serious enough to cause pain. Under a program of two or three years of very serious spiritual work, however, these errors are not permitted to lie dormant: they are roused up.

It is not only physical discords that lie dormant in most persons, but the ego itself because in many cases it has had very little opportunity to receive any attention. Those who have known little of honor and glory and who often feel like nobodies, which really all of us are as human beings, suddenly begin to blossom and find themselves in the midst of activities heretofore unknown. Then it is that the dear little ego is fanned and begins to feel important. With that comes the period of rebellion—the inability of the ego to maintain a proper perspective—and a period of struggle ensues.

In other words, during this second, third, or fourth year of very serious spiritual study, we can expect the worst of us to come to the surface, whether it is a physical worst, a mental worst, or even a moral worst. In many different ways the early years are troublesome ones because, if the temptations that come are not wisely handled, we can find ourselves, not only like Lot's wife looking back at the city, the state of consciousness, that she had left, but also walking back to those cities, to those places of outgrown consciousness which we have long since gone beyond. The goal looks so far away that we may become discouraged and decide to turn back. It is in these years, therefore, that we need to watch ourselves most closely to be sure that we are not overcome by our problems or by the situations that face us, but that we continue moving forward.

During this period of unrest, doubts and questions come to our thought: Am I on the right path? Is this my way? If we could but remember the changes that have taken place in our life or if we could just recall the blessings that we have witnessed in the lives of others on this Path, we would know that regardless of what may have happened to us, this is still the way. Unfortunately, in this period of doubt, most persons forget all the evidence they have had over the years which should have been sufficient to prove to them that this is the way for them.

And so it is that at this point those of us who aspire to the spiritual life must remember that the goal of the Spirit is not more or better matter. The goal is not merely adding more material good, not doubling or quadrupling our income, or turning a sick body into a well one. If, however, we believe that those things represent the goal and that judging by appearances we have failed to reach that goal, we may be tempted to leave the high road and turn away from what our real goal should be.

The spiritual path leads to God-realization, to God-government and God-control. Along the Way, and as a result of our progress on that Way, healings come to us: physical, mental, moral, financial, and healings also of discordant human relationships. These, however, are not the goal: they are but the added things. At some point in our experience they may serve as a temporary proof of the rightness of the Path, but in the final analysis they never are, because "neither will they be persuaded, though one rose from the dead." But these healings, nevertheless, do serve a purpose, and a good one, and they are necessary to the fulfillment of the teaching of Jesus Christ.

"I am come that they might have life, and that they might have it more abundantly." That is the promise, but there are footsteps leading up to the fulfillment of that promise, and these are some-times very, very hard, primarily because of the surrender that is necessary.

For the person who is merely seeking more harmony in his daily life, however, this surrender is not necessary. A little reading or an occasional call upon a practitioner or a teacher will give him sufficient help to make him comfortable so that he can go along avoiding most of the discords of human life, and leave the ultimate working out of his salvation to some future time, perhaps even to some future life. But for those who cannot rest in that, for those who have felt the son of God in their breast and who have had their footsteps turned to a spiritual path, there is no such thing as being satisfied with a little physical comfort, mental and moral stability, or financial security. There has to be the pressing onward to the ultimate goal, and that is where the surrender comes in.

We must surrender all desire to the *one* desire: to see God face to face, to know Him, and to let the will of God be made manifest in us. There must come the complete surrender of our personal selfhood, so that the Spirit of God can fulfill Itself in us in accordance with *Its* will, not with ours.

It is the will of God that we have life eternal; it is the will of God that we bear fruit richly. As a matter of fact, the Christ is planted in our consciousness for one reason, and one only: that we might be at peace; that we might have life and have it more abundantly; that if we are blind, our eyes may be opened; if we are deaf, our ears may be unstopped; in other words, that the grace of God fill us with an infinite abundance of spiritual good. Christ Jesus said not one word about using the spiritual path as a goal to acquire palaces and kingdoms and earthly treasures. Rather did he say, "My kingdom is not of this world."

The student of spiritual wisdom must pray, not for the kingdoms of this world, not for "the four temporal kingdoms." One of the reasons for our discontent is that the four temporal kingdoms have not been fulfilled in us as we had hoped they might be, and now we are being called upon to surrender our desire for those kingdoms—for the things of "this world," for the things for which we have heretofore prayed. Our goal must now be the purely spiritual one of attaining the kingdom of heaven.

The kingdom of heaven is a state of great peace and harmony; it is a place of many mansions where everyone is a master, and there are no servants. What a strange kingdom! A place in which there are all these great wonders, but no servants to take care of them. Each one is a master, and each one is his own servant. Unfortunately, however, some persons believe that heaven is a place where they will be masters with servants to wait upon them. It must come as a shock to many to realize that in their spiritual ongoing, there are no places of honor, greatness, or fame; there are no kings and princes; there is no upper ten or lower five. All these are one in Christ Jesus: there are no greater and no lesser. There is only a complete dependance on the Spirit of God.

There is a Spirit of Christ, and It will raise up our mortal bodies; It will be the bread and the wine and the water to our experience; It will take us out of those empty years of the locusts. There is a Spirit, but there is a price to be paid for It—a surrender. Spirituality cannot be added to a vessel already full of materiality. We cannot add the kingdom of heaven to our personal sense of self; we cannot attain the kingdom of heaven if there is an inordinate love of personal power, a love of glory, a love of name or fame, or a desire merely to show forth the benefits and the fruitage of the Spirit in the form of better human circumstances. Our vessel must be empty of self before it can be filled with the grace of God.

The Master Christ Jesus washed the feet of his disciples, touched the lepers, and served in any and every way to show that it was not he, himself, who had power, but that it was the grace of God that was operating through him, not a Grace in him alone, but a Grace that would operate in all those who were willing to leave their nets and empty themselves of self.

When a person realizes that it is impossible for him of his own self to do any mighty works, impossible even to have enough understanding to heal a simple headache, then, and then only, does he become an empty vessel through which the Spirit of God can do Its work on earth. It is when sitting humbly and completely aware of one's inability, even to know how to pray, that the Spirit of God can function and perform Its miracles on earth.

The Spirit of God is ever-present to lift us up out of our every infirmity, but it has to have a human consciousness to use as an instrument. There had to be a Jesus Christ to perform those miraculous and instantaneous healings in Galilee. There had to be disciples to carry on the healing work. God always acts through an individual consciousness, just as He acted through Moses, Elijah, and the disciples, and as He has acted through the mystics, metaphysicians, practitioners, and teachers of these later days. God operates through the instrumentality of individual human consciousness when individual consciousness is purged of its desire for self-glorification, for self-profit, or for whatever it is that "the four temporal kingdoms" represent to a person.

When we come to the point of serving as practitioners or teachers, we shall have to be courageous and completely purged of any personal sense because we will undoubtedly offend many of the very persons whom we wish to bless. In this ministry there can be no catering to anyone because of his position, wealth, or fame; there can be no catering to the grosser part of human nature. Every person will have to be brought to the same state of surrender, and, therefore, we may have to "pluck out eyes," "cut off hands," and point out, "This way is straight and narrow, and you either follow in the straight and narrow way, or you will not enter." This Path is not the pathway of popularity. We may make ourselves unpopular because we will be called upon to discipline, to correct, and to teach undeviating principles which the human mind resisted in the days of Moses and of Jesus Christ, and always will resist. The human mind had to have its golden calf even after Moses had revealed the nature of God; it wants a golden calf today because human nature does not like to surrender its golden calves, and the biggest golden calf it has is self—self-indulgence, self, self, self. The human mind wants anything but self-surrender.

Man has to be a hollow emptiness through which the Spirit prays, but when the Spirit prays in and through man, spiritual fruitage takes place in this world. It is the Spirit of God that performs the great healing works on earth through those people who are able to be still and silent, listening ever and always for the voice of the Lord. Into the emptiness inside, the Spirit of God flows, and spiritual fruitage appears.

Certainly in the early stages it may be painful when the Spirit is breaking up the humanness in us; certainly there will be disturbances in our existence. These we must accept with gratitude. This very pain and these very disturbances indicate that undersirable traits, qualities, and conditions are no longer lying dormant within us. Now they are being roused up, rooted out, and if we are faithful we will be purified.

CHAPTER XVI

THE SECRET OF THE WORD MADE FLESH

In the beginning was the Word, and the Word was with God, and the Word was God.

The same was in the beginning with God.

All things were made by him; and without him was not any thing made that was made.

In him was life; and the life was the light of men.

And the light shineth in darkness; and the darkness comprehended it not.

There was a man sent from God, whose name was John.

The same came for a witness, to bear witness of the Light, that all men through him might believe.

He was not that Light, but was sent to bear witness of that Light.

That was the true Light, which lighteth every man that cometh into the world.

He was in the world, and the world was made by him, and the world knew him not.

He came unto his own, and his own received him not.

But as many as received him, to them gave he power to become the sons of God, even to them that believe on his name:

Which were born, not of blood, nor of the will of the flesh, nor of the will of man, but of God.

And the Word was made flesh, and dwelt among us, (and we beheld his glory, the glory as of the only begotten of the Father,) full of grace and truth. JOHN 1:1-14

The Word becomes flesh, that is, the Word becomes the son of God in the consciousness of men. The consciousness of most men is dark so that it cannot receive or believe in the son of God. But to those who can receive, to those who have some measure of spiritual intuition, to them the son of God can come and be received, and because the son of God can be received even by one person in all the world, that makes it possible for all men, for us, too, to become sons of God.

All the mystics of the world have revealed that there is but one Selfhood, one Ego, one infinite Being. God created individual being, individual you and me, in the image and likeness of Himself, not through the act of human conception and birth, but He sent man forth into expression as the showing forth of all that He is and has— and this without any processes.

Because of this spiritual relationship with God, man is one with his Creator even though at some remote time he left his Father's house and decided to be something of himself, thereby becoming the Prodigal. He was not satisfied to share the Father's wisdom, His wealth, and His grace, so when he wandered away from the Father's house, from that divine *I*, he took unto himself the personal sense of "I," trying to make his way by means of his own efforts, wisdom, and strength, but failing—failing miserably. There in essence is the whole story of the human race. It is the story of the "natural man" who is not under the law of God.

That has been the experience of every one of us. Before we understood the nature of God and of individual being, we perhaps thought of God as some far-off being, probably sitting on a cloud or up in heaven, a sort of superhuman Father who rewarded us when we were good—if He happened to notice it—and who punished us when we were evil, which He always noticed. In those darkened days God was a kind of super-Santa Claus, who, if we succeeded in pleasing, might condescend to do something for us, and who, if we displeased, would hold us in some kind of darkness or inflict some punishment upon us.

In that darkened stage we had to rely on ourselves alone for our progress through life, earn our living by the sweat of our brow, go through life subject to all its laws—health, economic, and legal— many of them unsound and unjust, and live under the domination, sometimes of family and sometimes of government. We had no access whatsoever to anything of a spiritual nature that could solve our problems for us or be of any help in an emergency. We were human beings, unenlightened, unillumined; we were in darkness; we entertained a sense of a selfhood apart from God. God was a million light years away, beyond the stars; and in that sense of separation we believed that our sins and those of all our forebears were operating to keep us from God.

In our innermost hearts we felt dissatisfied and incomplete because we had not shown forth the wealth of the son of God, nor the health and perfection of life eternal. Feeling that absence, that sense of separateness and that incompleteness, we reached within ourselves and asked, "O God, where art Thou? Is there a God, or have I been deluded? Is there a supreme Being, or have I been fooling myself in trying to find One?"

This inner pleading testified to the vacuum somewhere within us, and this vacuum cried out to be filled. This vacuum, or sense of separation, may have appeared in us as sin, false appetite, disease, or poverty. What difference the form? However it appeared, it was really a sense of incompleteness, and this brought about within us a longing to be complete and whole. We may have interpreted this as a longing to be healthy, or to have a sufficiency of supply, or as a longing for companionship, but deep within us, our real longing was to be reunited with our Source.

Yet at that very same time this Word made flesh, this son of God, dwelt in us, but was shrouded about with so much darkness that we could not perceive It; we were not aware of Its presence. So in this spiritual darkness, brought upon us by our ignorance of the truth that within us is this Word made flesh, this Light of the world, we struggled by ourselves with whatever measure of human wisdom or human strength we had.

But whether we struggled for a healing or to be free of sin, false appetite, or lack, what we were really struggling for was to get back to our Father's house, to drop this sense of the personal "I," and once more rest in the assurance that we are not a prodigal. In that earnest longing and struggling, this false sense of self drops away,

and greater harmony appears. In our ignorance we call that a healing. It is not: it is the more-appearing of our divine Selfhood.

Paul rightly declared, "Neither death, nor life . . . shall be able
to separate us from the love of God." In reality we have never been
separated from God; we have never been separated from our good,
from our wholeness and completeness; but from the time we were
infants we have been taught about a personal "I," and we have,
therefore, entertained this false sense of self which claims, "I am
Mary," "I am Bill," or "I am Joel," instead of humbly realizing:

*"Be still, and know that I am God." I at the center of me is God,
and therefore, I live by Grace and by divine inheritance.*

To live by that divine inheritance does not mean that we do not
work. There is no provision in heaven or on earth for parasites. Regardless of the material wealth that we may inherit, we cannot sit
by and watch the sun rise and set without working, and in some way
making a contribution to this world.

So it is that even though we are heirs of God and, through our
spiritual realization, do ultimately derive our good from God, we
will work, and work more hours and more diligently than we did
when we were working merely for a living because now we realize
that we cannot manifest God's glory only eight or twelve hours a
day: it takes twenty-four hours every day to show forth God's grace
and God's glory. The whole of life becomes a matter of letting this
spiritual Influence flow through, but because we are united with one
another, everything that flows through from the Father to any one
of us is instantly shared by all of us.

Nothing can come into our experience except through an activity
of our consciousness. It is through our consciousness that we entertain a sense of separation from God, from good—supply, companionship, wholeness and completeness—but it is also through our consciousness, when we consciously make ourselves one with the Source
of all good, that we are restored to this realized oneness with God.

In his consciousness man either lacks or has. Within his consciousness he either separates himself from his good, or he meets up with his good. Whatever it takes, therefore, to fulfill him at his present level of life can come to him only through an act of his consciousness, and that act must be repeated again and again until eventually it culminates in conscious union with God.

Attaining union with God does not usually come at a single bound. It is more than likely to be the result of years of dedicated study, meditation, and service, the earliest stage of which might be called the First Degree. When we come to this First Degree, we begin to learn that there is a God and that we are so much one with Him that He performs that which is given us to do.

As we persist in following the teachings of the Christ, learning to forgive seventy times seven, praying for our enemies, and resisting not evil, we draw closer and closer to the realization of our true identity and the realization of the presence of God within us. But we cannot go into His presence with a cruel and condemnatory attitude toward life: we have to go in gently and peaceably, quietly and confidently, if we hope to hear that still small voice.

Gradually, we attain a conscious at-one-ment with the infinite Source of our being, a greater and greater awareness of Infinity. We become more and more aware that there is a Presence that goes before us to make "the crooked places straight." We feel that we are not alone, that within us there really is this Infinite Invisible. At times it seems almost as if It were within our chest, sometimes as if It might be sitting on our shoulder or standing back of us, but we are aware, even if dimly, that there is a Father, an invisible Presence and Power, and more and more we relax in It. All this is progress in the First Degree.

As we come toward the latter part of the First-Degree-experience, we begin to perceive that we are living more by Grace than by effort, we are living more by a power that is doing things for us without our taking conscious thought, and sometimes doing them before we even know there is a need for them. Something seems to be going before us and changing the relationships between us and the people we meet.

The end result of passing through this degree is the gaining of an absolute inner conviction that where we are, God is, that the place whereon we stand is holy ground, that there is a He that performs that which is given us to do, that there is a divine Grace that provides for our needs, "not by might, nor by power," but by the very gentle Spirit of God that is within us.

In spite of this continuing awareness of a Presence within, there is yet another barrier that separates all men from the realization and demonstration of God: the belief that there are two powers. In the early stages of our study of truth, we seek God as a power because in our ignorance we would like to use God-power over some other power. But the greatest attainment at this stage of our unfoldment is the realization of God as One, not as a power over some other powers, but as the only Power. It is when we begin to come into the realization of God as the only Power that we no longer fear external powers in any form, not even "the armies of the aliens."

In going through the First Degree, a transformation of consciousness takes place, and in proportion as we attain an awareness of God's presence and a realization of the Infinite Invisible, we begin to lose our hate, our fear, and our love of the external world. We no longer hate or fear germs, infection, contagion, epidemics, or accidents; we no longer hate, fear, or love form in whatever variety expressed: we are beginning to attain the realization of the non-power of all form. We do not fear earthquakes, hurricanes, tornadoes, cyclones, or floods: we understand that because of the infinite nature of spiritual Being these are not power. They are the "arm of flesh," nothingness.

Through the building up and strengthening of our realization of God as a Presence, as Law, as Life eternal, and as Peace, we are at the same time losing our fear of all material forms, whether appearing as condition or person. We are beginning to feel as the Master did before Pilate: "Thou couldest have no power at all against me, except it were given thee from above." Through our enlightened consciousness, we perceive that all the evils of this world are but shadows brought about by the universal belief in two powers, and we are losing that belief in proportion as God is becoming more and more real as a Presence and a Power.

The enlightened consciousness is a state of individual consciousness—yours and mine—when the fear and the hate of external forms begin to disappear. Undue love for the things of this world also lessens, although that does not mean that we are not to appreciate the beautiful things of life, experience them, and if it serves any purpose, own them. It does not mean that we are not to enjoy a beautiful home, if so be it is brought into our experience; it does not mean that we are not to enjoy wealth, if wealth comes our way: it means that we are not to be so attached to any form of materiality as to make of it a necessity, a something of importance in our life when it really is but a part of the passing picture.

Losing our hate, fear, or love of the external realm is not achieved by the mouthing of words or the making of affirmations or declarations, but only by the developing of our consciousness through the realization of a divine Presence which in the end we realize to be our own Self, the very *I* of our being.

At the beginning of our spiritual journey we were in darkness, in gross spiritual ignorance; we did not know the truth. Because of this we were living in material consciousness: our whole sense of life was materialistic; everything that we thought of was from the material standpoint; and power was placed in matter or in form, either for good or for evil. We were aware of ourselves as individuals living our own lives, fluctuating between successes and failures, all because we were limited to our own mind, our physical strength, and our personal sense of right and wrong.

One of the first things we learned was that we are not alone, that there is a Presence within us, a Presence greater than anything in the world, a Presence that in the beginning we call *He*, not for any particular reason because this Presence has no gender: It is neither male nor female; It is incorporeal and spiritual; It can never be seen, heard, tasted, touched, or smelled; It is known only as we experience It. We may say that we feel It, but we do not feel It through any sense of touch that we have. More correctly, we might say we are aware of Its presence.

We practice this Presence, which we later identify as God, by waking in the morning and recognizing that God gave us this day, that God rules the day as God rules the night, and that just as God governs all the forces of nature, so does He govern us.

As human beings we are not God-governed, nor are we under the law of God; and for this reason anything can happen to us— anything from slipping in the bathtub to running out in front of an automobile, or picking up a tiny little germ and being laid low in bed and ill for weeks. Anything can happen to us until we become aware of the Presence and begin practicing the truth within ourselves every day.

As we continue in this practice, an inner stillness takes place. We become more quiet within, more peaceful; we have greater confidence in ourselves because now we know that there is Something greater than ourselves working with us, in us, and through us. It may be that we hear the still small voice speak to us as clearly as any person might speak, giving us specific instructions in a language that we cannot possibly misunderstand. Sometimes we are aware of a great light within ourselves, and just the presence of that light changes our entire outer experience.

There are many ways that this Presence can announce and reveal Itself to us, but one way we can know whether it is a true spiritual experience is that there are always signs following. These may be in the form of the healing of some physical, mental, moral, or financial discord. The experience may bring about happier human relationships with others; it may increase our supply; or it may find employment for us. In one way or another, a spiritual experience is always accompanied by signs following—what in metaphysics is called demonstration.

While this process is going on, something else is taking place at the same time. Intsead of putting our entire hope, faith, and reliance on the external world and instead of living by the world's standards of life, we now begin to see that there is a spiritual Something that is of far greater importance than the material. There is a Spirit within us, and it is this Spirit that is playing the most important role in our life.

If some need arises in our experience that involves a sum of money, we do not immediately set about planning, scheming, or figuring out how we can obtain that amount of money, but rather we realize, "Wait a minute! 'Man does not live by bread alone'—by outer effects; man does not live by money alone." Then we drop the problem, and very soon whatever is necessary for its solution comes into our experience. It may cost money, but if so, the money will be provided; or it may even come without the need for money. It is not money that is the need: it is the word of God that is the need, and when the word of God comes, it either furnishes the money, or whatever is necessary without money.

During the days of our dependence on human ways and means, if we were having a physical problem, such as the heart causing difficulty, our whole attention would have been centered on correcting the functioning of the heart; but now, through this practice of the Presence and through meditation, something within says, "Man shall not live by heart alone, by liver, lungs, digestion, or elimination, but by 'every word that proceedeth out of the mouth of God!'" Now we are not thinking in terms of heart, liver, or lungs; we are not thinking in terms of digestion, elimination, or muscles: we are realizing that man lives by the word of God. As a result of that realization, either the organ or function of the body is repaired, or we are able to live comfortably without it.

Through inner unfoldment we learn in this First Degree that whereas before we thought we needed things on the outer plane and our whole life struggle was to attain more of these things, now we relax from that struggle and realize that "man does not live by bread alone."

As we took our first faint steps toward the Kingdom, we were led to this spiritual revelation: "Know ye not that the kingdom of God is within you? Know ye not that ye are the temple of God? Know ye not that the son of God, the Christ, dwelleth in you?"

These words came with some measure of conviction of their truth, and our heart answered, "This is what I believe, or what I would like to believe—that I am not alone in the world, that God has not sent me out into this world and then abandoned me. God has placed me on this earth that I may glorify Him. But how can I glorify God in any way, bound as I seem to be by my sins, my diseases, my false appetites, and my poverty? How can I glorify God in my struggle to survive, in my struggle to provide for my family? How can I glorify God?"

The answer is, "*You* cannot! But if the Spirit of God dwells in you, then you become the child of God, and are heir to all the heavenly riches."

Our first instruction in spiritual wisdom reveals that we are no longer to look up into the skies, and that the hills to which we look for our help refer to the high places in consciousness. When we return to the highest sense of our Self, to the Christ of God that is lifted up in us, we are looking unto the hills. Our vision turns within and upward into that altitude of consciousness where we can discern that the Word has become flesh and dwells in us.

When, in a flash, Saul of Tarsus on the road to Damascus was blinded to his ignorance, to his past, to everything that he had known before, and when all of his former beliefs were wiped out, he became a pure vessel, with his sight restored to him, a sight beyond physical sight—spiritual vision. He recognized that the Light shining within him was the Christ; he knew that the son of God had been raised up in him.

He dwelt alone with this sacred secret, retiring from the world to commune and tabernacle with this Word made flesh within him. He learned to be less concerned with the physical sense of life and its needs, wants, or fulfillments. Now he was lifted up in consciousness, and he was tabernacling in his mind with this Spirit that had been raised up, this Spirit born in the lowly mental environment of the humanly wise, but spiritually ignorant, Saul of Tarsus. And just as Joseph and Mary carried the Babe down to Egypt for several years, so Paul carried his Christ to Arabia, hiding there and letting It grow and develop in him until he himself became so consciously aware of, and one with, It, that just as the old Saul had "died," now the new Paul began to live less and less, as the Christ lived in him more and more.

Finally, the day came when the Christ could speak to Paul, "Begin your ministry. Go out into the world and preach *Me*. Preach to all men that *I*, the Word made flesh, dwell in you, and not only in you,

Paul, but in all those whom you address. Say to every one of them, 'The Spirit of God dwells in you.' And when your friends, the disciples, and others try to caution you to give this Word only to the Hebrews, for the Hebrews are the chosen of God, and only they are worthy to receive this Word, you will suffer their persecution; you will be tried for standing for the truth that the Word made flesh dwells in the consciousness of all mankind, whether Jew or Gentile, whether Christian or pagan. You will carry to the world the universality of the Word made flesh. You will break this bondage to one religion, to one teaching, to one teacher; you will reveal to all mankind that the Word becomes flesh, and dwells in the consciousness of all men, awaiting their recognition."

Paul went out into the world spreading the glad tidings to those of all religious beliefs: "I bring to you the message of the son of God. I bring to you the revelation of the Word made flesh that dwells among you as the Light of the world—as the Light unto your world. I bring to you the revelation that you are children of God. 'Neither circumcision availeth anything, nor uncircumcision,' neither fasting nor feasting availeth anything: you are already the children of God, for the Spirit of God dwells in you."

The Word made flesh is the son of God, or Christ, and It is in the midst of us for the purpose of performing the will of God. In this very moment there is within us the son of God, the Christ, and Its function is to heal and to raise us out of our "dead" humanhood, to restore the "lost years of the locust," to forgive us whatever sins we have committed while in ignorance of our true identity. This Christ is forever saying to us:

I am come that you might have life, and that you might have it more abundantly. Relax! Rest! You have sought Me. I was here all the time, but now you have found Me.

Now you know the folly of sin; now you know the stupidity of it; and now you know something even more important: there is no necessity for sin. No longer is it necessary to steal, no longer is it necessary to bear false witness, to scheme, to plot, or to take unfair advantage, for I in the midst of you am mighty; I in the midst of you am your bread and your supply unto eternity. I am the source of opportunity and of inspiration. I am the light unto your world.

I am the resurrection, and if your body has been wasted away by sin or disease, I will raise it up again. I—the Word made flesh, the Christ that dwells in the midst of you—I am here to raise up your body from the tomb of sin, from the tomb of disease, and even from the tomb of old age.

Do not let even the calendar defeat you, for I am the resurrection, and I am here to resurrect you out of that old body into a body not made with hands, a spiritual body, eternal in the heavens. You do not have to go through physical death to attain this new body: just dwell in the realization of Me in the midst of you! Morning, noon, and night, ponder Me, think on Me, dwell in Me, trust Me, rely on Me.

Know the truth that I am in the midst of you, and I am mighty. I am performing the function of God in you and through you. I in the midst of you am the mediator between you and your infinite Source.

Those things that I receive from the Father, I bestow upon you. The gift of Grace, the strength, the healing power, the redemptive power, and the forgiving power that have been given to Me of the Father, I in turn give unto you. Look unto Me and be saved! Believe in the son of God, and that that son of God, the Word made flesh, the Christ, is in the midst of you.

Since "before Abraham was, I am" here in the midst of you. I will never leave you, nor forsake you. Even if your parents forsake you, I will not forsake you. I will be with you unto the end of the world. I am to go before you to light your way and to prepare mansions for you.

Regardless of the trials or tribulations that face us on our human way, our recourse is to remember consciously the Word made flesh that dwells within us, and Its function. If we slip, Its function is to pick us up again; if we sin, Its function is to forgive us, seventy times seven.

After this truth has been revealed to us, we then begin a most difficult part of our journey because now comes that period when we have to make truth a part of our own being, and bring it to fruition in our individual life. The way to accomplish this is through practicing the presence of God.

Very soon this practice of the Presence becomes second nature to us, and we can hardly draw a breath without realizing that but for the grace of God, we could not draw it. The body of itself cannot breathe; the body of itself cannot stand on its feet. A body, separate and apart from consciousness, collapses and falls down. We cannot live a moment without the conscious realization of the function of this Spirit of God in us.

When the full significance of the meaning of the Word made flesh dawns upon us, and we realize that It is the mediator between God and man, we begin to see that this presence and power of mediation is in our consciousness, and therefore, all that the Father intends for us individually to have is ours by the grace of this realized, raised up son of God in us.

This continued practice of the presence of God leads to an inner silence and stillness, so that the turmoil of the world does not enter in, and when we sit down, we find ourselves in a meditation in which we come into conscious union with God, and we are witnesses now to the Christ that is living our life, beholders of Its glory.

We are no longer living by might or by power; we are no longer living by human wisdom, but by a divine Wisdom that flows out through us in what seems to be a human way. We live now, not by force, but by Grace, as if there were Something always out here knowing our need before we do, and supplying it. This comes about through the unfoldment and revelation that are attained in meditation when we have contacted that inner wellspring of life, that inner force which is our true Selfhood.

In relaxing from conscious effort, struggle, might, power, concern, worry, and fear, the glory of God can be made manifest through our personal life, so that all men may witness it and know that when the Spirit of God is come to individual life, that life becomes one of glory and of service. No one's life becomes glorified that he may go through life sitting on Cloud Nine: one's life is glorified that it may be a service and a dedication to the Creator of all, the Spirit of God that dwells in us.

During the First Degree, we come to the realization that there is this inner spiritual Substance, Activity, or Law, and that It is flowing out through our consciousness, becoming the substance of our new world. The man of flesh has "died," and in a measure that man who has his being in Christ is now beginning to come alive, resurrected from the tomb of material beliefs and risen into the realization of his spiritual identity.

CHAPTER XVII

THE MYSTICAL LIFE
THROUGH THE TWO GREAT COMMANDMENTS

The first stage of our spiritual unfoldment is an experience of coming more and more into a conviction of the Presence and Its availability in all circumstances and conditions. Simultaneously with this growing assurance, we also become aware of how much we are failing to live up to the stature of manhood in Christ Jesus and how far short we come even from measuring up to the Ten Commandments.

Realizing the presence of God and tabernacling with Him awakens us to our failings, and it is at this point that we enter the second stage of our spiritual life. Here it is that we begin consciously to try to live up to the Commandments, particularly those we have most failed to observe. It is not too hard for us to discover the degree of envy and jealousy that may be lurking in us, the bias and bigotry, the little lyings and deceits, the hypocrisies. These all come to light because the more we bring the word of God into our consciousness, the more we expose our own lack of godliness. This forcibly brings to our attention the necessity of developing a greater ethical and moral sense.

In this second stage of our unfoldment, therefore, we earnestly try to live up to our highest sense of right, depending on the presence of God to help us and relying on the inner Invisible to lift us to a higher degree of humanhood. We begin to think more about being benevolent and charitable, and about practicing brotherhood. Not only do we recognize the importance of caring for our own families and those needing help in our community, but we begin to think in terms of people in foreign countries, of aid for the distressed, or of providing education for those who at the moment cannot afford it. We turn our thought in the direction of living for others, helping them, and of bringing about better human relationships between management and labor or between members of different religious denominations. All this is an attempt to make the Ten Commandments an integral part of our daily life.

These Commandments were a part of a code of ethics given to the world by the Hebrews in the form of rules governing their religious conduct. Whether it was something concerning dietary laws, fasts, feasts, rituals, or one's personal life, everything was regulated according to laws which apparently proved so effective that they have been largely carried forward into the present Christian era and adopted by many people, despite the fact that Jesus emphasized only one of the Ten Commandments. To that one he added another from ancient Hebrew teaching, thereby giving the world the great Christian ethic embodied in the two great Commandments:

Thou shalt love the Lord thy God with all thy heart, and with all thy soul, and with all thy mind.
Thou shalt love thy neighbour as thyself.   MATTHEW 22:37, 39

The importance Jesus placed on these two Commandments did not imply that he considered it right and moral to violate the other Commandments—to steal, lie, cheat, defraud, bear false witness, kill, or commit adultery—because those to whom he was speaking understood that a strict adherence to these two great Commandments would naturally make obsolete and unnecessary all the others.

Herein lies the difference between living as a human being under the law and living as the child of God under Grace. In order to appreciate this difference it is necessary to understand why, and how, nine of the Ten Commandments could be dropped from a teaching and yet right and perfect conduct be maintained.

No one can live the Christ-life by willing or desiring to do so. Living this life is not a matter of will because, if he could, everyone would like to live without the temptation of sin or disease, everyone would like to be honest. Until God comes through and makes Itself felt in a person's consciousness, he cannot live by Grace: he must live under the law, and more especially the law of the Ten Commandments. Although living under the Commandments is only a step in human evolution, it is a necessary one in the experience of those human beings who have not yet been touched by the Spirit because the alternative is living in violation of them, and this inevitably leads to destruction.

Living in obedience to the Ten Commandments is very much like living in obedience to city, state, national, and international laws. If we live according to these Commandments, we will be able to avoid most of the troubles that afflict the men and women of this world: we will certainly stay out of jail and we will have more harmonious human relationships. This obedience, therefore, not only makes of us good citizens, but it takes us a step beyond that to the point where we are also good brothers one to another universally, and we thereby bring into concrete expression love and good will.

But now let us see what happens when we begin keeping the two great Commandments in our mind and in our heart, bound upon our arm, and even hanging upon our doorpost. To love God supremely means to place our entire faith, hope, confidence, reliance, and assurance in God, to acknowledge Him in all our ways from rising in the morning until sleeping at night, and to understand and rely on God as infinite Intelligence and divine Love. It is a relaxing into that assurance given in the Twenty-third Psalm, "The Lord is my shepherd; I shall not want," and a resting in it without mental agitation, without fear, doubt, or concern. There is no other way to love God supremely except to place ourselves wholly and completely in Him, under Him, and with Him.

Jesus knew that since God and man are one, there is no way of loving God without loving our neighbor, and the only measure of that love is that it be the same kind of love wherewith we love ourselves. Therefore, to live, doing to no man what we would not wish to have done unto ourselves, giving forth nothing to another that we would not willingly, gladly, and joyously receive, produces an effect beyond that which is involved in humanly loving God supremely and our neighbor as ourselves.

A third factor enters, and this is the great mystery. In loving God supremely and in acknowledging Him as the Principle of our life, the Source of our good, the Substance and the Law of our being, we are being unselfed. We are departing from the materialistic plane of life in which self-preservation is the first law of nature, a law that is completely antagonistic to the law of God and contrary to the spiritual life. The Master revealed that the highest form of life and love is to lay down our life—not to preserve it at the expense of someone else's, but to lay it down in the realization that in losing our personal sense of life, we gain life eternal.

This does not mean that we must let someone kill us, although it does mean that if it were a question of our life or another's, we would be called upon to lose ours rather than take the other's, hard as that may seem. Actually what it means is that in the acknowledgment of God as our wisdom, as our strength and the health of our countenance, and as the life, substance, and reality of our being, we are, by that acknowledgment, giving up a measure of our personal sense of life. There is no other way of finding life eternal than by laying down our personal sense of life.

In the personal sense of life we are almost always confident that any wisdom we express is our own; we are quite certain that the health of our body is ours; we glory in our mental and physical capacities because we believe that they are ours, different and set quite apart from the mind and body of others. On the other hand, as God is recognized as constituting the health of our countenance and the source of our intelligence, guidance, wisdom, and direction, we are thereby providing the necessary atmosphere and consciousness for the awareness and the capacity to understand the mystery of unselfedness.

Similarly, when we love our neighbor as ourselves, we bring about a state of being in which we watch ourselves more closely to see that what we do and think gives offense to no one, and in this connection it must be remembered that it is not merely what we do that may give offense, but even what we think.

Until this past century it was believed that as long as we kept any critical, destructive, carnal, or sensual thoughts within ourselves, we were not harming anybody because these thoughts remained locked up within us. The Master, however, knew, as all mystics know, that this is not true. The thoughts that flow out from us are sometimes more powerful than the physical acts, and it was because Jesus recognized this that he taught that it was not sufficient to resist the act of stealing, but that it was necessary even to give up inwardly coveting anything belonging to another because the nature of what goes on in a person's mind permeates the atmosphere.

It is hardly possible to be in the presence of a mystic or of a spiritually endowed person and not feel a sense of lightness, a joy, or a spiritual uplift. On the other hand, it is also hardly possible to be in the presence of a gross individual and not feel the heaviness, lust, animality, or greed that is emanating from him.

Adopting the attitude of loving our neighbor as ourselves does not mean to be anxious or worried about our neighbor, but it does mean to watch our thoughts and deeds toward him. There, of course, we come to the mystical point of maintaining in our consciousness the truth about our neighbor—the truth, yes, but not the truth about a human being; and here is the line of demarcation: it is not enough to believe that our neighbor is good; it is not enough to believe that our neighbor is our equal, or that our neighbor means well, because none of those things may be true of him.

It would be ridiculous to call certain people good, honest, and spiritual when their actions testify to quite the reverse qualities. Loving our neighbor as ourselves does not mean adopting a Pollyanna attitude and saying to a criminal, "Oh, you are a sweet person, and a child of God"; it does not mean looking upon some of our political figures and trying to realize how gentle and honest they are. All that comes under the heading of stupidity.

To love our neighbor as ourselves means to acknowledge that God is just as much the reality, life, mind, and law of our neighbor as He is of ourselves, whether or not our neighbor knows it or is acting in accordance with it. This does not mean looking at an evil person and calling him good, but it means looking at him and understanding that the same God that is our very being and our very breath is also that close and that near to him. It means to understand that God constitutes the nature of his being as well as of ours. Let it be clear that this does not mean looking at carnality and calling it spiritual; it does not mean looking at mortality and calling it immortality: it means looking through the appearance to the reality.

"If then I do that which I would not . . . it is no more I that do it, but sin that dwelleth in me." So, regardless of a person's degree of sin, we do not claim that he is a sinner, even though at the moment there may remain a sense of sin in him. In this way we are acknowledging God as constituting our neighbor, even those neighbors who do not yet know their identity or that which is the reality of them, or that which could release them from their discords.

We are not trying to live other persons' lives: we are trying to live our own lives in accordance with the two great Commandments. When we accept these as our guide and adopt them as our way of life, we have not only embarked on our spiritual journey but have made some headway on it: we have become followers of the Master and students of the real Christianity, of that which basically constitutes the Christ-teaching, and in that moment we have come out from the mortal sense of life and have made ourselves separate.

With our vision held high in the continuous acknowledgment of God as that which constitutes individual being, we are so completely unselfed that at some given moment the miracle takes place, the miracle known as the Annunciation which is the conception of the Christ in our consciousness.

By desiring or willing it, we cannot, of ourselves, receive the Christ. It is an act of Grace, but It comes in a moment of unselfedness, when we are loving the Lord our God supremely and loving our neighbor as ourselves. In that split second of unselfedness, room is made in our consciousness for the entrance of that Seed, the Christ, and then, as we nurture It silently, secretly, and sacredly within ourselves, telling no man, eventually the Birth takes place, and it becomes evident that we are a new being, that we have "died" to the old and been reborn to the new, that we have put off mortality and are being clothed upon with immortality.

This life of self-effacement is not a belittling of ourselves; it is not being overinterested in, or concerned with, ourselves. Rather is it practicing what was learned in the First Degree, watching our thoughts and inner feelings, keeping consciousness in line by means of the continuous acknowledgment of God, and holding our neighbor in our consciousness in the same light in which we would like to be held in the consciousness of our neighbor.

If we could, we would all prefer to be judged by whatever measure of spiritual light and divine sonship we have attained rather than as merely good human beings and certainly rather than as bad ones. If we could have our way, we would have all men overlook our human errors, and if we could rise high enough in spiritual consciousness, we would also have them resist any temptation to praise our human good. We would have them look through both the good and the evil, and behold God operating through and as us.

This is sowing to the Spirit and not to the flesh. This is the recognition of the spiritual integrity and identity of every person, so-called good or bad, in spite of appearances. It is a recognition of God as the central theme and true identity of all being, and then permitting that recognition to bring something new and different to light in the consciousness of those individuals.

Loving our neighbor as ourselves, then, is giving our neighbor that same recognition of godliness that we give ourselves, regardless of the appearance of the moment. That neighbor may be the woman taken in adultery or the thief on the cross, but we have nothing to do with that. What we have to do with is to love all our neighbors by knowing their true nature, just as we would be loved by having them know our true nature, in spite of what outward appearance may temporarily be evident.

In the loving of God and the loving of our neighbor there is an unselfedness which creates something of a vacuum, an absence of an awareness of the little "I," insofar as I, Mary, or I, John, or I, Joel, am concerned. That little "I" for the moment is absent, and in its absence conception takes place—the overshadowing by the Holy Ghost, the Annunciation, or the planting of the seed of the Christ within us.

From then on we walk quietly, sacredly, and secretly with this inner Presence until It comes into visible manifestation. And if we are wise we take It down into "Egypt" for a few years and hide It, until we are so thoroughly imbued with It, so thoroughly alive in It, that we can expose It to the gaze of the world and not be affected by the world's persecution of, or animosity toward, It, for the world always violently opposes any manifestation of the Christ.

The Christ in the midst of us foreshadows the death and destruction of mortality, and it is to that mortality that the human race wants to cling: mortality in the form of its personal good, in the preservation of its personal self, in the preservation of either its personal fortune or national survival at the expense of anything or anyone else. The nature of mortality is such that it resists anything that would dethrone that personal sense of self. So it is that if we were to tell our friends and relatives how to live without taking thought for what they should eat, that they should pray for the enemy more than they pray for their friends, or that they must forgive seventy times seven, we would bring upon ourselves their criticism, judgment, condemnation, and eventually, if they had the power, crucifixion, albeit not in the same form as Jesus' crucifixion.

In Scripture there is that nine-month period before Mary brings forth the Christ-child, in other words, before the visible evidence of Christliness can be brought into manifestation. Then there is the flight into Egypt to hide the Babe, a two-year period in which It could grow so strong that later, without wavering, Jesus was able to mount the Cross, knowing full well that the hatred and mental malpractice of mankind—envy, jealousy, bigotry, lust, carnality—are not power.

It takes those two, and possibly more, symbolic years in "Egypt," even after the Christ has been born in us, to come to the full realization of the non-power of the carnal mind, the non-power of human or temporal power, whether that of Pilate, of the Sanhedrin, or of any other Goliath.

In our first experience of Christ-realization we may be tempted in our enthusiasm to expose It to the world, but in so doing we may lose It because it is only by degrees that the Christ is enabled to prove Itself to us, first in minor ways, and then ultimately in the ability to stand before our particular Pilate or to rise out of any tomb of sorrow, disease, trouble, or poverty.

Being humanly good and living under the Ten Commandments is wise and necessary for all of us at a certain stage of our unfoldment, but for those who have embarked on the spiritual path, it is vitally important to take a further step, and that is to embrace the two great Commandments, consciously living them until that point of self-surrender, that point of vacuum where we make way for the grace of God to establish the Christ-presence within us. This is our path; this is our goal.

CHAPTER XVIII

THE FUNCTION OF THE MIND

After we have been in the First Degree long enough for its lessons to solidify in consciousness, we begin to realize that we ourselves are responsible for our character and for the harmonies or discords that are coming into our experience, and that it is within our power to prevent or remove the discords and inharmonies of life from being a part of our experience.

When we were living only as human beings, it was largely a matter of chance or luck whether the right circumstances came or the wrong, the right person or the wrong. The one thing every human being is sure of is that he is not responsible for the ills that befall him and, if he is honest, he will have to admit that he is not too responsible for the good things that happen either: they just happen.

When we realize that we ourselves have it within our power to determine our experience, that we could have prevented most of our troubles had we only known what we know now, and moreover that we can begin at any moment to change the entire course of our experience, we begin to take hold of our life and mold it in accord with our desires, not just accepting what someone thrusts upon us or what the world deals out to us.

As we sow, so shall we reap. In the human experience it is we, ourselves, who are forming our own life, and we are doing it either by living a materialistic kind of life or by beginning to understand that we can live by the word of God if we will but take the word of God into our life. We reap what we sow.

In the Second Degree a great principle is revealed: a mind imbued with truth is a law of harmony unto our life; a mind ignorant of truth results in a life of chance, luck, and circumstance, a life over which we have no control. We can control our life only in proportion to the truth we entertain in our consciousness. We ourselves can determine whether we want one hour out of twenty-four of harmony, or twenty-four out of twenty-four. We alone can determine how much of our attention we wish to give to truth, to every Word that proceeds out of the mouth of God.

In the early stages of the Second Degree we begin to apply and use principles of truth, taking hold of our life and governing it by spiritual law. If there is a problem of supply, we realize that supply is spiritual, within us; it is the very presence of God, for God is fulfillment. We work along this line; we remind ourselves of truth, and mentally apply every statement of truth we know to the erroneous appearances that present themselves. If we have a task to perform and it seems to be too hard for us, we turn within and remember that He perfects that which concerns us. As we relax in that remembrance, before we know it, our task is performed.

It is in this second stage that our humanhood mounts and improves, and we are coming closer to where we can be like the scribes and the Pharisees, claiming that we are righteous and virtuous, good men and good women, and proud of it—and of course we are trying our best to make everybody else over in our own image and likeness.

It is not long before we begin to think that we of ourselves are doing all this and that we are very clever and capable. We are ridding ourselves of all our discords and bringing about harmony, and we think that this mind of ours is really powerful. It is then that we may begin to believe that mind is God.

There are many persons who use the word "mind" as synonymous with God, but the very fact that we can use our mind is in itself proof that mind cannot be God because it is hardly possible that anyone could use God, and moreover since the mind can be used for both good and evil, it cannot be God, for God is above the pairs of opposites.

When the secrets of the mind were first revealed, it was evident that the mind could be used for both good and evil. But some of those who learned these secrets could not maintain their spiritual integrity, nor did they have sufficient humility to be servants. To these people conversant with mind-power and its potentialities, the idea presented itself that inasmuch as they knew how to work with thought, thought and mind must be power. Mind, according to them, therefore must be God; and thought, the instrument of God, must be power. This led them away from the spiritual path; they dropped out of their particular wisdom school; and some of them became founders of what are known as the black brotherhoods. These brotherhoods were made up largely of men who had originally been part of a spiritual teaching, but who, after discovering the powers of the mind, left that teaching and formed brotherhoods where they could make use of mental powers for their own glorification and personal profit. Unquestionably, many members of these groups used mental power for what to them was a good purpose, but too often these mind-powers were used primarily for selfish or ulterior purposes.

Many books have been written on the subject of witchcraft, voodooism, and malpractice, some of them containing authentic accounts of actual experiences which testified to the fact that while these people had touched the realm of mind, they had not yet touched the realm of Spirit. The ceremonies, rites, and rituals of most of the primitive races of which I have any knowledge were, and are, based on the power of the mind. Participants in the primitive ritual dances shriek, holler, and scream, and paint their faces in grotesque fashion, all for the purpose of frightening the spectator, instilling fear in his heart, and a dread of some terrible power close at hand. Every trick of the art of suggestion is used.

The higher we go in spiritual awareness, the more we learn about the mental realm, not because we seek that knowledge, but because it is revealed to us. It is like being on a mountaintop where, having reached the summit, we can see from that height down into the valley far better than those who are looking out from the limited perspective of the valley. Those who are on the spiritual level can see into the mind, thereby becoming aware of things that those living a materialistic and mental life can never know because they are too close to the picture and too much involved.

A knowledge of the secrets of the mind gained through spiritual wisdom is entirely different from the knowledge gained through the human mentality. Moses, for example, had been initiated into all the secrets of occultism at the Court of the Pharaohs, and when he returned to Egypt after his I-AM-THAT-I-AM revelation, he and Aaron performed mental tricks such as transforming the rod into a serpent and turning the water of the river into blood. This was pure mental manipulation. It all took place on the mental plane and was in no sense spiritual.

What we must remember always is that even when such tricks are used by spiritual-minded men, they are still mental. They may play a part in the life of the spiritual disciple who rises high enough, as is evidenced in the experience of Moses, but they will do so only for one reason. Moses made no use whatsoever of these mental tricks when he was at the stage of leading the Hebrew people, but in the presence of the Pharaoh and all his magicians, how do we know but that he may not have felt himself called upon to prove to them in their own language what he could do?

A person of developed mentality can withdraw consciousness from any part of his body, and have no sensation there. In India, this mental control is a form of yoga which teaches such complete control of the body that a person can virtually do anything with it that he wants, depending on the degree of his practice and determination.

In our humanhood we are usually subject to the whims of the body: it tells us when it feels pleasure, when it is in pain, when it is cold, and when it is hot, and we do not seem to be able to do anything about it except change the outer conditions in an attempt to make it happy. As we rise into the mental plane, however, the body does not exercise that much control over us, and often instead of its telling us, we can tell it how to act and feel. This is because we have arrived at the place where we realize that heat and cold are not properties of the body: they are properties of the mind. The body does not know when it is hot or cold; it does not even know whether it is alive or dead. The mind of man does know, and therefore the mind can be trained to reach that point of development where regardless of how hot or how cold the body is, the mind does not report it.

Men of spiritual illumination learn everything there is to be known about the mind and the body, but they do not use this knowledge for performing tricks, for show, or for a display of power. If an occasion should arise when they need to use it secretly and sacredly for some demonstration of dominion, or if there is ever a time when they feel the necessity of using it in public, they might do so. Normally, however, those of spiritual illumination do not ever resort to an exhibition of mental power, although it is true that the spiritually illumined know how the mind operates and how it can be manipulated.

The mind does have a rightful purpose in our experience. At the present time, the scientific world is beginning to agree with the findings of spiritually developed men and women that mind is the substance of this physical universe. The universe that we know with the physical senses is not a material universe: it is a mental universe. This material body is not material: it is a mental creation, the mind-creation of the second chapter of Genesis.[1]

The substance of body is mind. In and of itself, the body is dead; it has no life, no sensation, and no intelligence; it cannot move itself about. It is our mind that governs our body, and therefore our body can behave or misbehave, according to our mind. When we perceive this, we can understand that as long as we are functioning on the level of mind, we are functioning on the level of either good or evil, so this cannot be God. God is neither good nor evil: God is Spirit.

In the Second Degree, then, we learn that the truth with which the mind is imbued becomes tangible as the health of our body, as the abundance of our supply, and as the harmony of our experience.

[1] For a more complete exposition of this subject see "Transcending Mind" and "Unconditioned Mind" in the author's The Thunder of Silence (New York: Harper & Row, 1961; London: George Allen and Unwin, 1961).

Whereas before we were spiritually blind, in ignorance, and governed by circumstances, conditions, environment, and prenatal experiences, now we are being governed by the truth that we entertain in our consciousness. Truth is the substance and the law of harmony, but this truth does not dangle around in the air: it must be embodied and incorporated in our mind.

If we use the mind for personal and selfish ends without considering the effects upon others or upon the world, we are heading for trouble, because as we sow, so shall we reap. If, in using our mind for our own gain or satisfaction, we injure anyone, that injury will return to us. There is no denying that we can use the mind in any way we want to use it—erroneously, selfishly, or personally, and without due regard for the rights of others—but this may prove extremely dangerous and may be fraught with dire consequences.

As long as the mind is governed by truth, there will be no selfishness in it because we will not be directing the mind toward specific ends, but only toward attaining a greater awareness of truth, and letting this truth change our consciousness.

Entertaining truth in consciousness is not for the purpose of being able to buy expensive automobiles, palatial yachts, or magnificent homes; it is not for the purpose of reducing a fever or getting rid of a disease: the purpose of entertaining truth in consciousness is to spiritualize mind and body, to bring to our awareness the light of truth so that our whole being may be transformed from a materialistic sense to a spiritual sense. By the truth entertained in our consciousness, by this renewing of our mind, we are transformed from the man of earth into that man who has his being in Christ.

But this truth must be the truth about God. There is no truth about man; there is no truth about supply; there is no truth about health; there is no truth about safety. The only truth there is, is the truth about God, the truth that God is the substance of our body, our business, and our life. God is the cement of our human relationships: God is our fortress and our high tower. In Him, not in material or physical structures, do we live, and move, and have our being.

God must be in everything we do throughout our work in the Second Degree—God. By dwelling in this consciousness of God as our being and nature, gradually all hate, fear, and love of the outer world disappear, and their place is taken by a realization of the Spirit within.

Every word of truth that we embody in our consciousness becomes the breath of life to us, even the very activity of the organs of our body. We do not have to think of any of our bodily functions: all we have to think of is of God as the activity and the law unto our being, and then all action is performed harmoniously and perfectly in accordance with divine law.

Originally, the mind was—and it must again become that for which it was created—an instrument of awareness and knowledge. For example, through our mind-faculties we can know that God governs the weather, but with our mind we cannot make the weather good or bad, although by realizing God as the very nature, substance, and activity of weather, we can bring harmonious weather into visibility. Using the mind to create something or to draw some person to us would be taking the mind out of its natural orbit, and we might thereby bring forth something that could become a Frankenstein to us.

When the mind is used for the purpose of knowing the truth, that truth then becomes the law of harmony unto our experience; it sets us free from every sense of limitation: physical, mental, moral, and financial. The truth that we entertain in our consciousness takes over our life, eliminating discords and inharmonies and bringing about peace, harmony, and security.

It is in this Second Degree that we decide whether we will serve God or mammon, and if we decide to serve God, we must determine how many hours a day we will serve Him. Eventually, those who follow this Path learn that there is not a moment of the day when their mind is not stayed on truth. They do not have to state truth consciously: they are living it. It is much the same as living an honest life. Honest people live honestly: they do not entertain in their thought ideas of dishonesty, but that does not mean they have to go around declaring, stating, or affirming that they are honest. If they have attained an honest state of consciousness, they merely live honestly.

In the unfolding of our spiritual consciousness, which means our progress or journey from a material sense of life back to the Father's house, we may have to know and affirm truth for hours and hours and hours to break the discordant appearance. We have to live with this truth until, through our meditations, there eventually comes a time when the contact with our Source is so well established that we never have to use the mind again for the purpose of knowing the truth: truth springs up from within our own being and utters itself to us. We do not declare it any more: it declares itself.

When the Voice utters Itself through us, the healing is instantaneous and complete. So it is that when we have studied truth, worked with it and lived it, filled our consciousness with truth day and night, then one day in our meditation, we find that whenever it is necessary for a truth to appear, we have only to close our eyes, turn within in an attitude of "Speak, Lord; for thy servant heareth," and then truth comes up from within and announces itself to us. When that happens, there are signs following.

At first we fill our consciousness with truth until the mind is transformed from a material to a spiritual base; then we stop using our mind as a mental power to make something happen, and let it become an avenue or an instrument of awareness through which to receive God's grace. Ultimately we live by the Grace that flows from the Spirit within, and that becomes apparent to us through the mind.

From the time of our entrance into the First Degree, we worked toward the goal of the God-experience, but whereas in the First Degree we concerned ourselves only with practicing the presence of God and with meditation, in the Second Degree we begin to apply every word of spiritual truth we can to our daily living, thereby spiritualizing the mind until eventually our mind no longer reaches out for some kind of a weapon—whether mental, verbal, or physical —but automatically goes within for a word of truth.

At that stage of consciousness, regardless of what problem presents itself, we reach into our consciousness for a word of truth with which to meet it. Whereas the human mind would think of running to a policeman, to a law court, or to some other kind of a human weapon, we rush back inside ourselves for the truth with which to meet the situation. We are now learning not to use the commonly accepted modes or means of life, but to rely upon the word of truth that is within our consciousness. Eventually we will draw from within our own consciousness enough truth to change our entire world because we are learning in this Second Degree that our consciousness embodies all the truth that has ever been known from the beginning of time.

For more years than can be numbered, religion has had as one of its objects the conversion of individuals in the hope that, if all the people of the world could be converted, a new world would emerge. What most of these zealots have failed to realize is that by the time everyone had been converted, a new generation would have been born, and they would have to begin the same work all over again.

The Infinite Way reveals, however, that the conversion of the world or even of a whole generation is not necessary: it is only necessary that a sufficient number attain the ability to go within and draw their spiritual good from that Withinness, and then the next generation will be born into this new consciousness. It is out of the understanding that good and evil are impersonal that the state of consciousness of the next generation is being built. The state of consciousness that we are forming, therefore, is not merely your consciousness or mine. Can consciousness be limited to time or space? Is not every word of truth that is transforming our state of consciousness also, in a measure, transforming the state of consciousness of the entire world? Once truth is brought to light in individual consciousness, the next generation will be born into the same state of consciousness that we have developed.

Consciousness cannot be limited. God is individual consciousness and God is infinite; therefore, our consciousness is infinite. Through the realization of this Infinity, a composer could shower the world with original melodies, or a writer could invent new plots and ideas for the next hundred years. This complete reliance on infinite Consciousness does not entail going out into the world for anything: it means going within ourselves, bringing forth all things needful as the effects of a spiritual impulse, and then beholding how this Infinity forms Itself on the outer plane.

The part the mind plays in all this is at once apparent. Through the activity of our mind it is we who go back into our consciousness, into the center of our being, and draw forth spiritual truth. Thereby we are enriching our entire life—our body as well as our mind.

The earth has to be fertilized; it has to have water and sunshine; and in proportion as it gets these, does it bring forth abundant fruit. So with us. The mind must be enriched; it must be fed with spiritual meat, wine, and water; and the only place it can get these is from the Soul, from the deep Withinness. As we bring this nourishment up and let it feed our mind, we are building that mind in us which was also in Christ Jesus, and that mind becomes the substance of our body. Whatever the nature of the food we feed our mind, that is the nature of the quality of our body since our mind is the substance of our physical body. Every time that we turn within and bring forth a word of truth, we have released it into consciousness, and we have not only fertilized and enriched our own state of consciousness but we have enriched the state of consciousness of the world.

Mind, in and of itself, is neither good nor bad. Mind is unconditioned. Behind our mind we stand, and we have the power to fill our mind with good or with evil, with abundance or with lack. We can fill our mind with truth, leave it empty, or we can let it be filled with the mesmerism of the world. Mind is unconditioned, and we are either letting it be permeated with the rubbish of "this world" or with wisdom, with material or with spiritual thoughts.

Because the mind is an instrument, it can become aware of truth in its entirety, whereas if it relies wholly on what is already known, it never can rise out of its self-imposed limitations and learn what is awaiting its opening. As long as we do not limit our mind to what we hear or read and as long as we are willing to go back into our Self, we can be taught of God—given wisdom, safety, and direction. This, however, does involve a surrender of the little self and the ability to be still and know that the *I* at the center is God; it involves a willingness to listen and let God direct and illumine the mind.

When we have progressed in the Second Degree to the point where we have spiritualized the mind, where we understand the mind to be an unconditioned channel for God's wisdom, and have learned to be still, then when problems are brought to us for solution, we are not concerned about thinking thoughts, but go within and let His voice utter itself, let ourselves be instructed from within, and let His power come through.

Although it usually takes students from five to nine years to encompass the Second Degree—not a quick process—they do not have to wait those long years for the fruitage to appear. The fruitage begins to come very quickly: it is only the *full* attainment that does not come so quickly.

"Choose you this day whom ye will serve." Shall we serve the discords and inharmonies of this world along with some of its pleasures, or shall we rise above both its discords and pleasures and learn the secret of "*My* kingdom"?

In the First and Second Degrees, most of us do attain harmony of body, pocketbook, and of human relationships, but this is only a step on the spiritual path because we have not yet discerned the real nature of immortality, eternality, and infinity, of completeness and of perfection. That lies ahead of us—but not until we have encompassed these two degrees.

"In quietness and in confidence shall be your strength. . . . Be still, and know that I am God." *I*, that *I*, way deep down inside us, that *I* comforts us, that *I* is the Presence, that *I* will instruct us. Then we will never have to use our mind as a power, but this rich spiritual food which wells up from within will feed our mind and become the substance and activity of our life and our body.

CHAPTER XIX

ATTAINING DIVINE SONSHIP

When we have encompassed the First and Second Degrees, a new dimension of life, an entirely different area of consciousness, opens up to us. In that moment there is something within us that is no longer a quotation, an affirmation, or a recalling of truth: it is an experience. We have entered the Third Degree, where we no longer live by the standards of this world, where the values are different, and life is governed not so much by what the outer law is as by what our inner integrity is. It is at this point that we pass from law to Grace.

As human beings we live under man-made laws which continue to operate as long as we remain in ignorance, and until we are awakened, we are held in slavery to all kinds of mental and physical laws.

As we come to an awareness of a spiritual Presence within us, we gradually become immune to these laws because as we pass into the third stage, the Presence lives our life, and It cannot be influenced, nor can It be acted upon by physical or mental laws: It is immune to them for they are only theories, superstitions, and the universal belief in two powers. In proportion as the son of God is raised up in us, these laws do not operate, and not only are we not receptive or responsive to them, but we aid in nullifying them for others who may come to us.

When an immunity is developed to material and mental laws, we live in an entirely different world because then we do not have to take the law into consideration, nor do we have to be concerned about things. Having found the kingdom of God and dwelling in it, something else is taking over the responsibility for our entire experience. The government is on His shoulder, on this divine Son which in the Third Degree is now raised up in us. In our humanhood It was dormant; It stood by and could do nothing. Regardless of what wrong was done to us, we had to resign ourselves to it unless our human wisdom or strength could provide an escape for us, and in most cases it could not.

In the awareness of this transcendental Presence, however, we have entered a state of consciousness where we do not have to fight and oppose error, or continuously try to destroy it. We are now in a state of consciousness where error does not touch us—we are not even aware of it. We are not just experiencing more and better human things and conditions, but a new factor has come into our life, a new joy.

Probably the only way that this can be explained is that in our humanhood we experience pleasure or satisfaction because of something that takes place out here. For example, learning that some activity has been successful or awakening on Christmas Day to find ourselves blessed with beautiful gifts arouses joy in us; but, on the other hand, failure or the absence of gifts might bring sorrow.

Our joy as well as our sorrow is usually prompted by outer occurrences, whereas from the moment that this transitional experience begins, joy, which is an integral part of our being, bubbles up from within without any external cause, and when sorrow comes, it is recognized as "this world" and is quickly dissolved.

In the Third Degree we do not try to demonstrate anything in the outer world: we are seeking only that inner release or peace which, in itself, is the demonstration and the attainment of our goal. It is not to be attained for any purpose, but only for itself, and it produces an effect in the outer experience that follows just as daylight accompanies the sun. The sun does not rise and then produce light: the sun itself constitutes the light. Just so, we discover that there is no God to give us health, supply, or companionship; there is no God to give us anything, but there is God, and when this Spirit is consciously realized, It is the very substance of our outer experience.

As the sunshine does not give us light, but is the light, so the grace of God within does not produce something in the outer plane: the grace of God within is the very substance of the good that is to appear outwardly. There is no such thing, therefore, as the presence of God and a discord; there is no such thing as the presence of God and lack or limitation. God is the peace, God is the comfort, God is the supply.

Spirit and Its outer activity are one; Spirit and Its formations are one; Spirit and Its creation are one. Spirit does not create in the sense of their being a Spirit *and* a creation: Spirit is the substance that appears outwardly as form, not as the form of what we see, hear, taste, touch, or smell but as spiritual form. The impressions received through the senses represent our concept of that spiritual Presence that is here.

In this third stage, we outgrow and undo all the work of the first and second stages. We stop depending on a God, and while this may sound incredible to those not yet advanced to this stage, it is not too difficult to do because, with the experience of the Christ, everything is provided for us before we know we need it. The Christ imparts wisdom, provides protection, and bestows love, and there is no need to depend on anything without: there is always That which is going before us to make "the crooked places straight"; there is always That which is walking beside us as our safety and security.

Such heights of consciousness are not experienced in the first two stages. There we have only our own thoughts, hopes, and the assurance of the mystics who have written the Scriptures and the metaphysics of the world. These are a staff upon which we lean, and they stand with us until we receive the Experience.

With the advent of the Experience, however, all of this changes. Very slowly it begins to dawn in consciousness that we are no longer the person we were because now we are not depending on some remote God, thinking or talking about a far-off God, and certainly not trying to influence Him. Not only are we not trying to be good, and of course, anyone who advances into the Third Degree could not be bad, but now there is no awareness of goodness because there is nothing with which to compare it: there is no temptation to be bad. In fact, nothing from without now acts as any kind of a temptation to us.

It is like the mathematician so well-grounded in his science that he never for a moment is tempted to believe that twelve times twelve is one hundred forty-three. There is simply a complete awareness of one hundred forty-four. The mathematician would not be able to understand those of us who are always faced with the temptation that two times two is not four, and three times three is not nine.

It is difficult for anyone living in this consciousness of the Third Degree to understand a person who steals or lies, or who attempts to gain his ends by false advertising. What must be going on in a mentality that engages in such practices when there is no need for them? "The earth is the Lord's, and the fulness thereof," and therefore, is not all that the Father has ours? Yet in this higher consciousness, we never consciously think of these truths; they never enter our mind except when someone presents the opposite picture to us, and there is the need to assure him of God's loving, omnipresent care.

When we come to the third stage, which is reached by passing through a series of initiations, each marking a transition from a lower state of consciousness to a higher one, there is no sowing and there is no reaping: there is only a state of divine being, the fourth-dimensional consciousness which, when attained, enables us to live by Grace. When the son of God is raised up in us and is alive, we need take no thought, for It is of the essence of Omnipotence, Omnipresence, and Omniscience; It is the All-knowing, the All-powerful, the All-presence, and It does these things for us.

In our humanhood we are a sleeping entity, but when we awaken, what do we find? We find ourselves in His image and likeness; we find that there is a God, that God cares for His son, and that you and I are that Son. We are consciously one with God; and then we can give ourselves up to be crucified, sent to war, or to anything else that the human mind wants to do to us, and we will walk right out of the tomb, free and clear—we will walk right out of the situation. Why? Because the son of God is spiritual and, therefore, is not subject to the laws of cause and effect, nor is he subject to karmic law.

In this Third Degree we are no longer good or bad, we are no longer well or sick, and we are no longer rich or poor: we are just a state of divine being, and it is not that we are that of ourselves; it is that This that has taken possession of us is it. There is then no personal responsibility for supply or for health: our only responsibility is to live in God.

When this experience of living in God first comes to us, it is disturbing because, just as in our first stage we were "dying" to the negative sense of life and being reborn into a more positive sense, now we are "dying" all over again. This is not only an annihilation of our undesirable humanhood, but it is also an annihilation even of our good humanhood, and at first it is frightening and disconcerting as veil after veil drops away, and we come face to face with naked truth.

The first flush of enthusiasm on the spiritual path brought to us a sense that being healthy is a proof of our spiritual understanding, and being wealthy is, of course, another great proof of the degree of that understanding. But in the Third Degree we rise into the consciousness where there is no health and there is no wealth. There is neither good health nor bad health; there is neither virtue nor vice; there is neither honor nor dishonor; there are neither high people nor low people; there are no greats, near-greats, or not-so-greats: there is only a spiritual state of being which is described as "My kingdom," My consciousness, the Christ-consciousness—and that is not a state of improved humanhood.

In our first stage of spiritual development we were improving our humanhood merely by virtue of our greater awareness of a spiritual Presence. In the second stage we were consciously improving our humanhood so as to measure up to our highest concept of goodness, virtue, integrity, loyalty, and fidelity, using the mind as an instrument for the activity of the Spirit. But in the third stage all this is taken from us. In this degree we cannot rejoice in our benevolences, in our health, or in our wealth because now we see that we do not have any of these of ourselves. The Christ, the spiritual Son, is our life, our health, our wealth, and the source of our good. This spiritual Selfhood, this Messiah which is within us—this is our good, the source of it, the experience of it, the expression of it. In this there is no little human "I" left.

The final experience is the annihilation of our human self, of its good qualities as well as its evil; it is "dying daily" until even the best of humanhood is gone, and spiritual identity is revealed. Death to the materialistic concept of life and a rebirth of the Spirit—this is what takes place through our spiritual unfoldment and progress on the Path.

When the transition takes place, sometimes slowly or sometimes in a flash, it always leaves us with a trace of our old self. This is a difficult period because we have glimpses of what spiritual living can be, and yet at the same time we have the frustrating experience of not being able to live in the Spirit continuously. While our old un-illumined self does not dominate the scene, its shadow still lingers, and we are often tempted to indulge in the old habits and modes of life. So there is a need for great patience until the son of God has been more fully raised up in us.

The Master, himself, even after having made the transition from being a Hebrew rabbi to being the Christ, was tempted three times, which indicated that there was enough of personal sense left to tempt him by saying: "With this power, you can make yourself great. Show this power; show the world that you and God are on such intimate terms that He will not let anything happen to you. Show the world that you have all the supply in the world because you are so close to God; show the world that you are a saint."

But these temptations were overcome because of Jesus' realization of the nature of each temptation. He did not try to reform himself; he did not say, "Oh, I am weak; God has left me." He did not try to blame it on anything: he recognized instantly when he commanded, "Get thee behind me, Satan," that this was the impersonal satanic suggestion of a selfhood apart from God. This was truly a temptation to believe that he and his Father were not one, that there was an "I" and a God, and that he was some favorite of God. He recognized this as an impersonal mesmeric suggestion, an impersonal evil, or impersonal tempter. He refused to accept an "I" who could be good or bad. He did not accept an "I" who needed food, clothing, or housing; he did not accept an "I" who required healing. He knew the truth, "I and my Father are one," and that that I would never leave him or forsake him; It would be with him to the end of the world.

In that revelation and realization the total "death" of the man of earth took place, bringing about his complete rebirth in Spirit as Christ-consciousness so that thereafter he knew himself as the Christ, the son of God. Then Jesus, the son of man, was "dead," and the Christ was risen from the tomb of mortality, of mortal identity, and stood revealed as individual, infinite, eternal individuality.

Jesus Christ was not absorbed in God: he remained as individual identity, as he does to this moment, just as all the mystics who have attained conscious union with God live now, live here, and are available to every individual who attains even a touch of Christhood.

When we rise high enough, we, too, tabernacle with those who have left human sight and are on the level of Christ-consciousness, for we are of one household, in one place, and of one Father consciously realized.

In Christ-consciousness there is divine harmony, and this divine harmony, in some measure, makes itself evident in various ways in our experience. Because of the activity of the Christ in consciousness, we witness healings in our bodies and minds, healings in our human relationships and in our economic condition. We have seen how the activity of the Christ lifts our individual experience out of the world of sickness and health, swinging back and forth between good and evil, and even though we may not attain the fullness of the Christ, at least if there is "a thorn in the flesh," we forget "those things which are behind," and live as much as we can in this higher consciousness.

When we first set out on this Path, let us not forget that we already are the Christ, but that the Christ is so heavily veiled that we cannot behold the real Self. Every moment of our journey the veils are dropping away from us—the claims of humanhood—until eventually we stand forth and see ourselves as we really are, sons of God, united in a brotherhood with all mankind, wherein there is neither Greek nor Jew, bond nor free, where all are one in Christhood.

Nevermore can we be evil any more than we can be good; nevermore can we be sick any more than we can be well; nevermore can we be dead any more than we can be alive. Henceforth we are the sons of God, the offspring of God, God Himself incarnated as individual being, God Himself made manifest.

CHAPTER XX

THE MEANING OF INITIATION

Initiation is an act of Grace bestowed on individuals at a certain time in their unfoldment, lifting them into the master-state of consciousness. There is far less opportunity for a student to attain initiation in the Western World than in the Eastern because in the West we are brought up from childhood with the idea of equality. We are taught that we are all equal, and therefore we do not have the correct understanding of the role of a spiritual teacher, or what spiritual consciousness is. We do not realize that while we may have political and economic equality, we are far from being equal in spiritual development.

We of the Western World do not lend ourselves to becoming students of a spiritual teaching. Oh yes, we are very eager in the first year or so to jump up from the status of a beginner into being at least a master, and then going on from there. Attaining the spiritual life, however, does not come so quickly: it is a life of continuous dedication to that which is greater than we are.

Personally, I do not believe that a student can consciously prepare for initiation, nor have I ever seen anyone who had initiation as his goal achieve it. Rather the goal must always be the attainment of that mind that was in Christ Jesus without any thought of receiving initiation or experiencing the effects of initiation.

As the student takes his first steps on the Path leading to illumination, he learns to meditate on the indwelling Spirit. Initiation carries him from one step to another into the awareness of the Presence, on and on and on, purifying him to the extent that he no longer wants God to destroy his enemies, but is willing always to forgive and love them because he knows that it is only through their ignorance that evil is being expressed. He is purified to such a degree that he no longer wishes to gain his ends by any personal sense of might or power. In way after way his life becomes so purified that it is lived in dedication to others.

The world loses its attractions for him, not because he planned or willed it so, nor because he studied to bring it to pass. Rather has an experience taken place within him. The Spirit of God has begun to come alive; his Soul-center is being opened, and instead of indulging in the pleasures of the world, he now finds himself more at home with persons who are spiritual-minded and with books of an inspirational and spiritual nature. He has not yet reached the Absolute, but having been elevated above human consciousness, he is now partaking of the nature of, and living in large measure in, the divine Consciousness, being fed and clothed by It. The activity of this Spirit is making of him a better human being and is making of his human life, a better life.

Now comes the period that is described in the mystical literature, both of the East and of the West, as "dying daily." This is the experience of putting off mortality and putting on immortality. It is an experience in "death," an experience that comes to very few, but when it comes, it carries them further along the Path up to illumination.

On the spiritual path we have to "lose" our life before we can gain spiritual life, that is, we have to lose our physical sense of life, that sense which believes that we are alive because the heart is beating or because the lungs and the digestive and eliminative tracts are functioning. We have to come to a point where life is living the body, not the body living the life. At present it is not we who are living our life. The body tells us, "I have a cold"; "My heart is not functioning properly—or my liver, or my lungs." It is constantly telling us about all the things that are threatening our human sense of life.

How stupid can we be? Life is eternal. The life of God is eternal. The life of God is infinite. There is only one Life, and therefore that eternal Life must be your life and mine. The very life that we are living is infinite and eternal, and it is not dependent upon the action of the body: the action of the body is dependent upon life. Such a realization leads us to the period of transition where we move from existence in the body to an existence which is external to body, and yet which governs the body.

Before this transition is complete, usually so much good has come into our experience that we think we have entered the land of milk and honey. We have become accustomed to good health, and if we have not achieved it, at least we would like to experience it. Probably sometimes we envy the people who are forty, fifty, or sixty years of age, and have never had a day of illness in their lives. We wish we could be like that, but it is not to be so—not on the spiritual path.

To most persons this is as far as they go on the Path in any one lifetime, unless they have made some progress in a previous existence and are now ready to go beyond it. It is a shock for them to discover that when all is apparently going so well, that is just when their real problems begin. Now the really deep ones come—problems of life and death.

Sometimes I find myself smiling a little sadly when I read in my mail of the number of people who want initiation. I wonder what would happen to them if they came up against real initiation and had to go through some of those fiery trials that are included in every initiation of the spiritually illumined. How many Lot's wives there would be to turn around and look back at the good old city!

It is not usually taught that before there can be an ascension there must be a crucifixion. It is comforting and comfortable to accept the theological belief that Jesus was crucified for us, and that therefore we can experience the ascension without the crucifixion. That we should never believe. No, to experience the ascension, we have to take all the footsteps that Jesus showed us including the temptations and the crucifixion.

These temptations do not come only when we are lowly mortals. Jesus' three temptations in the wilderness took place after he was well-established in his spiritual life. Knowing that he had glimpsed the secrets of life and could do many miraculous things, now came the temptation to use this power. How could such a thing have happened to Jesus Christ at his advanced stage of development? How could he have been tempted to glorify himself, to enrich himself, to use personal powers? If we study this experience of Jesus, we will understand why it is that just when we think we are entering the kingdom of God, our trials begin, and our temptations.

The temptation of Gethsemane came to Jesus when he was a fully ascended Master, and that of Golgotha when he was already a Saviour. Even he did not attain the infinity of his being until after the Crucifixion, the Resurrection, and the Ascension that finally lifted him completely above material sense or finite form.

Had Jesus succumbed to those temptations, there would be no Christian teaching today because he would have failed the tests required of him for his initiation. Every initiate on the way to the Absolute reaches the place where he is tempted to accept the fortune that is awaiting him, if only he wants to reach out for it; every initiate is tempted to accept the world's fame. These temptations come to all those on the spiritual path, and usually at a time when they have reached the place where they are good human beings and are about to shed their humanhood.

With a small degree of illumination, it is not too difficult to achieve fame or to gain fortune. Many opportunities open to those who have attained some measure of spiritual light, and it is when these temptations in the form of such opportunities present themselves that a choice must be made: whether to bend every effort toward the acquisition of wealth and fame or to renounce all ambition to be numbered among the great and powerful. While there is nothing wrong about name or fame that comes of its own accord without seeking it, those individuals who use the knowledge or power that has been given to them for that purpose lose their way on the spiritual path. All of humanhood must be renounced, and every person on this Path must "die" and come to this point of absolute realization:

Of my own self, I am nothing. There is a Spirit within me that does the work; there is a Presence; there is a Power.

I am a beholder of this invisible Presence and Power at work. I watch how It goes before me and witness the miracles It performs.

When this spiritual way of life begins to change our nature and we find ourselves being cut off from society, we do not always realize that we are going through a transitional period and that once this transition has been made and we are completely isolated from our former associates, we will be led into the companionship of those of our own spiritual household. But as long as we are still tabernacling with the world, we are not going to meet those of our own household. It is only when we have "died" to the world that suddenly out of this whole universe one person crosses our path whom we recognize as a kindred soul, and then another and another.

If our lives are cluttered up with the social activities in which our friends and relatives have involved us, however, we are not free to enjoy the companionship of that one, two, or more who eventually cross our path, nor are we free to make the journeys that are sometimes necessary to be in their company because we may not always find that one, two, or three in our own community. It is true that we may see these companions only once in a year or once in three years, but that will not make any difference because this is a spiritual companionship that takes no thought of time or space, and even if there were years in which we were physically apart from those of our spiritual household, upon the next meeting we would be wholly at-one.

The student who is at the stage of witnessing his friends and relatives drop away, and for that matter the whole world, sometimes becomes fearful and lonesome and begins clutching at something or someone, and very often he is clutching at the wrong thing or the wrong person. And why? Because he cannot take aloneness, and if he cannot endure aloneness, he cannot enter into this life.

As spiritual truth begins to reveal itself in a person, a silence descends upon him, an inability to speak and to be a part of the world's gabble, gabble, gabble, and this of course makes everyone feel that he is odd. Even those who are starting on the Path cannot quite understand that desire to be still, that total inability to say anything and yet to impart and even to receive, and so this, too, which is another form of that inability to endure aloneness and quietness, breaks up many a student's progress on the way.

Many do not realize that the "my own" which "shall come to me," referred to by John Burroughs, is contingent upon an attained state of consciousness which is absolute stillness and peace. When that is attained, all a person has to do is to be a beholder and watch the whole world come to him. Most persons go through life frustrated because their own does not come to them: their own companion does not come, their own opportunity for service, their own opportunity for showing forth God's grace. They do not realize that "my own" will not come to a human being. It will not come except by being still and knowing that I is God, and then letting the awareness that the I of our being is Omnipotence, Omnipresence, and Omniscience perform Its work.

This can be attained only in the degree that each one of us realizes that I am I, that I am Consciousness, that I am the Consciousness which brought me and every individual being forth into expression, even including the trees and all that is. This does not mean that we have conscious dominion over things in the external world; it does not mean that we can "mentalize" anybody and everybody and thereby bend them to our will. The indulgence of human thought in the direction of control is domination and often ends in tyranny and destruction—usually self-destruction—and is such a form of egotism that it almost borders on insanity.

When we realize that all dominion lies in not exercising that conscious dominion which in the end becomes domination, it is because we know the truth of the I-AM-ness of our being. To know that since I is God and that I is the very I that I AM, then that I AM has dominion over everything on the earth, above the earth, and beneath the earth. To be still and know that I am God makes way for a divine Presence to go out before us, prepare mansions for us, and draw unto us our own When we know the I, we will know that I is the creator, but there must be no egotism connected with that. That, too, is one of the great temptations.

Very few initiates succumb to these temptations and fall by the wayside after a certain point in their development, but up to that time, even though the teacher knows that the aspirant is ready, the aspirant does not always fulfill that readiness, largely because personal sense is still in the saddle.

As long as there is any personal sense of self, we try to protect it, and whenever anything seems to threaten it, we rise up to do battle. Such a reaction may cause us to fall by the wayside because on the spiritual path we are not permitted to take up the sword. Judas, who was so close to the Master as to be his treasurer, retained enough of a sense of personal selfhood that he wanted to be "top banana," he wanted to be the most important disciple, and as soon as any of the others seemed to gain the favor of the teacher, he rose up to protect his position.

The personal sense of self that has left in it even a trace of ambition, envy, or jealousy is enough to trip up a student at any stage of his development. Until he has completely lost all sense of self and there is no further possibility of falling away, every initiate faces the temptation of fame or money, and if it is not a mad ambition for money, it may be just the ambition for enough money to ensure security. These are the devil-tempters. The enlightened consciousness has no need for safety or security and no need to be concerned about a future, but until one has attained that state of consciousness, the temptation is certain to be present, and there is always the possibility that the initiate may yield to it.

The fabric of every temptation that assails us consists of some form of personal sense. It is only with the final illumination, that final experience of God incarnating as individual man, a revelation that has come to so few people in all the world, that personal sense is dead. At this stage of unfoldment there is none of the human self left. Fame means nothing, fortune means nothing, safety means nothing. Does God need safety? Does God need security? Impossible!

But students on the Path have not attained that final revelation of God incarnated as the Self, the revelation that enabled the Master to say, "He that seeth me seeth him that sent me." How few there are who can make the statement, "You are looking at God"! And until they can do that, there is some measure of personal sense remaining that could cause them to fall. After that, when all personal sense has been eliminated, when there is no "I," "me," or "mine," there is only God, there is only the Light Itself, and this is Self-supporting, Self-maintaining, and Self-sustaining, needing no help from any human source.

The final step for every initiate is the command to "die." No one attains the heights until he reaches a complete surrender of self, a willingness to give up the human sense of self, give it up completely—if necessary to jump off the cliff into the ocean, to swim out to sea, to keep swimming and never turn back, to do what the Master commanded: "lose" his life, "die" to his human sense of life.

The "death" of the self is explained in different ways in different teachings. In the older teachings, in addition to the story of Osiris and the Phoenix rising up out of their own ashes, there are accounts of the crucifixion of six spiritual masters before the time of Jesus, each of whom rose again. In the wisdom schools the final attainment was always dependent on the "death" of the student. Every student of a wisdom school was required to go through a "death," be "buried," and "resurrected"—raised up again—before he was given the spiritual status of a master. In the ancient Egyptian teachings, as well as those of Greece, there is always the "death" of the master, followed by his resurrection and rebirth. Many fraternal teachings include, as a part of their ritual, the "death" of the initiate, and his being raised up again. This "death" of the self is exemplified in the Master's experience by the Crucifixion, the Resurrection, and the Ascension above all personal selfhood.

Crucifixion can be an actual physical crucifixion, and resurrection can be an actual resurrection from the grave, but not necessarily so. They may be symbolic to show the "death" of the self and the raising up of that divine Selfhood which we are, out of the dust of that corpse, out of the tomb. In other words, the crucifixion, which is the "death," or the crossing out of the self, may come in any dark night of the Soul when the last trace of selfhood is being swallowed up and there is nothing left but the light of the divine Selfhood—no vestige left of any "I," "me," or "mine," just the *I* that is the *I* of us.

Whether during this particular lifetime on earth or in another, the day must come when we "die"—not in the sense of a physical death as the result of disease, age, or accident, but a "death" to all human sense. We can know how rapidly we are "dying" by the degree to which we insist on the preservation of our human self which is said to be the first law of nature. If we are at the stage of consciousness where we would shoot to death a burglar who had entered our home, we have not yet "died": we are still in human-hood, still living a life of self-preservation. If we believe that in the event of any conflict our country should throw a bomb before the other country does, we have not yet started on the spiritual path: we are still under the law of self-preservation. The connotations of that law are terrifying to contemplate. It is another way of saying that our life is more valuable than that of others.

On the spiritual path, and particularly as we rise high enough above and beyond all personal sense of self, we are able to under-stand that when the Master commanded his disciple to put up his sword it was as if he had said, "I know that they are going to crucify me, but what is the difference whether I die, or this soldier dies? Is it not the one Life? Is it right to kill him in order to protect me? Life is life, whether it is his life or my life. I have taught you to lay down your life that you may find it. I know what my fate is, but do not take someone else's life to protect my life because then all that I have taught you is lost."

Only in the degree of our self-surrender, only in the degree of what we give up, will we ever find our Self, and if we think to preserve or save our life by taking that of another, we have given telling evidence that we have not advanced very far spiritually. It takes only a little spiritual light to see that the life of one person cannot be more important than that of another, for life is life. The truth is that my life is your life, and your life is my life; and when you die, I die; when I die, you die.

We are never on the spiritual path until we have risen above the pairs of opposites, above good and evil, above "me" and "mine," above "thee" and "thine," until we have risen to the place in con-sciousness where there is One. When there is One, and One only, we can feed the multitudes and have twelve baskets full left over, we can heal the multitudes, we can forgive the multitudes, but not while there is a sense of a little self that is seeking for itself.

That which originally caused us to be cast out of our spiritual home into a material sense of the universe was duality—the belief in a selfhood apart from God with its belief in, and fear of, two powers. It is not in someone else that this belief is overcome: it is overcome in us, and by us.

The overcoming is never the overcoming of something out here: it is always the overcoming of a belief that has been accepted in our consciousness. *The overcoming is within our own consciousness.* The longer we postpone that overcoming, the longer will we postpone the day of our final initiation when we become the master of our experience.

No one attains the spiritual heights except those who have been in the lowest depths. When we are going through our darkest human experience, very few of us actually believe that God is with us. Most of us are convinced that He has forsaken us. But God has never forsaken anyone—not even those in the lowest depth of sin imaginable. God is just as much omnipresent with the sinner as with the greatest saint.

When Moses was leading the Hebrews through their forty years of wilderness-experience, I doubt that many of the Hebrews around him would have acknowledged that God was present; but Moses himself surely must have known during all those forty years that the place whereon he stood at any given moment was holy ground. Had God not been with Moses, would there have been an end to those forty years in the wilderness and the next step into the land of milk and honey?

Elijah, too, must have had a little feeling, for a time at least, that perhaps God was not present when he was out in the wilderness and was being so persecuted. But if God had not been present, ravens would not have fed him, or the poor widow, nor would he have found cakes baked on the stones in front of him. Regardless of the problems through which Elijah went, had there not been Omnipresence, Elijah would perhaps never have been heard of again. What an inspiration it is to us when at the end of his trials and tribulations, God reveals to him, " 'Yet I have left me seven thousand in Israel, all the knees which have not bowed unto Baal'—I have saved out your completeness, your perfection, your harmony, and your mission in life." God always saves out for us, too, our completeness, perfection, harmony, and mission in life.

If God had not been with Jesus, even on the Cross, could there have been a Resurrection? Separate and apart from God, does man have powers of good, powers of resurrection or ascension? It is important for those of us on the spiritual path to recognize that wherever there is the restoring of the lost years of the locust as in the case of Elijah, Isaiah, and Joel, wherever there is an experience, such as the ministry of Jesus Christ culminating in the Resurrection and the Ascension, there must be Immanuel, God with us, there must be Omnipresence, even though there have been those intervals in which the appearances were not outwardly testifying to the Presence.

Watching Paul in his persecution of the Christians and in his many attempts to eradicate them completely, it would have been hard to believe that God was with him. If we had been part of that Christian band, we would have looked on Saul of Tarsus as a devil. But he was not so great a devil that God was not with him. In fact, God was with Paul awaiting recognition and realization even in the years of his ignorance, in the years of his persecutions and what the Christians would have called his deviltries. God was with him when he received the light and when he became a major factor in the founding and teaching of the Christian faith.

Peter and John were imprisoned, but God must have been with them in the prison, or else there would have been no escape for them. But there was an escape, and there was a whole ministry awaiting them because of Omnipresence, and not so much because of That as because of their recognition of It.

There is no one anywhere, at any time, without Omnipresence. There is no one anywhere, at any time, who does not have the fullness of the Godhead within him, regardless of what crosses, trials, or tribulations, regardless of what years of ignorance, sin, fear, or evil may be his lot. And but for these trials there would be no rousing out of mortality, out of humanness, out of evil humanhood, and later on there would be no rousing out of good humanhood, although eventually, both of these steps must be taken.

In the beginning of our spiritual experience we are merely coming out of the mortal or erroneous sense of life, usually into a good sense of human life—healthier and more abundant. But that is not the ultimate of life: the ultimate of life is spiritual realization.

To attain that spiritual realization, the primary responsibility of the student is the practice of meditation. It is in meditation that he loses the self with a small "s," and gains the Self with a capital "S." It is in meditation that he is developing, enriching, and unfolding his inner Self, but not while the human mind is busy with the ambition or desire for attainment.

The preparation for spiritual attainment, if there is any, therefore, is to forsake a goal. Let us suppose that initiation came to a student at this moment, and then he was told never to appear in public again, never to let himself be seen, but to find a cabin in the woods somewhere, and pray. How would he feel if he were a master and nobody else knew it, and he could not even wear a robe? Everyone who has attained that high realization has been given something to do that, while he was doing it, made it impossible for him to have name or fame. The Master Christ Jesus was not known as the Saviour or the Messiah during his own lifetime: he was a simple rabbi walking up and down the streets and villages of Palestine. Later, he was given the honor of being the Saviour, but only later.

Certainly, then, a prime requisite in the preparation for initiation on the spiritual path is the understanding that the aspirant is ready to be unknown and to be nothing. If he is instructed to sit in silence the rest of his days, he will sit in silence. If he is bidden to go off somewhere and pray for the world, he will do that, and above all things, he will never let his neighbors or friends or anyone else know that he is a person of spiritual attainment. That is a denial of attainment.

A real master does not look anything like a master: the real master is more like the servant who comes knocking at the door, asking, "Can you give me a little food?" and if we have the vision to recognize him as a master, there is a great blessing in it for us.

The more of a master one becomes, the more of a servant he really is. There never has been a real master who called himself master; there never has been a master who did not realize that he was not a master, but a servant, a servant to all who came unto him heavy laden, to all who came seeking the Light. He who has attained the consciousness of a master becomes the servant of everybody, and a person with such a high state of consciousness could never stoop even to have a lurking desire to set himself up to be bowed down to and worshiped.

When a person is identified by the title of master or *guru*, it is only a means of signifying that individual's spiritual attainment. The person we see is not the master. What constitutes the master is his divine Consciousness. Did not the great Master tell us in effect, "Do not call me master, do not call me good: there is but one Master, there is but One good"?

No one can take credit for attaining the spiritual heights because no one has done anything to deserve or earn it, even on the lower levels. I can remember the time of my entrance to the spiritual path when the first signs given me were that I cared no longer for smoking, drinking, or playing cards. I could not even go across the border and put a two-dollar bet on a horse. All of that disappeared. How foolish it would have been if I had taken credit for this, and boasted about how noble I was when I had nothing at all to do with it. These things were simply taken from me: there was no credit accruing to me.

As one goes higher on the spiritual path, he attains a humility and a complete freedom from worldly fear. Almost with the first spiritual experience, the fear of death disappears because in the realization of life eternal, it becomes of relative unimportance whether he lives on this plane or on that. No one attains spiritually while a fear of death remains in consciousness. But there again, how could a person possibly take credit for not fearing death, when it is something he did not accomplish, but something that was done for him by the Grace that was given him.

In order to attain the spiritual heights, every initiate must go down into the depths and go through a period known as "the dark night of the Soul," which may last months and months. This is a time of anguish, a period of barrenness in which he is torn apart and feels certain that God has forsaken him, that he is unworthy, that he has made a mistake, or that he has committed a sin, and God has therefore cast him into outer darkness. The reason for this desolation is not that God has thrown him off: it is only that a greater, deeper light is coming, and there must be an emptying-out process before that greater light can come.

There are many "dark nights of the Soul" on this Path until the final one. The final one, of course, is the real night of the Soul, and that very nearly costs some their life before they can pass through that particular experience and come out into the full realization of the light.

This "dark night of the Soul" culminates in the "death" of personal selfhood and the lifting of the initiate into the master-state of consciousness. In this experience the initiate may witness a tremendous light, a filmy cloud, or a pillar of cloud, descending as if from above and taking form on earth as an individual. In other words, he beholds God incarnating Himself as man, and in this vision I, God, is now I, man: the Father has become the Son, and now I am that I AM. I am He; I am He that should come.

With this revelation there exists forever after what the world calls teacher, saviour, or *guru*, but which is really the light of God manifested as man, and the power shown forth is the power of God which appears to others to be the power of a man. That is why so often an individual has been set up and glorified as God: it was not seen that it was not a man who was God, but that God was the man. There is quite a difference! A man is never God, but God becomes the man.

While it is true that there have been only a few full and complete God-incarnated-as-men on earth, there have been very many who have appeared as God incarnated on earth in a measure, and some in a very great measure. Otherwise the works they have performed could not have been performed because they were always works that a man could never have done. No man could have left as his contribution to the spiritual literature of the world the Gospel of John, the Advaita Vedanta, or any of the great original teachings that have become the spiritual heritage of man.

The Absolute is not a teaching but an experience. When it is given in words in a book, it is a revelation, but still not a teaching. Nobody can *teach* anyone to become the God-incarnated man, but after it has been revealed, it can be taken into consciousness, and the measure of the readiness of the student will be the measure of his experience of it.

Although there are some few in the history of the world who have come to earth so highly endowed spiritually that they have received the impartation of the Spirit directly by Grace without the intervention or help of a teacher, the vast majority of those who have attained the realization of the Absolute have attained it through a teacher.

What might be called the first revelation of the Absolute is accredited to Krishna, and while there are no proofs of his attainment, nor are there any manuscripts attributed to anyone by the name of Krishna, this name recurs again and again and again in religious literature, and is always in some way associated with the revelation of God as individual being, God as the only I AM, and that God, or I AM, constituting individual being.

We have no knowledge of how many attained this consciousness in the days antedating written accounts, but probably one of the first authentic records of such an attainment is that of Melchizedek. With Melchizedek there was no teaching; he taught nothing to anyone; and if he did impart his experience of the Absolute, there is no record of it. Our only information is that there was such a person as Melchizedek, he to whom even Abraham, the father of the Hebrew nation, paid tribute, that is, acknowledged as greater than himself— Melchizedek, never born and never dying. Has anyone but God Itself never been born and never died? No, only God is from everlasting to everlasting; therefore, it was the awareness of his identity as spiritual being, as God, as the I AM that was fully revealed as Melchizedek.

Moses, too, on the mountaintop, at the very height of spiritual revelation, received the awareness that I AM is God. He never taught the Absolute, however: he attained It. The teaching he gave to his followers was a very relative one. To try to reveal to them what he had attained was an impossibility, and the most he could do with his followers was to attempt to teach them to be good human beings, and this by means of The Ten Commandments.

Isaiah and John, also, undoubtedly attained the Absolute, but they never taught It: they merely revealed in their writings that they had attained It and Its truth. In one way or another, a teacher can show that he has attained the Absolute and can impart It in a measure, but he cannot teach It because It is not a teaching: It is an experience.

With Shankara, the experience of the Absolute became more of a teaching. While he probably did not achieve it in the same degree as Moses and John, and certainly not in the degree which Melchizedek attained, still he was able to leave behind him a wealth of writing which became the foundation of the Advaita Vedanta, the only absolute teaching of India.

Whenever an individual attains conscious union with God and realizes in some measure the I-ness of his being, he is in the Absolute, he is then the divine Consciousness expressing Itself. When this happens, he either decides that he has finished with this particular phase of existence, lays down his body, and departs, continuing his life in an incorporeal form, or he is given some specific mission on earth and continues working to accomplish that mission until it is fulfilled, because the Consciousness which he now is perpetuates him as long as the need remains for his earthly experience.

Moses took his people right to the Promised Land, and probably must have felt that that ended his ministry. Elijah undoubtedly completed his mission because he ascended and rose beyond visible manifestation without having to go through disease or accident. Jesus must have felt that his work was done because in the presence of his disciples, he "lifted up his eyes to heaven, and said . . . I have finished the work which thou gavest me to do." John was given the mission of preparing the manuscript of the Gospel of John, so that that revelation might be preserved, and Shankara was enabled to complete his work of presenting the philosophy of the Advaita Vedanta of India.

Each one who attains some measure of the realization of the

Absolute has a work to perform, and part of that work is imparting the Absolute to those few who are able to receive It. Not all are able to accept It because it takes, first of all, an evolved consciousness, and secondly, it requires the ability to leave all to follow the work. Scripture speaks of leaving mother and father, and sister and brother, for *My* sake. There are not many people who have done that, nor many who are, or would be, willing to do so. There are not many who, if asked to leave their "nets" and follow the Christ, would actually give up their jobs and leave their families to follow that *Me*. That does not mean, however, that there are not such, nor does it mean that it is not happening, because it is.

"Many are called, but few are chosen." There are many who receive some spiritual light, but instead of instantly saying, "Ah, I must follow this to the end," they usually are content to rest in the additional comfort gained. They accept the increased human good and are satisfied with it, rather than seeking to find the principle that brought it about.

Spiritual evolution comes about not in one lifetime: it comes about over a period of many, many lifetimes. There are those who receive some measure of spiritual light, but aside from using it to gain better health, more abundant supply, or more satisfying companionship, go no further with it. This, however, gives them such a firm foundation that in their next parenthesis they go higher, and it is possible that in the one following that, or the one after, they will attain the highest initiation and receive the illumination of the Absolute.

CHAPTER XXI

"THE SPIRIT OF THE LORD GOD . . . HATH ANOINTED ME"

Once the mystical realm has been touched, we live in a world where things happen that never happen in the human realm. It was in this realm that Jesus was living at the time of the Transfiguration, and it was through his conscious oneness with the Father that he was able to show Moses and Elias to the disciples, thereby proving to them that these prophets had never died.

In the mystical realm there is no past, present, or future: there is only *now*. The form that we think of as our body is not externalized reality, nor is it outside of our being: it is a mental concept or image in thought. The spiritual form as which we exist today is the same form as which we existed yesterday, and it is the form as which we will exist forever. The *I* of us and of all God-substance are one and the same, and even the body is made of that same pure substance. *I* is incorporeal and spiritual; *I* has form, but it is not a dense form: it has no thickness and it has no weight. It is really a "light" form. To begin to perceive this is to understand that our present existence is of the same spiritual nature as our pre-existence was and as our future existences will be.

As we unfold spiritually, we are no longer quite as aware of physical form as we were before. Instead of noticing the physical appearance of a person we meet, we quickly look into his eyes because behind those eyes sits the *I*. We have learned by now that a person can never be found in any part of his body: in his feet, legs, torso, or even in his brain. It is in meeting the eyes that we meet the person.

The further we go in spiritual development, the less awareness we have of, and the less importance do we impute to, outlined physical form. We begin to perceive other forms of beauty, real beauty, intelligence, even love and life shining out of a person's eyes, or around his lips. We hear something in his voice and catch glimpses of something deep within him.

As our state of consciousness evolves to a higher level, we even rise above that and become aware of an aura or an atmosphere, and regardless of what the physical appearance or the speech of a person may be, we are either drawn to the atmosphere flowing out from him, repelled by it, or we are indifferent to it.

Everyone carries his atmosphere with him, and there is no way to hide it or cover it up. For a person of spiritual discernment, it is not too hard to sense whether those with whom he comes in contact are simply good human beings or whether they have developed spiritually to any degree. Something tells us when that spiritual development is present in a person. The person himself cannot tell it because, if he does, that is a denial of it. But we can feel it and are attracted to it. In fact, such a height of spiritual elevation can be reached that a person with a highly enough developed spiritual consciousness can see the entire body of a spiritually illumined person disappear and, in its place, there will be nothing left but light. It may be either a light around the body with the body invisible, or the entire body may be a body of light. This is a momentary thing; it does not last for long, but it does happen.

Nobody can say, "I am spiritual, and my body is light," and then expect that others will be able to see that light. No, even when a person has attained the place where he is a body of light, no one else can see that body as light until he himself has attained the degree of spiritual illumination that makes it possible to witness what is there.

At the time of the Transfiguration, Jesus was at the stage of his unfoldment where he was no longer a man: he had become the Way, the Truth, and the Life—incorporeal and wholly spiritual—but as far as those in his immediate environment were concerned, he was still walking around in what the universal human mind interprets as human form. His friends, relatives, and followers had not risen in consciousness. They still remained on the human plane, so they, therefore, were able to cognize only materiality.

During the experience of the Transfiguration, Jesus had with him the most highly developed of his disciples, and inasmuch as by this time they were perhaps too far advanced spiritually to be taught much more of the letter of truth, they were with him on the Mount only for inspiration, meditation, and illumination.

Through his meditation and through his going deeper and deeper within himself, he was able to raise his disciples the extra notch that was necessary so that their human sense was "dead," and as he became more deeply immersed in the Spirit, the fullness of his spiritual body, his light-body, was made evident to them. They had "died" to their finite sense and had been lifted to a state of consciousness where they could behold him as he really was.

Every practitioner who has worked spiritually, or even one who has used mental arguments, has been lifted up above mental argument to a place where it stopped, and quietness began. Such a practitioner has witnessed something much like the Transfiguration even though he may not have been aware of it. In response to a call for help from some person, he may have so far forgotten the person and the condition in his knowing the truth about God that all of a sudden he came to the end of the mental argument and for just a flash—one tiny bit of a second—something happened: it was as if he had seen spiritual man, and then he knew that everything was all right.

He may not have realized what had happened, but in that blinding flash he lost all sense of corporeality and saw man as he *is*. He did not see him with his eyes: he perceived him with his inner vision. He saw with inner spiritual discernment, and with that inner spiritual discernment there was that second's glimpse of the real man.

So we continue with our spiritual development and unfoldment. We catch a glimpse of spiritual man, sometimes even of spiritual form, and eventually we arrive at the place where it is almost a daily experience to see some person, usually a patient or a student, in his spiritual identity.

The Transfiguration is not an experience of two thousand years ago. It is a continuing experience that always has been and always will be. It is an experience in which individuals so lift themselves above the physical or mental state that they become less aware of the corporeal form, and more aware of what is shining through that form. Thus we have Transfiguration, and we have it here, and we have it now, available for all who have eyes to see.

The Spirit of the Lord is upon me, because he hath anointed me to preach the gospel to the poor; he hath sent me to heal the broken-hearted, to preach deliverance to the captives, and recovering of sight to the blind, to set at liberty them that are bruised.   LUKE 4:18

That is the mystical experience. But before that happens, we are human beings, separate and apart from God, mortals who have no God-contact, who are not blessed or reached by God, and not even known to God. When we first feel that divine Presence, however, we are ordained; we are no longer human beings, no longer mortal: we are now the sons of God. We are still the son of man insofar as those who see our body are concerned; we eat and drink, use transportation, and carry on our normal daily activities, but we are the son of God in that those things are the least part of our life. The major part of our life now is the presence and power of God, the same Presence and Power which Jesus said anointed and ordained him to heal the sick.

When a person comes to that place where a transition has taken place in his consciousness and he no longer looks out on this life and sees men and women, good and bad, sick and well, but is able to see through the human picture to the spiritual reality, that one is spiritually ordained.

There is no need to tell this to anyone, to advertise, or to voice it because when the Spirit of the Lord God is upon a person and he has received light, there is something within his consciousness that communicates itself silently to others. They feel comfortable in his presence, and they ask him to pray for them.

It makes no difference where he lives, whether in a tiny village or a big city, as the word spreads, he will be called upon for comfort, healing, and eventually for teaching. His work will grow because the moment anyone has a healing, he is quick to tell his friends and relatives and to write to those in other cities and states. The teacher may never receive honor in his own city; he may remain hidden in his home and not even his next-door neighbor realize the work that he is carrying on, but he will be known far and wide. Nothing spreads quite so rapidly as the news about a healer who can heal.

The Master was wise when he said, "Go and tell no man." No person should ever advertise in any way the spiritual light that has come to him, or give testimonies about it, but he does give a cup of cold water in this spiritual Name whenever the opportunity presents itself. An indication of the degree of spiritual light that has come to anyone is his willingness to be anonymous, to stay away from the activities of the world, and to be drawn only where he can be of service.

If we sincerely love truth, we will give ourselves unstintingly to the search. Whatever is necessary to do, we will do: if it is to buy books or teachings, if it is to give time, if it is effort, if it is devotion, if it is meditation, whatever is necessary to give, we will give. Every part of our life must be dedicated to God; our first fruits must be given to God, for God is not to be attained with a little spare time or a little spare change. It takes the whole heart, the whole Soul, the whole love of one's being, and above all things, it takes secrecy. We let not our right hand know what our left hand is doing. We do not tell our neighbors or our friends and relatives that we are seeking God because when we have found Him, they will know it without our telling them.

Every person who goes into spiritual work must be certain that he has been called and ordained of the Spirit and that he has not engaged in this activity simply because of a human desire. To desire a spiritual activity is a wrong desire: to want to meet God face to face, to experience Him, to want spiritual light and illumination—this is the only desire that is worthwhile. Human ordination does not make a man spiritual, nor does it make of him a healer or a comforter. Only spiritual ordination from the Father within can do that. What happens to a person after the light comes rests with God, not with man.

The spiritual teacher must wait until he knows within himself that the Spirit of the Lord God is upon him and that he has been ordained to heal the sick, to lift up, to redeem, to forgive; and he must also be very sure that he is ready to pay the price.

Few people realize the price that has to be paid for engaging in spiritual work. Many still have the idea that it is a part-time job, or that a person in this ministry works for an hour or two a week giving lectures and classes, and then hires a big firm of income tax specialists to make out his income tax. That is nonsense. Spiritual work demands a seven-day week, and usually a twelve- to eighteen-hour day. As a rule it means the loss of one's family, and it always means the loss of one's friends because in spiritual work no one has the leisure necessary to enjoy friendships or for time-consuming social dilly-dallying.

If a person is not prepared to leave this world and all his friends, even his family if necessary, he obviously has not been ordained and has no right to embark on this activity, because in spiritual work no one's life is any longer his own. The truly spiritual teacher belongs to his students and patients. If he is unwilling to have a telephone at his bedside and be awakened at any hour of the night, or if he does not go about almost with a walkie-talkie, he does not belong in the work because he must be at the beck and call of telephones, mail, and telegrams or cablegrams seven days a week. There is no time out for weekends or vacations, and it is extremely rare for the person in this work to have even an occasional holiday.

Sometimes the price is paid in the coin of loneliness. No matter how many students the teacher of spiritual wisdom may have or how many friends, in his spiritual life he will have to be content to live all alone in the center of his being. He may be physically present with many people, but he is not otherwise present. The price is high! Everyone who has been successful in this work knows how very high it is; and the price one has to pay in loss of family and friends, and in loneliness, does not take into consideration the hatred that is brought down upon the person who stands for truth—sometimes the persecution, and always the misunderstanding. Nobody can quite see another's motive because he is not seeing through the same state of illumination, and what someone else is thinking and doing very often looks wrong to a person who is on a different level of consciousness.

So the questions that must be answered by us in the depth of our consciousness are: Do we love the Lord God with all our heart and with all our Soul, and for no other reason than to want to know God? Do we want to make that dedication and devotion to God our life, and leave the healing and teaching to the Christ within us? This we must answer in our hearts. Only a love of God, a love of being in God's company—away from people, not with people—must remain.

Above all things, if we have any desire whatsoever for the spiritual life, we must realize that we cannot at the same time have a desire for some outer activity. Our only desire must be for God Himself: to love Him, to know Him, to commune with Him—and not for any reason. If we have a reason, we will erect a barrier. No one must ever go to God for a reason. To go to God to commune with Him, that is enough. Then, if we are entrusted with spiritual work, that is just one of the added things.

On the day when the Christ touches us, that is the day of our mystical experience. We do not become mystics—we may never become mystics on this plane. This experience of the Christ may be only the preparation for the day when we will be mystics, but we will have the mystical experience, and it will be followed by others, as long as we are living in the awareness of the Presence.

In the assurance of the Presence we rest, not on our human wisdom, our human health, or human strength: we rest on It, and It is almost like resting back on a cloud, so tangible and so evident is It. It is much more valuable, much more powerful, much more present, and much more satisfying and reliable than any human relationship has ever been.

That is the *I AM*; that is the Christ; that is the son of God. When the son of God is conceived or born in us, from then on, if we nurture It, if we keep reaching toward It, relying on It, keep turning within and acknowledging Its presence and power, It develops and grows. We have to take It down to "Egypt" to hide It because if we tell our friends and neighbors about It, they may ridicule us to such an extent that we may wish such a way of life had never become a part of our experience; but as we keep It secret and sacred, one day It becomes evident by Its fruits.

It never becomes evident as a tangible thing. Nobody will ever come up to us and say, "Oh, you have the Christ." But very often people do come up to us and ask, "What are you doing lately?" or "What are you reading or thinking? You seem to be changed, and things seem to be improving for you." There is no recognition of the Christ as such. What has happened is that the Spirit of the Lord God is upon us, and now we are ordained to speak the truth, to heal the sick, and to comfort those in need of comfort.

After this first glimpse comes to us, this first awareness that there is a Presence within us which really does miracle-working things, from then on we behold It at work. "He performeth the thing that is appointed for me. . . . The Lord will make perfect that which concerneth me."

In the very moment we attain a realization that we are no longer alone, that there is a Presence and a Power within us, we have touched the mystical experience, the experience of a transcendental infinite Presence, a transcendental Something that cannot be explained. It goes right to the roots and the marrow of our bones and bodies and makes us every whit whole. It cements relationships. It takes persons out of our lives, too, who cannot be a part of a spiritual life.

There are many persons who have mystical experiences, but they are not therefore mystics: they have merely accidentally had an experience that was never again repeated. Mystics are those individuals who have attained conscious union with God and who can attain this union almost at will—although not completely so because it is not a matter of human will power. Those who do actually attain the mystical consciousness recognize it for what it is, and they thereafter live in that consciousness at least in some measure most of the time, and in the fullness of it at frequent periods.

Many a time some students have felt that they have had a spiritual experience, but have found later that it was either an emotional or an occult one, stemming from the mental realm and not the spiritual. But when we have a genuine spiritual experience and the Presence becomes very real to us, and there is an inner stirring or awakening, there are always signs following so that we cannot mistake the way. If some question remains in our mind as to the validity of the experience, obviously we have not had *the* experience, for when that occurs there is no question.

God is positive. God never leaves us in doubt. He may make us wait. In fact, in the spiritual life there are often long periods of waiting, waiting between one step and the next, between one unfoldment and the next, or between one experience and the next. Spiritual experiences do not come every day of the week, just by turning something on and turning it off, or by closing the eyes for meditation.

Each spiritual experience is like a plateau, and our progress on the Path like a series of plateaus. We reach a particular plateau, and then stand there, seemingly making no progress, and all we can do is wait. There is nothing to do but wait. Just as a rosebud cannot be hurried into a rose, but must take its normal natural time to unfold, so must a spiritual experience.

So we have an experience, and it is deep and rich; it is bright; it is light; and it gives us a vision beyond anything we have ever known before. We live with that, and we work with it, and we dream with it, and all the time whatever work is given us to do is performed. Then it seems as if everything is taken away, and there comes an emptiness, a vacuum, a sense of absence from God, a sense of separation, but this is only to make us ready for the next step or plateau, for a still higher experience and unfoldment.

These experiences are not given to us lightly, nor do we earn them lightly, nor can we ever deserve them. They come by Grace, and each one places a demand on us that we fulfill life at the level of that realization until by Grace the next one is given us. We cannot doubt these experiences, nor can we ever tell of them. This may be surprising because many books have been written about initiation and about the lives of the great masters. But do you believe that any one of these accounts is authentic? Do you believe that any master has ever revealed the inner secrets of his spiritual life? In all the history of the world could there be a manuscript or a book fully revealing the inner life of a mystic? Can such an experience ever be expressed in words?

Even though the mystical experience may not come to you in its fullness, it is not likely that you are on this Path without the possibility of having some measure of spiritual experience. The very fact that you have been led to a spiritual path would indicate that there is something in store for you of that nature. When it does come, regardless of how small the experience may be, or how great, do not share it with anyone because to do so is virtually to ensure that it will not happen again, and that it will not bear fruitage.

If you have a spiritual teacher who has played a part in bringing you into the light, you may share your experience with your teacher, and thereby be led into a greater expansion of consciousness because your teacher knows how to hold your experience secret and sacred, and deepen and enrich it. But no one else—not a parent, not a wife, not a husband, not a child, not a friend—should ever share the depth of a spiritual experience—no one but your teacher, if you have one.

Those who have never had a spiritual experience do not speak this language, and they therefore have no way of understanding what we are talking about. Friends and relatives think we have gone off center, and they begin to doubt our sanity. So it is the part of wisdom to remember that spiritual experiences are not a subject to be flaunted before the world to bolster one's ego or to make one seem great in the eyes of others.

Many persons believe that the spiritual experience will increase their health and wealth, or increase their powers, making itself evident in some human way. But the Master did not accumulate wealth, and in his own days on earth he was never accepted as a saviour. He was a very much misunderstood person, and a much persecuted one. He never attained name or fame while on earth, nor for hundreds of years afterward.

A mystic is never known as a mystic to anyone except the few who have the ability to discern the spiritually real behind the appearance. A real mystic will never set himself up as a great teacher or as the head of anything because that is not the nature of the mystic. Left to himself, a mystic would prefer to live separate and apart from the world and carry on his work in secret.

The mystic wears no robe; the mystic wears no halo: the mystic is a simple person with an inner light and with enough wisdom to keep that light hidden from the outside world—not to seek place or position by means of it, but always willing to share it with those who recognize and desire it.

If we have a spiritual experience or have been given a spiritual message, the world will beat a pathway to our door. If we have the light, if we are the light, we shall never need to announce it: the world will seek us out. It is far better to wait until we are ordained of the Spirit, and then let those who have seen the son of God raised up in us come to us, and let us share with them whatever measure of light we have.

CHAPTER XXII

THE MYSTICAL MARRIAGE

Every mystic eventually achieves such a oneness with the Spirit within that forever afterward there is a union with the divine Consciousness. That which is human and that which is divine meet: the human element is dissolved, and all that is left is the divine. The two become one. This coming together in oneness is called the mystical marriage, the spiritual marriage. This Marriage is symbolically described in some mystical literature, such as the Song of Solomon, as the union of the male and female, brought together by a love that transcends love in any human sense. It has no sensuality in it because there is no corporeality about it, and yet this relationship that develops between the spiritually endowed individual and God can be described only in terms of love.

In the consummation of the mystical marriage, the Father and Son become one: "I and my Father." There is a close, intimate relationship between the two. "He that seeth me seeth him that sent me." There are no longer two: there is only one. It is no longer Jesus, son of Joseph: it is now Jesus, the son of God, the Christ, or Jesus, the Christed one.

In many spiritual teachings the names of the disciples are changed at a certain point in their unfoldment. Their former names identified them with a physical body and a human ancestry. Thus it was that Simon was called Simon Bar-Jonah, meaning Simon, the son of Jonah, but when he awakened to his divine sonship, his name was changed to Peter. He was no longer identified with his human ancestry: he now took on the name of his spiritual ancestry, the Rock.

Today in some spiritual teachings when a certain point in the student's development is reached, the teacher gives the disciple a new name, symbolic of the "death" of his humanhood, and signifying that he has "died" to his past history, he has "died" to his mother and father, sister and brother, and has been reborn of the Spirit. To everyone who attains the mystical experience comes this changing of name and of character, even though it may not be outwardly known. Those to whom it happens do not tell the world about it, but when it happens, they know it.

The bestowing of the Robe is also a mystical experience, and everyone who comes into the mystical consciousness has felt that Robe descend upon him. He would never refer to it: it is an inner spiritual experience—not an outer robe, but something to be worn spiritually as a garment which one places around himself to separate him from whatever is left of human sense in his consciousness.

"I can do all things through Christ which strengtheneth me. . . . I live; yet not I, but Christ liveth in me." Here is the mystical marriage: Paul and his Christ. They are wedded, they are one. Paul does nothing without his Christ. The Christ thinks through him; the Christ works through him; and this is the fruitage of the Marriage.

Every mystic not only experiences this dual relationship of "I" and the indwelling Christ, but each one, at certain times, transcends this relationship and becomes that higher One. He loses sight of his human identity. The Master revealed that he had attained this high state of complete union when he said: "I and my Father are one. . . . Before Abraham was, I am." This is the Master speaking from his Godhood, from those moments when he had transcended the duality of the Marriage and had become the He that is greater than any human identity.

Mystical literature gives accounts of those who, at some time or other, transcended the sense of a Presence always within them, and became the Presence Itself. There must inevitably come a time in our spiritual journey when we realize our *I*-ness, and then we are that One, and the other one has disappeared from view. So far there is no record of anyone's attaining that level and remaining on it permanently, although this does not mean that it has never happened. It means only that when that state is attained, the person's work is finished here, and he leaves this plane of consciousness.

The ultimate of the mystical experience is conscious union with God. It is a state of inner communion so intense and so lofty that the person disappears and exists then only as the infinite *I*, while at the same time maintaining his individuality as a person. There is no absorption into God at any time, even in the moment of conscious union.

In the period just before the full and complete union, there is sufficient oneness so that the mystic perceives his oneness with all life:

I am the life of the grass; I am the life of the tree; I am the life of the ocean. I can look up from under the sea and see the sky, but at the same time I can look down from the sky and see the sea. I can look out from a tree and see the birds, and at the same time be the bird that is sitting on the branch of the tree. I am the life of all being.

I am consciously sitting on a star, or inside of a star, looking out at this world, while at the same time looking up from the ground at the star. I am the life of the stone, and at the same time I am looking up from the ground at the stone.

I am here, and I am there, and I am everywhere: I permeate all creation. I can see in every direction at once, and always as if my Selfhood were centered in just one tiny spot, and yet in every spot at the same moment. I am the life of every person around me. I am the mind, I am the law, and I am the power of Grace unto them. I am the way, and I am the truth, and I am the life.

Always in the end the spiritual aspirant discovers that the kingdom of God is within him, and realizing that, pondering it, almost understanding it, step by step he is taken along both the mental and the spiritual path until one day the parenthesis is erased, his initiation is complete, illumination comes, everything drops away, the Light is there, and he realizes:

I *am That. That which I am seeking, I am.*

Then comes a complete inner release from personal selfhood, from human sense, and *I* stands revealed within as his identity.

PART THREE

LIVING

IN THE CIRCLE

Living the Mystical Life

CHAPTER XXIII

LIVING IN, THROUGH, AND BY THE SPIRIT

The attainment of the fourth-dimensional or illumined consciousness is the secret of harmonious, abundant, and gracious living, living without strife or struggle, completely free from the material sense of life. This freedom of the illumined is really a freedom from ignorance because only the ignorant can cleave to the belief that life is dependent on things and people in the external realm. Is not the whole material sense of life characterized by a faith, hope, and reliance on the external? To believe that life is dependent on a heart and sustained by food alone, or that strength is dependent on the development of muscles, in short, to believe that life is subject to, or dependent on, any thing or any thought is material sense.

The truth is that life governs the external realm, but to come into agreement with that, we must understand that our body and our mind belong to us, and that it is *I* that governs that mind and that body, not the mind or the body that governs us.

In the degree that we realize that *I* governs the mind and *I* governs the body are we illumined and free from the domination of mind and body. The mind is given to us as a thinking apparatus so that we can think what thoughts we want to think. We have a mind and we therefore determine what is going to occupy our mind.

But inasmuch as we are human antennas, we often find ourselves thinking the thoughts that everybody else is thinking. That is why at times fear overwhelms us, a fear that is not our fear but the universal fear that we pick up through our everyday contact with the world. This that comes to us by way of the universal mind can be fear or it can be doubt, it can be almost anything; and until we are aware of the *I*, those things will continue to intrude into our experience and dominate us. But that domination will become less and less, the more we realize the *I*. There must be that recognition of *I—I*, Self-complete being:

I am the embodiment of all that God is. Because of my oneness with my Source, all that is true of the Source is true of me, for I and my Source are one.

Even when we come to a place where we are convinced of this truth, this is not yet illumination. Illumination does not take place merely by reading words and agreeing that they are beautiful, and hoping they are true. Illumination is that moment of realization when we know that whereas before we were blind, now we see.

Illumination is the attainment of that fourth-dimensional consciousness in which we no longer see materially, hear materially, or believe materially, but in which we see through the appearance, just as we would see through the appearance of a mirage on a desert.

The human being, living in the third dimension, sees an ailing body or a disturbed mind, and longs to do something about it, whereas the fourth-dimensional consciousness sees through it. This does not mean that this higher consciousness has no awareness of the existence of such things, but to the fourth-dimensional consciousness *they do not have existence as reality*. That is the difference. Even Jesus Christ saw the crippled man, but while his physical eye took cognizance of this condition, his inner eye saw through the appearance to the man's Christhood.

The fourth-dimensional consciousness sees the discords as well as the beauties of this world, but when it sees these, it does not become hypnotized, enthralled, or excited by them. This enlightened consciousness sees both abundance and lack as but temporary phases of human existence—here today, and perhaps gone tomorrow—full well realizing that it makes little difference what the appearance is because the reality is still there. And what is the reality? The reality is consciousness. If through our consciousness we manifest a certain amount of supply or abundance, and if for some reason it is wiped away, what difference does that make, if we still have the consciousness that brought it forth?

It is much the same as stripping a tree of its fruit. What difference does it make as long as we have the tree? If the tree is still intact, in due season it will have another crop of fruit because that is the nature of the tree. And so, too, it is the nature of our consciousness to produce and reproduce itself, to multiply, so that regardless of what may be taken away, the consciousness of it remains, and tomorrow it will begin producing again.

The substance of the fruit is consciousness, and whatever consciousness contains, consciousness can bring forth. Inasmuch as God is our consciousness, our consciousness, therefore, contains infinity, so the measure of our bringing forth the fruits of consciousness must be infinite. If, on the other hand, we believe that we have a consciousness of our own, we measure our fruitage in terms of our education and experience, and since these are limited, they cannot bring forth infinity. The fourth-dimensional consciousness is satisfied to have that mind which was also in Christ Jesus, but it requires illumination to be able to realize that, and until that illumination comes, we will continue to judge by appearances and thereby hold ourselves in limitation.

When the fourth-dimensional consciousness is attained, even in a measure, life begins to flow more by Grace than by effort. Things come more easily and more abundantly than ever before, because with illumination comes the realization that the *I* of us, individualized as our consciousness, embraces infinity, and good flows forth from our consciousness into visible expression. The more we abide in the truth, "I have meat to eat that ye know not of," the more we bring infinity into expression.

The only way we can arrive at a state of complete Self-reliance is to attain such a measure of the fourth-dimensional consciousness that we are content to know, "I and the Father are one, and all that the Father has is mine," and then close our eyes to the outside world. There has to be this inner conviction: "If there were not a soul in the world, I and my Father are still one. If I were a million miles from civilization, I and my Father are still one, and my unfoldment must come to me from within." As we abide in that, we are free of dependence on "man, whose breath is in his nostrils."

Illumination brings freedom from dependence on persons and things, and the only perfect human relationship there can ever be is one in which we do not look to anyone for anything. It is impossible to want anything from anybody and not have friction develop. No matter how close two persons may be, the moment one of them wants something from the other, a defense mechanism is set up, and conflict ensues. There is no way to enjoy perfect human relationships except to want nothing from anybody. Then we have normal, happy relationships because we are free to share without thinking of any return. We will never be free of needing money, companionship, or a home until we reach the stage of illumination in which we have no desire for any of those things because they are all in-built, all included in the consciousness which we are.

We do not try to demonstrate persons, things, or conditions because if we succeeded in gaining any desired object, we might be afraid to let it go, and on the spiritual path we must not be afraid to let anything or anyone go. In fact, at least once a day there should be a period of releasing this world and everything and everyone in it. We have no right even to try to hold on to the truth that we learned yesterday. If we could empty ourselves every day of all we know, we would make way for what God has to reveal and what man has never so far even yet received. If we are trying to hold on to anything or anybody, if we continue to live on yesterday's manna, we are living wholly in material consciousness, and we have no measurable amount of illumination. The manna falls day by day, and the more receptive we are, the greater the measure of it that we receive.

The three-dimensional consciousness thinks always in terms of that which has concrete form. On the other hand, the fourth-dimensional consciousness sees the form, but looks through it and finds concreteness in the Invisible. The real substance is in the Invisible, the Invisible which is the *I AM*, the invisible *I AM* which we are, the invisible Being, the invisible Life, the invisible Omnipresence which we are. All this seems so intangible that we cannot grasp it with our mind, and that is our safety and security, because if our mind were able to grasp it, we can be assured that that is not It.

The fourth-dimensional consciousness, Christ-consciousness, or our consciousness when it is illumined, does not have to labor or struggle: it has to be only a state of receptivity. It is always receiving by Grace; it is always receiving nourishment because of the ever-presence of that invisible meat, bread, wine, water, substance, law, and activity. "I have meat!" There is more power in the realization that we have meat that the world knows not of and that we embody within ourselves the divine Substance of all form than in all that we could attract to ourselves in the external world, because with this inner realization, supply will multiply itself over, and over, and over again, as the plants keep multiplying leaves, flowers, and fruit. It is just a continuous state of multiplication once we realize Withinness: within us is the kingdom of God, the kingdom of Allness.

Desirelessness attests to the degree of illumination. By the degree to which we no longer desire persons or things from the outside world, can we measure our progress. Our progress spiritward can also be measured by watching our own reactions. The less we feel called upon to use a power, the higher we are going spiritually. The less use we find for powers, even God-power, the closer we are drawing to the realm of *Is*.

God *is*! There is nothing we can say, do, or think that is going to make God do anything. The kingdom of God is a spiritual kingdom: it is not of "this world," and the more we try to use spiritual power for the purpose of attaining the things of this world, the further we are from the attainment of spiritual enlightenment. We are free in proportion to our freedom from seeking for powers, even spiritual powers, and to the degree that we can relax in non-power.

"Resist not evil" is the realm of the Fourth Dimension. In the third dimension, humanhood teaches, "Resist the devil, and he will flee from you." Not so the fourth-dimensional consciousness in which the command is "Resist not evil." The more we relax in this assurance, the more we are in the Fourth Dimension, and the higher is the state of our illumination.

Illumination frees us from the fear, hate, or love of any form in the external world. The nature of God is light, or enlightenment, but since we can never know light except through our consciousness, it is only our enlightened consciousness that constitutes our God. Consciousness, the universal Consciousness, is individually expressed, and our consciousness is that Consciousness, but not until the moment of illumination. Up to that moment, we are "the natural man [who] receiveth not the things of the Spirit of God"; we are not under the law of God, "neither indeed can be."

Only when we reach the stage where we realize God as our Consciousness have we reached the stage of immortality. The difference between the continuity of life after death and immortality is that the continuity of life after death is just a continuation of the same state of consciousness that existed prior to death, whereas *immortality is the expansion of consciousness to the point of infinity*.

The human being is born, matures, deteriorates, and dies—all this as an existence separate and apart from God, all this as a personal selfhood that has in it no element of spiritual law, spiritual life, or spiritual creation, all this as a purely animal life. That is why, even when the heart has practically stopped beating, it can be kept active by means of a drug, but it is not the God-life that we are sustaining with a drug: it is the animal life. God-life cannot be affected by drugs: human life can be.

What a difference there is between the "natural man" who lives like a vegetable and is fed by food alone and the individual that we are when some measure of illumination takes place and we no longer live by bread alone, but "by every word that proceedeth out of the mouth of God"! What a difference there is between the individual that we are when we are not being fed just by books, but being taught of God—when inner light is coming to us directly from within, when we find ourselves experiencing Grace that we have not earned or deserved, but yet which comes to us!

The degree of our illumination will determine the degree of our freedom, freedom from personal sense, freedom from living on externals, freedom from outer dependencies, freedom that enables us to tabernacle and commune with our inner Selfhood, not only blessing us, but eventually making us forget ourselves and using us only as instruments for the blessing of others.

Spiritual freedom comes with illumination, and with that illumination, no more power is given to the things or thoughts of the outer world. At some period in our study or meditation, the light dawns, and whereas before we knew the truth intellectually, now we feel it, now we see it, and now we live it.

It is a great miracle when we can look out at all the people in the world, those close to us as well as those far away from us, and realize that we can tabernacle together, be friends, and can live in the same house, but always, under all circumstances and conditions, "I and my Father are one." There is that sense of oneness, that circle of joy and of sharing, and yet with it a separateness and a lack of dependence.

It is usually much easier to be free of places and things than to be free of persons; but to be able to see everybody in the world and have no sense of need or attachment, to see each one free as an individual unit maintained in oneness with his Father—this is the height of freedom. This is the supreme freedom. It is one of the last freedoms to be attained, and certainly the greatest freedom that can come on earth. When we have attained our freedom from persons, or freedom in our spiritual oneness, we are then united with everyone on a spiritual basis, and this is a relationship unlike any other in all the world. The strange thing is that in attaining that freedom, we find ourselves bound to people throughout the world, drawn to them, and they are drawn to us—in freedom, always in freedom.

There is the Spirit of God in man, the Spirit of life, of abundance, and of wisdom; there is the Spirit of God's presence in man. There is the Spirit of God in us; there is the Spirit of love, of peace, and of comfort. There is the Spirit of the divine kingdom within you and within me.

I live by the Spirit of God, not by external things, thoughts, or persons, but by the Spirit of God.

This is the real meaning of the life of Withinness, the mystical life that lives in and through the Spirit, rather than in and through the material world. It releases us from all attachment to the outer universe: we have no fears, no hopes, no ambitions. We are living in the Spirit, through the Spirit, and by the Spirit. And this is living the mystical life.

CHAPTER XXIV

THE MASTER ALCHEMIST

Too many Occidentals believe that the mystical life is not only impractical, but largely a figment of the imagination. In this age, however, the way of mysticism is being shown to be, not something mythical, mysterious, or occult, but spiritual, and a far more practical way of life than any yet devised in the human realm. It changes life from the everyday humdrum human experience with its trials and tribulations and its ups and downs to an entirely different kind of life, one lived from within, and yet not lived by us, but rather lived through us—a life in which we pass from living by taking thought and by our own effort to living by the Spirit.

The Master Christ Jesus taught his followers to "resist not evil," to cease from strife of all kinds whether by the sword or the law, and to give twice as much in return if something were taken from them. Such a teaching sounds very impractical for this day and age, but as a matter of fact, it is far more practical than living a life dependent for its security and safety upon an army, navy, and air force: not only would we be relieved of the staggering expense of maintaining them, but we would also be relieved of any danger from an enemy because in this way of life there are no enemies. It would be as impossible to live with this transcendental Presence and have an enemy as it would be to live with It and then find oneself in danger from snakes, wild animals, starvation, or any other form of physical or mental discord.

This is a very difficult idea for the human mind to grasp. What the unillumined mind sees, hears, tastes, touches, and smells seems so real, and the material and mental universe looks so real, that nothing could be considered quite as ridiculous as to stand before the highest temporal authority of the day and calmly state, "Thou couldest have no power at all against me, except it were given thee from above," or to say, "Destroy this temple, and in three days I will raise it up." The human mind is simply unable to understand such an attitude. But that is the human mind. The unconditioned mind, the illumined mind, the mind that comprehends the meaning of the word *I*, that mind is an instrument for the activity of the divine Consciousness.

When we can rise to the fourth-dimensional state of consciousness, we do not need anything anyone else possesses: we then live not only in freedom from fear, for there is nothing to fear, but in peace, security, and freedom from every discord of human experience. As the Master's consciousness becomes our consciousness, and as we enter that circle of eternity, we too can know:

Within my own being I have the kingdom of God. It is not outside, or in the heavens: the kingdom of God is within me.

In this moment of quietness I hear God say, "Son, thou art ever with me, and all that I have is thine. I have meat the world knows not of. I am the meat, and the wine, and the bread. I am the resurrection. I am life eternal."

All of this is within me; all of this is embodied in my consciousness. All of this constitutes the Withinness of my own being.

I myself embody the kingdom of God and all that is therein. I do not have to curry the favor of "princes" because I embody my bread, meat, wine, and water unto eternity.

Within me there is a Presence that says, "I will never leave thee, nor forsake thee. I will be with thee to the end of the world. I am thy bread, and thy meat, and thy water."

This Kingdom is already established within me, and I need not look outside my own being for anything.

Such a relationship with our Source makes our relationship with every person one of love and sharing. It is literally true now that we do not need anything that anyone else has and that no one needs anything that we have because within our own being is established this infinite Storehouse, this infinity of Good, this allness of God. As we continue to look within, It pours Itself forth as we need It, abundantly and with twelve baskets full left over to share with others.

The key to living a complete and fulfilled life lies in the realization that there is a mystical, transcendental Presence within us that has already provided our infinite supply unto eternity, that contains within Itself our companionship unto eternity, and that has within Itself the power of fulfillment.

What a miracle takes place in our lives when our sight is removed from looking upon a person as a possible source of something and the realization dawns that all that we can ever need of infinite abundance from everlasting to everlasting is within us! What courage and strength are ours! We are no longer living on our intellectual power, our physical power, our inheritance, or by virtue of our business or employment: we now live because we know that there is a mystical Presence called *I* within us, an *I* that is our eternal substance and to which we can look to fulfill Itself and to multiply.

But just as we have no way of proving that an apple tree has life, for we have never seen its life, so we can never see, hear, taste, touch, or smell this invisible Withinness. We will always be able to witness Its fruitage, however, just as every spring we see the inner invisible life of the apple tree flowing and manifesting, producing buds, blossoms, leaves, and eventually fruit. Looking at the tree in full bloom, we have little difficulty in believing that that tree has a beautiful and an abundant life, a life that functions even during those seasons when the tree appears to be dead and barren. Life is invisible, and although we never see life, we do see the fruitage of it.

So it is that although we never see the Christ of our own being, nor will we with our eyes ever see the Christ of another's being, the Presence is easily and quickly recognizable in those who live in the constant awareness of Withinness: there shines forth an inner peace, integrity, and joy that are at once apparent. More than that, there is the necessary measure of abundance in their life as well as the health, protection, and security.

At some point in the initiate's progress on the Path, he feels this invisible Presence stirring, and It either speaks to him in the still small voice, or in some other way gives him the assurance that It is with him and that It will never leave him:

Live and move and have your being in Me; live and move and have your being in the realization that I am here, that I go before you to make straight the way, and to prepare mansions for you.

I go before you to multiply the loaves and fishes.

I go before you to be the cement of love between you and all whom you meet in your business, professional, and family life.

I am He that is your rest and your abiding place.

Be still and know that I in the midst of you am God, an invisible Presence, to human sense intangible, but tangible in expression and practical in life.

When this moment comes—and I would not give anyone the impression that until that time there are not many periods of doubt, frustration, and sometimes even false hopes—and after it comes, there is another period when there are many joys and many successes, and then occasionally in between there are doubts and frustrations because the *fullness* of the realization has not yet been experienced.

Until such time as that fullness dawns, we have the benefit of teachers and the companionship of one another, and then in the dawning of that fullness a whole new life opens, a life of dedication, filled with new joys and new experiences. Hidden capacities and hidden talents come to light as this realized Presence opens up a new pathway in life and new vistas of experience.

Until illumination takes place, we do not live a full life or even a

God-protected life because we are living separate and apart from God—not that God is absent from us, but if God is not consciously known it is just as if He were not there. It takes the experience of illumination—*darshan* or *satori*—to awaken us to the invisible Presence and Power that will live our life for us, instruct, teach, guide, direct, support, maintain, and sustain us. This is not accomplished by our directing or ordering the Presence, but rather by relaxing into that Presence and letting It make the decisions as to what direction we are to go, or in what capacity we are to function, and when and where and why. This entire activity remains on the inner plane without taking conscious thought, and yet the fruitage appears in the outer life.

At this stage of our life we come into what might be called a life of prayer, a praying without ceasing. From early morning to night, and sometimes in the middle of the night, we are living constantly and consciously in the realization:

Thou within me art mighty. Thou within me art the presence and the power in which I rest. Thou art my bread and my meat; Thou art the inspiration of my life, and its fulfillment.

There is a constant communion going on with this inner Grace, and before we know it, we are bearing witness to experiences in our life that we did not consciously set in motion and which we recognize to be the result of Grace, an act of God brought into our life without any human volition or human will. When this begins, our faith and confidence deepen; we relax our fears about tomorrow, next month, or next year in the assurance, "What more can I have than the divine presence of God Himself within me, the Source of all, the Creator of all, the Maintainer and Sustainer of all? And all this is walking around within me!"

Such an assurance would enable us to look every man, woman, and child in the face as much as to say, "You will never have to fear me. I have access to a divine Source that you know not of. I have meat the world knows not of. Keep what you have; enjoy what you have: I have no designs upon it."

The miracle is that we would never be called upon to say or even to think this because now that we have this infinite Source within ourselves, no one could ever come into our presence without feeling that he does not have to put up a mental wall of protection against us. Lines of anxiety and concern disappear from our face: it shines with the confidence and certainty of our own abundance, and with our willingness to share. Our eyes are pure: no longer does desire look out from them; no longer does fear haunt them. Our whole bearing testifies to the fact that we have found Aladdin's lamp.

"Aladdin's Lamp," usually placed in the category of the fairy tale, is really the truest story in all the world, built on truth, but written in such a way as to conceal the truth from those too gross to perceive it. This is the story of I, the I that is within our own being, the son of God, the Presence which is the power of resurrection unto our body, business, home, and family. Whatever temple in our life has been destroyed, the I will raise it up again. This I that is within our very own being, this is the Aladdin's lamp—and we do not have to rub it; we do not even have to tell it our desires. It knows our need before we could possibly utter it, and it is Its good pleasure to fulfill it. Our only part is to remember that we have the hidden Aladdin's lamp; we have the power of alchemy.

Every one of us has a Master Alchemist within his own being, and Its name is I. This I will take the dross of human nature and refine it. This I will take ignorance and provide the necessary knowledge in its place; It will take the grossest, most material human nature and evolve it into the Christ; It will take the lowly fisherman or the tax collector and make of him a spiritual disciple.

Ponce de Leon went out searching in time and space for the Fountain of Youth, and all the while he was carrying it in his own breast. There is no greater fountain of youth than I AM: I is the fountain of youth; I is the fountain of life eternal.

Did not the Master say to the woman of Samaria at the well in so many words: "If you knew who I am, you would ask me, and I could give you water that would bubble up into life eternal"? And I can— this I that is in the midst of us, if only we know who I is, and what I is. If we could know the I that is at the center of our being, we would have the wellspring of life eternal, the fountain of youth, within our very own being.

The mystical life has to do with the secret of our true identity. "Whom do men say that I the Son of man am? . . . Whom say ye that I am?" If we have risen to the spiritual level of a disciple, we will respond with, "Thou art the Christ, the son of the living God. Thou art the beloved of the Father. The Father is in you, and you are in the Father, for you and the Father are one, even as I am in the Father and the Father is in me. And you are in me, and I am in you, and we are one in the Father."

This completes the circle. When we realize that because of this I that we are, because the I within us is one with God, and because there is only one God, and therefore only one I, we are one with every spiritual identity in the world of the past, the present, and the future. We are one with all spiritual identity, whether on the level of the saint, the human being, the animal, the vegetable, or the mineral.

We are one with Infinity by reason of our oneness with the I that we are. The I that I am is the I that you are, for there is only one I, the Father in heaven; and He is your Father and my Father; He is the I of your being and the I of my being. Therefore, when I am one with my Father, I am one with you, one with your spiritual identity, with your love, with your life, with your truth, but not only with you who are human beings, but with you of the animal world, the bird world, the vegetable world, and the mineral world. We all know one another because of our oneness with the I that we are.

There is nothing fictional about alchemy, the turning of dross or base metals into gold. That is not fiction: that is fact. When this alchemy takes place in us, when that catalyst, the divine Spirit, touches us, It transmutes the base and useless part of our nature into the gold of our spiritual nature, into the purity of divine Consciousness, and then in some degree we are less human than we were, and more divine.

CHAPTER XXV

LOSING "I"-NESS IN *I*

There are very few persons in all the world who are really interested in living spiritually or in attaining the spiritual goal, and certainly there are even fewer who have any conception of what it means to "die daily" and be reborn of the Spirit. Many must inevitably fall by the wayside, but those few who understand that true greatness, true wisdom, and true success lie in the very opposite direction from that of glorifying the self or pushing forward the personality, and who remain and persist, will reach the highest degree of spiritual consciousness, spiritual awareness, and spiritual unfoldment.

To submerge the personality and make it subservient to that which is greater than itself is well-nigh impossible for most persons and gives rise to inner conflicts which may deflect them from the path leading to the goal. Through meditation and the practice of the Presence, however, the mind is stilled, and an awareness of this Something greater than themselves is developed. Eventually, a state of complete quiescence in which there is no thinking or planning is reached, and the human will yields to the divine will.

This surrender of the human will to the Divine can be more readily understood if we use the analogy of a cube of ice floating in a glass of water. The ice rests in the water, cradled in it: it has no power to move itself. Only the water can propel it from one place to another. The ice itself is inert, immobile, passive, its every motion dependent upon the movement of the water. Let us think of ourselves as the ice, and of Consciousness as the water, while we wait in silence and stillness for the movement of Consciousness. In other words, we must wait patiently for the will of God to make itself known; we must be as completely quiescent as the piece of ice.

Such a state can be achieved only when all desire has been surrendered because desire nourishes the personal sense of "I"-ness. As long as there is a desire, there is a projection into the future; as long as there is a regret, there is a return to the past, both of which are dead, without substance and without life. Yesterday and tomorrow, therefore, must be discarded in nowness. Now is the only life; now is the only reality; now is the only time.

There can be no desire, not even the desire to give, for that, too, feeds the sense of "I"-ness and bloats the ego. There must be a complete resting, as the ice rests in the water, or as the sap flows up from the roots of the trees into the branches to form the buds, flowers, and leaves of the tree. The ice has no concern or worry: it lets the water move it where it will. The tree has no concern or worry about whether there will be enough rain or sun in due season: it waits patiently; it does not try to interfere with the normal and natural flow of life.

So, too, we must not interfere with the free flowing of life by injecting "I"-ness into the already completed picture, an "I"-ness which manifests as fear of the past or dread of the future: concern, anxiety, desire.

The difference between living the life of "I"-ness and the spiritual life is the difference between permanent success and some temporary sense of success. The "I-me-my" life is limited and hampered by that very "I"-ness which is dependent upon personal experience, education, the personal sense of what is right or wrong, or on what is timely. In the degree, however, that we can relax in an inner silence, quiet, and peace, we can be led of the Spirit, influenced by an infinite Wisdom, an infinite Intelligence, and an infinite Power. Then our actions really become the carrying out of the divine will, not our will. This ability to be still and to let divine Grace move us leads to a God-governed, God-directed, and God-impelled life.

At first it may not be easy to make the transition from the ordinary "I"-life to the life of spiritual guidance and protection, but actually it takes only a few months of meditation and really serious practice of the Presence to come to a place where we can accept divine guidance, the divine will, and divine movement.

To begin with, the retiring into a quiet state should not be of more than two or three minutes' duration at the most—probably only one or one and a half minutes would be better—but this should be repeated as many times in the day as possible, and it should be repeated at night any and every time that one may awaken from sleep, and then again early in the morning. If we make a habit of turning within, even for that one minute, we are preparing our consciousness for the experience of receiving divine Grace.

Living as human beings has cut us off from the kingdom of God which is within us, and what we are doing in our periods of silence and quiet is maintaining a contact with this Withinness in which our entire good is already established. The kingdom of God is within us. It is within us in all Its fullness, completeness, and perfection. This means that the fullness of life, its completeness and perfection, is already established within us from everlasting to everlasting. If we were to live a thousand years on earth, our completeness for that length of time is within us: fulfillment, infinite supply, infinite wisdom, infinite Grace—Infinity Itself. It remains for us to open out a way for this Infinity to escape and find expression.

But how do we open the way for infinite wisdom, eternal life, and divine love to flow out from us? First of all, we must begin to acknowledge that Infinity is, and if we acknowledge that It already is, and is within us, we should give up all attempts to get or achieve anything from outside ourselves. Instead, we should center our attention on letting It escape from within our own being. Then, every time that we close our eyes, even if it is only for fifteen seconds, it is to acknowledge:

The kingdom of God is within me. Lord, let It flow forth into expression.

After that moment of acknowledgment, we return to our work, whatever its nature, and are active in what we have been given to do today. We take no thought about tomorrow, All we are called upon to do is to live in this moment, and to live in the assurance that the full Christhood, the fullness of spiritual being, is established within us.

This is making a transition from the human sense of life in which we look to others for our good to the spiritual life in which we look within ourselves, and let God's grace flow out from us.

No one can expect or be expected to prove this beyond the capacity he has attained: no one should try to walk on the waters until he has been given an inner assurance that he may attempt it. If the still small voice tells him to take a step which at the moment he cannot humanly see as right, it should be taken only after the contact within is so certain that there can be no question but that the Voice, and not the human will or desire, has spoken. When the Voice speaks, It never leaves a person with the responsibility of doing something alone through his human strength and wisdom, but It is always beside him, performing that which It gives him to do.

In the early stages it may appear that this frequent turning within is not producing any fruitage, and that is why so many persons lose heart and give up. It is like the hundreds of people who have taken piano lessons and who today would be able to play quite acceptably had they only had enough perseverance to continue practicing the scales and exercises which would have developed proficiency in the art; but instead they became discouraged and lost interest when, in a comparatively short time, they found that they could not perform with the facility of a concert pianist. So also, in the spiritual life when results do not come quickly, some of us stop making an effort.

The spiritual life differs so completely from human experience that when we embark on this course, we are really setting out on uncharted seas, not that others have not been there before us, but the log of someone else's journey does not always point the way for us. We have to have the patience to move forward slowly, yet with steadfast purpose. Above all things, from this moment on, we must never accept any sense of limitation, we must never feel that any good is beyond our capacity or reach, or that any heights are too high to attain, for there are no limits to the I which we are, after we have made contact with It.

In proportion as we understand that we are one with the Father, in that proportion do we understand that all that the Father has is ours: the mind of God is ours, the life of God is our life, the Soul of God is our Soul. There is only one Spirit, one Life, one Soul—and that is yours and mine.

And God said, Let us make man in our image, after our likeness: and let them have dominion over the fish of the sea, and over the fowl of the air, and over the cattle, and over all the earth, and over every creeping thing that creepeth upon the earth.   GENESIS 1:26

That dominion was not given us as something of ourselves, but by virtue of the I that we are, the I that is within us, the I that constitutes our individual being. That is why we can rest as if we were a piece of ice floating in the water, and let the water move us, let the water be the substance of our being, its activity, quality, and quantity.

The substance of the water and the substance of the ice are the same, H_2O, and all that is true of the water is true of the ice. Whatever qualities water has, ice has. These are not two separate substances, these are not two separate qualities: ice and water are one—two different forms, yes, but they are one in essence, one in substance, and one in quality. The ice does not turn to the water for anything that the ice does not already have, but its movement is dependent upon the activity of the water.

That same relationship exists between man and God. It is true that God is invisible to human sight, but nevertheless God is the substance of which man is formed and the substance as which he lives and moves and has his being. The qualities of God are the qualities of man, and yet God is always the greater, for God is the creator, the law, and the activity of man.

To understand this makes it clear that in our spiritual identity all that God is, we are. There is no need, therefore, to turn to God for something: there is the need only to recognize this relationship of oneness, and then create within ourselves a vacuum, so that we can realize:

My being is constituted of the quality, the substance, and the essence of God; and it is the law of God that governs, guides, directs, and instructs me.

The nature of our being is the same as the nature of God-being, for we are one. Relaxing in that oneness, we permit the Invisible to govern, uphold, sustain, move, feed, clothe, house, direct, and instruct us. This is different from thinking of ourselves as something separate and apart from God, having to ask God or attempting to influence Him: this is the difference between successful spiritual living and unsuccessful living of any type.

God's grace governs us. God's grace is our sufficiency, but that Grace is not brought into our experience by praying to God in the sense of asking, pleading, or seeking for it. Rather does it come by relaxing into an atmosphere of receptivity.

At this very moment let us turn from the human picture which is presenting itself to us and realize that we live and move and have our being in God. Wherever we are, let us relax in the Invisible. We cannot see, hear, taste, touch, or smell It, but through faith, through an inner conviction, we can understand that the place whereon we stand is holy ground, that where the *I* of us is, God is, that the kingdom of God is within us, right where we are, and then, feeling that, relax.

The God that made and formed this universe is certainly capable of maintaining and sustaining your identity and mine unto eternity. Then why not let God's intelligence move us as It will—feed, clothe, house, direct, resurrect, restore the lost years of the locust, and return us to the Father's house—let His will be done in us without any idea at all of its being necessary to tell Him what we need, or what we would like, without any idea at all of advising God as to what we should have, or what we think we should have, or even what we would like to have?

Let us acknowledge God as infinite Intelligence and divine Love and be satisfied with that:

I am satisfied to be what You want me to be, to do what You want me to do, to be where You want me to be.

I live and move and have my being in Your consciousness. You are closer to me than breathing; You know my needs before I do. It is Your good pleasure to give me the kingdom, and I can rest and relax in You.

We must relax in His consciousness; we must relax in His Spirit, His wisdom, His judgment, and His will. A person who does that is developing a healing and redeeming consciousness because he is not seeking a God-power; he is not acknowledging a power that has to be overcome: he is living in God-power. That is going back to the fullness of mysticism in which we learn that evil has no existence at all except in the mind that believes in good and evil.

The healing consciousness comes only to those who arrive at a state of consciousness in which they can live consciously at-one with God, in full and complete confidence that God is infinite, needing no help from anyone. In this God-consciousness there is nothing for God to battle, nothing for God to overcome.

The mystical life rests on the premise that in the presence of spiritual consciousness neither material nor mental power is power. That is the healing consciousness, and in its presence human power of every kind dissolves. All spiritually illumined individuals are in agreement that they know nothing of the nature of any power with which to overcome sin, disease, lack, or inharmonious human relationships, but they also testify that in proportion to their attainment of an inner stillness, without any sense of needing a power, the discords evaporate.

The realization that God is the one infinite all-power and that neither material nor mental power is power is what constitutes spiritual consciousness. Spiritual consciousness is not something mysterious: it is not a consciousness of might, power, or human effort, but the consciousness of *My* Spirit. Spiritual consciousness acknowledges that God alone is power; it is a consciousness that is not divided, a consciousness that sees with a single eye, and sees but one Power, one Presence, one Being, one Cause.

Spiritual consciousness is our individual consciousness when we no longer give power to physical force or mental force, but understand

God as the only Force, and then live the command of Jesus Christ, "Resist not evil." We do not consciously direct spiritual consciousness: it performs its function in us and through us, and we merely become aware of what it is imparting to us.

For example, our hand, of itself, cannot go up and it cannot go down; it cannot give and it cannot withhold. We must move the hand. We must direct it. If we are living on the physical or mental level, then we can do this for good or for evil; but if we have attained even a measure of the consciousness that God alone is power, then the hand is moved, not by us personally, but by the divine I that we are, and never for evil, never for destruction, never for harm. We are not consciously moving it: we are letting it be moved by the Consciousness which is God, the Consciousness that we are.

This is true also of our body: we can move it where, when, and how we want to, and we can move it for good or evil. The choice lies within us. But in proportion as we come to the realization that God is the only consciousness, we will find that our body is being moved. We are not consciously moving it: it is being moved, but never toward sin, never toward disease or old age, and never toward death. It is being moved in accord with the grace of God, and when the time comes to pass from this human scene for greater experiences, it will be a passing, not a pushing out.

God is the one and only infinite consciousness, the all good. My consciousness, and everything within the realm of my consciousness is God-governed, God-maintained, God-sustained, God-fed. God, divine Consciousness, is the substance of all form: there is no evil form, there is no destructive form, no harmful form, no injurious form, for God is the substance of all form.

All form is of the name and nature of God. All form is of the quality and activity of God, and exists under the law of God. As we understand God to be the substance of all form, in the clarity of our inner vision, we will know that there can be no destructive form, no injurious or harmful form. We do not deny that there are germs, but we know that a germ cannot be injurious or destructive in the realization of one Power, one Intelligence, one Love, and one Life.

Regardless of the name or nature of the problem which is brought to our awareness, we have to begin with the truth that God is one—one Presence, one Being, one Power—and all that God is, we are. God-consciousness is our consciousness, and nothing can enter that consciousness which "defileth . . . or maketh a lie." In this truth of oneness, of one Being, one Presence, one Power, there are no opposing powers.

When we rest in that truth, it picks us up and transforms the mind, the body, and all that is called our life or outer experience, which is not really an outer experience at all but an experience that is taking place within us, in that inner world that is the only world there is.

This consciousness of truth, which is attained through meditation, becomes the illumined consciousness. We may have a realization about one facet of truth, and we may bring forth mighty works with that, but let us never believe, when we have had a realization of truth, even to the extent of illumination, that we have gone the full distance. We have only started on the Path. Afterward, there come realizations of other truths, more and deeper realizations, and actually this goes on forever, and as far as I know, it never ends. This must be so because of the infinite nature of God.

God is forever imparting Itself to us, infinitely. The beginning of wisdom is the understanding that all that we are seeking is already established within us, and that we are seeking only to bring it forth from within our own being. This will prevent us from worshiping something or someone outside our own being. As we realize the nature of the I within us, fear will lessen and eventually fade away because then we will neither fear nor worship anything or anybody external to us.

In the brief periods of meditation which we should experience as many times a day as possible, our first thought must be:

God made this day, perfected it and decreed its activity. His will is done in me today.

Even if we have time for nothing else, we will have made a contact with the Presence and prepared the way for the infinite glory of

God to express as us. In that short meditation, we have acknowledged the presence, the power, the life, the wisdom, the perfection, and the protection of God. We have fulfilled Scripture by denying ourselves as if we of ourselves were anything, and we have made ourselves receptive and responsive to the spiritual influence in the realization that we alone do not live our life, but that Christ lives our life.

There are not too many persons who are at this moment fulfilling their spiritual purpose and activity, or even any activity which approximates it. They therefore must do whatever is given them to do today and let the future take care of itself by acknowledging God today, even while scrubbing the floor or preparing a meal. Acknowledging God in these activities that seem so far removed from a spiritual activity brings God into actual expression, and leads them from one activity to another, and another, and another, until they are being fulfilled spiritually.

Wherever we may be today, in a prison, in a hospital, or in a mental institution, in the most luxurious home or the most poverty-stricken one, we disregard the appearance.

What the appearance is has nothing to do with our oneness with the Father; what the condition of the person may be has nothing to do with it; whether we are sick or well, living or dead has nothing to do with that realization of oneness, and cannot alter it. Those conditions are the appearance, but the *I* of us is picking us up where we are at this moment, and from now on, *I* in the midst of us will lead, direct, govern, feed, clothe, and house us.

To attempt to leave the place where we are now through human means and while in the same state of consciousness would serve no purpose because without a higher consciousness of truth we would eventually return to the same place where we are at this moment. As we abide in the truth that *I* in the midst of us is one with God, our consciousness becomes enriched, deepened, broadened, and filled with spiritual truth. Gradually—sometimes slowly, sometimes quickly —truth comes alive in us, and as this truth which we are fills our consciousness, it literally appears outwardly as greater harmony in our experience.

We must live and move and have our being in the consciousness that we are one with the Father, and that all that He has is ours, here and now, where we are. As we continue to disregard the appearances, not trying to change or improve them, but standing fast where we are, we let the Spirit move us as we are prepared for It.

CHAPTER XXVI

"MY KINGDOM IS NOT OF THIS WORLD"

To live in *My* kingdom is to live in the circle of eternity. "This world" is the world of mankind, but *My* kingdom is of an entirely different nature. *My* kingdom is not the realm of physical health. *My* kingdom is not the realm of material riches. We all know what constitutes physical health, but what is the health of *My* kingdom? What is the health of the spiritual kingdom? What is God's state of health, and the state of health of the son of God?

We know of what material supply and material wealth are constituted, but what are heavenly riches? What does it mean to be "joint-heir to all the heavenly riches"? What are the heavenly riches to which we are heir, and yet which we are not enjoying in the human scene? They cannot have anything to do with such things as money, investments, or property because "*My* kingdom is not of this world."

On the spiritual path, therefore, there is no use in going to "My kingdom" to get something for this world. We must seek first the kingdom of God; we must learn how to pray so that in praying to a God of Spirit we are praying only for heavenly riches, spiritual health, and spiritual companionship.

As long as we are trying to get material riches, physical health, or human companionship, that is what we will get, and it will some-times be good and sometimes evil, sometimes right and sometimes wrong, because all materiality is made up of the belief in two powers —good and evil. But if we keep our consciousness aligned with spir-itual reality and keep our desires in the realm of spiritual form and spiritual well-being, we shall experience the joy and the peace of spiritual oneness.

To seek to know the nature of heavenly riches, of spiritual health, and of spiritual companionship is not seeking for anything of a ma-terial or human nature: it is a resting in the Grace of the spiritual kingdom. The word "Grace" cannot be translated into such things as money, houses, or families. We have to leave the word "Grace" right where it is, and if we do not understand the meaning of Grace, we can always pray that God reveal His grace to us.

Getting rid of problems before we have attained spiritual wisdom merely opens the way for another problem, or seven problems, until we are compelled to learn to pray aright. For example, if a headache or any other ill can be removed without advancing us in spiritual understanding, what will have been gained except a temporary period without a headache? Sooner or later, another headache will come, and eventually we will have to take our stand and realize that this problem will be with us forever unless we are given the necessary wisdom with which to meet it. Just as Jacob wrestled all night long with the angel, praying that he would not leave him until he had received his enlightenment, or the spiritual truth necessary to the overcoming, so must we be steadfast in prayer.

Only our problems compel us to seek spiritual good. For the most part, human beings are content with good health, a sufficiency of supply, and moderate happiness in family life, and after these needs have been satisfied, many persons feel that there is little more to be desired from life. Those of us, however, who have had problems thrust upon us, not by God, but through our ignorance of God, and have had to go through some very trying experiences, know that but for those problems we would never have risen above the level of be-ing good human beings.

To live the spiritual life and to pray aright means that insofar as possible we put the problem aside, and begin with the realization that God's kingdom is not of this world, so it is useless to pray for anything in this world. Let us therefore learn to pray for those things that are of *My* kingdom, and to seek only the grace of that Kingdom.

Our function on the spiritual path is to learn what the kingdom of God consists of. Isaiah said, "Cease ye from man, whose breath is in his nostrils: for wherein is he to be accounted of?" The human being is that "man, whose breath is in his nostrils." Why, then, should we take thought about making that man better, healthier, or richer? Why take thought about him when we can take thought about the son of God? But first we must know what the son of God is.

The ancient Greeks taught: "Man, know thyself." And what is this Self, but the son of God in us. There is a part of us, an area of our consciousness which is the son of God, and yet how few of us have any knowledge of this part of our being or any acquaintance with our innermost Self? How can we know that son of God in us? Only by turning within where the kingdom of God is, taking the time to be alone to seek the kingdom of God within. If we have to beg God, then let us beg God to reveal Himself, to reveal the son of God in us, to reveal the nature of His grace and of the spiritual kingdom, and the nature of the heavenly riches to which we are heir.

As we give ourselves to the seeking of this spiritual kingdom, we discover that our outside world falls into place by itself; things begin to happen; and suddenly we awaken to find that the grace of God has brought us something of an unusual nature in the form of a healing, an enriching, a supplying, a companioning, or the teacher whose function it is to open our eyes. But these will not come while we are praying for them. They come, not by taking thought or by praying for them, but by dropping them out of our thought and letting God take care of our needs in His own way while we center our attention on what the kingdom of God realized is. All the enduring things of the material realm are added unto us when we do not pray for them, when we seek only the Kingdom, when our thought is no longer on the things of this world, and is centered on the spiritual kingdom.

When we have progressed sufficiently far on this Path, doubtless we, too, as was the Master, will be tempted to use spiritual power, and it is then that we must resist the temptation to perform miracles, and be guided by the Master's spiritual wisdom not to glorify or cater to the self. If we could turn stones into bread, we would not need God, and those of us who are on the spiritual path would rather be an hungered than to find ourselves not needing God. It would be tragic to come to the place where we believe that we have risen so high that God has no place in our life. Rather, then, than attempt to perform a miracle that will make a show of our power, we will put away the temptation to pray for persons, conditions, or circumstances and make our life of prayer one of spiritual seeking, a seeking for spiritual enlightenment and spiritual Grace, one of praying for the understanding of the nature of spiritual riches and spiritual fulfillment.

What is fulfillment? What does "in thy presence is fullness of joy" mean? How does that fullness express and interpret itself? What is the fullness of God? When we seek the understanding of that spiritual wisdom, all things will be added unto us, and they will appear in due course without our taking thought: we need only do everything that is given us to do every hour of every day and do it to the best of our ability, keeping our mind centered on God, the things of God, and the realm of God.

As has been pointed out before, one of the cardinal principles of spiritual living is that, to the transcendental consciousness, temporal power is not power whether it is of a physical or a mental nature. Only the grace of God is power, only the realized consciousness of oneness, of one power and of the non-power of all else other than God. Prayers have failed because they have largely been an attempt to overcome a temporal power which in reality is not a power. Such prayer is like trying to overcome the mirage on the desert or like trying to overcome two times two is five. How can we use a power over a non-existence?

The human world is filled with temporal powers: disease, money, politics, war, and preparations for war. To persist in the age-old prayer of "God, overcome our enemies," or "God, overcome those atomic bombs" is to waste precious time and energy because such prayers have never succeeded and never will succeed.

The struggle physically and mentally, and finally the attempt to use God to overcome the evils of this world, must fail because they are not power and do not need to be overcome. It is only our acceptance of the universal belief that evil is power that causes us to linger in evil conditions. The instant we accept God as Omnipotence, our problems begin to fade away.

When we realize that the Christ-kingdom is not of this world, and yet that that Kingdom is the only power in the world, then, when we are presented with an evil appearance, no matter who or what it may be, we stop and ask ourselves, "Is this spiritual power? Is this evil power of God? Can there by an evil power coming from God? Is not any such claim of power, therefore, only temporal power?"

The whole teaching of the Master was the revelation of the non-power of that which appeared as power. To the blind man, he said, "Open thine eyes": he knew that there was no power to keep them closed. To the man with the withered hand, he was able to say, "Stretch forth thine hand": he knew that there was no power to stay the hand. Jesus' entire ministry was a revelation that what is called "this world," while it exists and he was given the mission to dissolve it, does not exist as power: it exists only as an appearance. That realization enables us to sit back in quietness and in confidence and realize:

God alone is power. This, that has been troubling me and that I have been battling, is an appearance that I am retaining in my thought as a mental image: it is not really a thing. I cannot win a battle over nothing, but I can relax in quietness and in confidence, and realize that this picture with which I am confronted is nothing but a picture—not a person or a condition, even though it may appear as person or condition.

As soon as we recognize evil as temporal power, we can inwardly smile and realize that this means no power because *that which is not of God is not power.* God has given us dominion over all that exists, and therefore, this that appears as effect is temporal. All power is invisible. This danger that is so very visible and apparent cannot be power and cannot be of God.

And as we sit beside a person who is ill, and realize, "I will not give power to this disease, this sin, or this false appetite. This is temporal power which means it is no power, and I will not believe in it," we shall find him getting better, and then we will know that we have proved, if only in a small way, that temporal power is not a power in any form.

The spiritual life is not the *overcoming* of evil but the *recognition* of the *nature of evil*: evil is not ordained of God; evil has no law of God to sustain it; evil has no God-existence, God-purpose, God-life, God-substance, or God-law: it is temporal, the "arm of flesh," or nothingness.

As long as we are praying for a God-power to overcome evil, we are resisting evil, but when we are anchored in the truth, we relax in the realization that this thing that is facing us is a mirage, not a power, and that we need not fear what mortal man can do to us, or what he can think or be. All fear of mortal power is dissolved—temporal power, material power, the laws of infection, contagion, calendars, or age—because we know that nothing in the realm of effect is power. All power is invisible, and that which is appearing to us as power is a mental image in thought, a picture, a mistaken concept of power.

Knowing this truth will make us free, but while we are knowing it our thoughts and action must conform to the truth we are knowing. We cannot be denying the power of effect and the next minute indulge in it, or to put it more bluntly, we cannot deny the power of effect and then hate somebody or fear somebody because he is a part of that effect.

If we are unable to do this one hundred per cent, or if occasionally we fail, we must not be disheartened. It is hardly possible for anyone to change overnight from a material state of consciousness to a spiritual state of consciousness, or to become wholly and completely spiritual after only a year or two of study and meditation.

Let us be grateful that from the moment we have set foot upon the spiritual path and begun to practice living this way, in some measure, we are attaining that "mind . . . which was also in Christ Jesus," and in that measure, however small, we are demonstrating outwardly the fruitage of it. The point is not that we expect to attain Christ-hood in a single bound, but that with every day of this kind of prayer and meditation, we are attaining some measure of that Christ-mind. As we look out at the temporal universe, let us realize:

This world is not to be feared or hated or loved: this is the illusion, and right where the illusion is, is the kingdom of God, My kingdom.

My kingdom is the reality. This, that my eyes see or my ears hear, this is the superimposed counterfeit, not existing as a world, but as a concept, a concept of temporal power.

My kingdom is intact; My kingdom is the kingdom of God; My kingdom is the kingdom of the children of God; and My kingdom is here and now.

All that exists as a temporal universe is without power. I need not hate it, fear it, or condemn it: I need only understand it.

As we are able to understand the nature of the temporal universe, the forms of this world will begin to disappear: forms of sickness, sin, false appetites, and lack and limitation. All these will drop away, and in their place will be harmonious conditions and relationships, and these will be the showing forth of our higher state of consciousness.

Our world is the externalization of our state of consciousness: as we sow, so shall we reap. If we sow to the flesh, we will reap corruption: sin, disease, death, lack, and limitation. If we sow to the Spirit, we will reap life everlasting.

The word "sow" can be interpreted to mean "to be conscious of." If we are conscious that the spiritual kingdom is the real and that that to which the five physical senses bear witness is without power, temporal, the "arm of flesh," we are sowing to the Spirit and will reap harmony in body, mind, purse, and human relationships. If we continue to fear "man, whose breath is in his nostrils," if we continue to fear infection, contagion, and epidemics, we are sowing to the flesh; whereas, if we realize that all power is in the Invisible, we are sowing to the Spirit, and will reap divine harmony.

My kingdom, the Christ-kingdom, is the real, and it is power. All that we see, hear, taste, touch, and smell, the temporal kingdom, is the illusion and is not power.

The spiritual path is a training ground where we gain the conviction that the temporal world is presenting merely a picture of temporal power, and temporal power is not power. The Invisible alone is power, the Invisible which is the *I* we really are.

Let us carry that idea into our consideration of the body. Because our body is visible, there is no power in it; it cannot be well or sick: the power is in the *I* that we are. If we believe that this body has power, we are giving power to the temporal universe. Looking out at a finite world and a finite body, we can change our entire experience by realizing:

Since you are effect, the power is not in you; the power it not in this body: the power is in me. I direct my body, and my body cannot talk back to me. I talk to it, and I assure it that I am its life, I am its intelligence, I am its substance, I am its law—that I which I am—and then the body has to obey.

Such a practice turns us away from looking for material good. We are not thinking in terms of a better physical body: we are "absent from the body, and . . . present with the Lord," and our whole attention is turned in the direction of spiritual harmony, not better human relationships, not better health, and not just more dollars, but to the peace and harmony of *My* kingdom:

My kingdom reigns here, not human good and not human evil— My kingdom, the kingdom of God.

If there is any human evil here, any sin, any hatred, envy, jealousy, or malice, what of it? It is not person, and it is not power. It cannot manifest, and therefore it has to die of its own nothingness. It is temporal, and it is impersonal; it is forever without person in whom, on whom, or through whom to manifest. It is the "arm of flesh," or nothingness.

Divine love, not human love, is the only power operating in the place where I am. Divine wisdom, not human intelligence, is the only power operating in my life.

Thus, more and more our attention is centered on God's kingdom and His grace rather than on form and effect, and then as we are absent from the body of form and effect, that body, form, and effect appear harmoniously.

CHAPTER XXVII

LIVING ABOVE THE PAIRS OF OPPOSITES

From the time of the second-chapter-of-Genesis creation, man has lived in a world of two powers, fluctuating between good and evil, and often experiencing more of evil than of good. As he gains the concept of one power, and one alone, and perceives that there is neither a good power nor an evil power, he is no longer fascinated by either the good or the evil of human experience, and he becomes less identified with sensations that arise from one or the other.

Man gradually learns to look upon evil without emotion, without attaching it to anyone, one might say almost without sympathy. He recognizes the nature of the appearance, and instead of accepting it as real, he accepts it as an appearance or as an illusory experience. This is not always easy to do, and it is far easier to see the illusory nature of an appearance of evil than it is to see the illusory nature of an appearance of good; but, easy or hard, the attitude must be attained and maintained that if the good is not of God, it will not be permanent, and therefore there is no use in rejoicing over it.

It is obvious that this attitude takes a great deal of pleasure out of the human aspects of life, just as it takes a great deal of misery out of it, but it does replace those human emotions with an inner conviction that behind this visible scene there is a spiritual reality, and at any moment it can come into full view.

When a call for help comes, our first and natural human reaction is the desire to change the evil appearance to a good one. If we are to succeed in spiritual living, however, we must very quickly bring to conscious awareness the truth that the object of a spiritual ministry is not to change disease into health, for health is only one of those temporary conditions that become disease tomorrow, next week, or next year, and not to decry the evil and try to bring about the good; but rather to turn away from the appearance and keep our gaze on the Middle Path, realizing that right where there is an appearance of either good or evil, there is spiritual reality.

An evil appearance of today can change into a good appearance tomorrow, and, as we so well know, every good appearance can soon be turned into an evil one: the peace on earth one day is only a momentary pause before another war; perfect health today is only a temporary condition which germs or the calendar can change. In the human picture we are on a merry-go-round that goes round and round and round; in the human picture we sway like a pendulum between sickness and health, between lack and abundance, between war and peace, going back and forth, but never getting anywhere.

But the pairs of opposites do not operate in *My* kingdom: *My* kingdom is a spiritual kingdom in which everything is intact; *My* kingdom is under the direction, protection, maintenance, and sustenance of its divine Principle, God. In *My* kingdom there is no darkness. That statement would seem to imply that darkness is evil, but by the time we reach the Third Degree, we have risen to the spiritual stature of the Psalmist who said that "the darkness and the light are both alike to thee."

Darkness and light are the same. In the eyes of God there is no difference between them. In the spiritual kingdom there is neither light nor darkness in any physical sense: there is only Spirit, a Light which has no similarity whatsoever to what we know as light.

Light in the spiritual sense is the illumined consciousness, not illumined by a light but illumined by wisdom. "Whereas I was blind, now I see" does not refer to blindness or to an absence of sight. It is the figurative way of stating that whereas before we were in ignorance now we have attained wisdom. Ignorance is frequently referred to as darkness, and wisdom as light, but there is no actual darkness or light about them.

It requires months, sometimes years, of spiritual experience before we can realize that in *My* kingdom light and darkness are the same, and that we are not trying to change darkness into light, or to get rid of darkness in order to get light. Darkness and light are one. Grasping that concept is a big leap for anyone, but for the person ignorant of spiritual wisdom and untrained in metaphysics and mysticism, it is an even greater leap—almost an impossible one—to grasp the idea that disease and health are one. They are really just opposite ends of the same stick. When we can state with conviction, "As far as I am concerned, darkness and light are one. I am not seeking to get rid of one to get the other: I am seeking only to realize spiritual wisdom, spiritual truth, and the divine Presence," then we shall begin to perceive the spiritual nature of this universe.

It is when we are trying to get rid of something, or to get something, that we have left the spiritual universe for the universe of human concepts. Neither disease nor health has any part in the spiritual life: all that exists in the spiritual life is God, Spirit infinitely and eternally manifested as individual incorporeal being.

Incorporeal being cannot be known through the senses of sight, hearing, taste, touch, or smell: it can be experienced only in our consciousness, but once that experience comes to us we shall really understand that darkness and light are one. And what is that one? Mortal illusion, *maya*, appearance. Whatever we are aware of through the senses—sickness and poverty today, or health and wealth tomorrow—is an illusion. We are not beholding reality until, through our spiritual awareness, we behold incorporeal spiritual being.

When we can look out upon this human world and ask, "What has it profited the world all its wars?" and receive the answer, "Nothing," we are beginning to reach the goal. Hand in hand with this question must come a second one, "What has it profited the world all the days in which there has been no war?" and this, too, must receive the answer, "Nothing." Spiritually, it is not war or peace we are seeking: it is the government of God, spiritual government, divine government. And where does this take place? In our consciousness. That is where it must be realized.

No matter how many solutions are offered today to the problems of the world, tomorrow they will break out in new and more serious forms. The end of all this shifting back and forth will come only when we perceive the nature of spiritual power, and realize that spiritual power has nothing to do with good conditions today or evil conditions tomorrow. Rather does it have to do with our understanding that we are not seeking to change the conditions of matter but to realize the omnipresence of Spirit, that we are not seeking to turn sickness into health or war into peace: we are seeking the government of God, the revelation and the realization of God as our consciousness.

This changes our whole mode of life. Under our old way of living, the best that we could hope for was to turn some evil condition into a good one or some negative condition into a positive one, and even though there was the ever-present fear that it would not be permanent, we were always striving for those temporary moments of health, of peace, or of harmony.

The revelation and understanding of one power helps us to arrive at the consciousness where we do not seek to change the negative to the positive. In the realization of one power, we not only stop seeking some material power with which to meet our need, but we stop seeking a spiritual power.

Since there is but one power, then, there is nothing on, against, or for which to use this power. What in essence does this really mean? What does it mean to reach a point in consciousness where we relinquish all thought of using God as a power? Have we not thus really released God from responsibility? And is not that exactly what we all must learn to do?

God is forever about His business. God is the creative, maintaining, and sustaining influence of the spiritual universe. God governs His universe by Grace, and this not tomorrow or next week. The divine Grace that has been in operation from everlasting to everlasting will continue from everlasting to everlasting without our bribing or trying to influence God, without our praying, pleading, or doing anything else to persuade God to do His own work. God is, and this includes the truth that God is forever about the business of being God.

Our function in prayer and meditation is to "know the truth," and the truth will make us free: know the truth that there is but one power; know the truth that "thou couldest have no power at all against me, except it were given thee from above"; know the truth that in the kingdom of God, light and darkness are the same. This constant, consistent, and dedicated knowing of the truth will develop a state of consciousness that does not shift back and forth between the evil and the good: it holds itself at least with some measure of stability to the spiritual path and to spiritual realization.

God is, but in order to realize that God is we have to rise above time and space because in *Is* or *Is-ness* there is no time and no space. God's *is-ness* is from everlasting to everlasting; therefore, nothing is ever outside the jurisdiction of the is-ness of God; nothing in the spiritual kingdom has ever gone wrong. Our whole state of consciousness has to change from a material base, from its functioning in two powers, to a resting in the is-ness of God.

In the entire kingdom of God there is nothing of a changeable nature, nothing of a discordant or inharmonious nature, nothing that needs healing or improving. In that state of consciousness we are no longer hypnotized by appearances, nor are we compelled to try instantly to change the evil to the good, or to try to hold on to whatever good appearance there may be. This does not in any way affect our outer life. As this spiritual realization comes to us and our life becomes more harmonious, we are no longer dealing with a good appearance that was once evil: we are now dealing with the spiritual reality that has come into view.

Sometimes students are not happy with the detachment that must come to them as they continue on the spiritual path. Often they feel as if they were losing something worthwhile in life. Their treasured art objects, their pets, and their lifelong friendships are not quite so important to them as heretofore. The world is becoming more objective to them—their body and even their life. In looking out at this world as a beholder, much of what constitutes a great part of human life, that is, emotion, is lost.

It is true that there is a reorientation of human values as students go forward in the spiritual life: they are not quite so hurt by the negative aspects of human life, but neither can they rejoice so much over the good things as they once did. Feelings and emotion do not enter into daily life to the extent they formerly did. As these things drop away, however, there are gains that far outweigh the losses.

When we become beholders of life, we do not look out at life and wonder what is going to happen. We behold what God is doing. The beholder on the spiritual path awakens in the morning and realizes, "This is God's day; 'this is the day which the Lord hath made.' What is God going to do with this day in its relationship to me? What experience will the activity of God bring to me this day?"

In that objective and detached way we go through the day with the expectancy of something just around he corner, the feeling that whatever God brings to pass in this hour, the next hour, and the hour after that is the product of God, and the effect of the activity of God. We now come into the experience of an unchanging harmony. We are at that point where we are no longer as concerned with outer effects as we once were; we have come to that place of looking at the appearance whether good or bad, and realizing its illusory nature.

Concerning ourselves with the nature of the appearance indulges and perpetuates the hypnotism. Morning, noon, and night, we must maintain within ourselves a spiritual balance in the realization that in the kingdom of God there is neither good nor evil: there is only Spirit; and in the kingdom of this world the appearance of evil and the appearance of good are equally illusory. If we wish to bring about a spiritual demonstration of Christhood, we cannot concern ourselves with the momentary appearances, but must hold fast to the spiritual truth within ourselves.

Although the kingdom of God is invisible and incorporeal to human sight, it is tangible and real to those who have the spiritual vision to behold it. Only through spiritual awareness, through spiritual consciousness, through the fourth-dimensional consciousness, Christ-consciousness, can we behold spiritual identity. We cannot see spiritual identity with our eyes, but just as God can look through light and darkness and behold them as one, so can the spiritually illumined look through the appearance of good or bad humanhood and behold Christhood.

In a mystical teaching we have no right to look at a human being with the idea of changing evil into good, disease into health, or lack into abundance. What we must do—and it is imperative that we do it—is to look through the appearance and realize:

Unseen to my human eyes, this is the Christ, the son of God. I do not seek to change him, improve, reform, or enrich him. I look through the appearance, and remember that even though I cannot see it, here is spiritual identity.

For those who have been trained to see the unreality of erroneous appearances, this may not seem to be too difficult to do, but the reason most of us do not have greater success in looking through the appearance is that we do not apply this principle when we see good human appearances. Why should there be rejoicing over a healthy, wealthy, successful, or happy appearance when the whole picture can be reversed in less than an hour?

It is not easy for anyone, not even for the spiritual student, to be able to look at himself, his friends, or his relatives when they are the healthiest, the wealthiest, and the purest, and realize that this is only an appearance, but that invisible to human sight is the Christ, the spiritual son of God, the Reality. If a person is able to do that, however, he will always be tabernacling with the spiritual identity of his friends, relatives, and students. It is the very love of God flowing through him that is closing his eyes to appearances and showing him the Soul of every person, of those who are good as well as those who are bad—the same pure Soul which is God.

In proportion as we can be in this world, but not of it—in it, and yet not be fascinated by the human identity of persons, but realize that every person is really the Soul of God made evident on this earth—we shall be living in "My kingdom." This takes a developed inner vision which sees the presence of God in every person.

It is amazing what miracles take place when we give up all attempts to make bad people good or sick people well, and begin to dwell in this realization:

God, reveal to me Thy spiritual Selfhood; reveal Thy spiritual Son; show forth the son of God in every individual.

With this vision we begin to see and to feel spiritual sonship all around us. People act differently toward us and we toward them because we are no longer treating them as we think they deserve to be treated. We hold no one in condemnation because we know that it is only his ignorance of what he is doing, his ignorance of his divine sonship, that makes him act as he does. Crimes against society and individuals—lying, stealing, cheating, defrauding—can be committed only as long as we think that you are you, and I am I. All that stops the minute we discover that we are brothers with the same Father, and that we belong to the same family and live in the same household. At once this makes the world less real and *My* kingdom more real, revealing the universe as a spiritual kingdom where nothing has to be attained by force.

This is the mystical life: we look not at the good human appearance and rejoice in it, but look through the good, as well as through the evil, human appearance, and behold Christhood. We can do it. We all can do it. True, it requires some discipline and some training because what we are trying to do is to overcome the effects of hundreds of generations of those who have left us as a heritage the belief in two powers. We are casting aside both the good and the evil to behold the spiritual, casting aside both good health and bad health in order to attain the realization of that Christhood which is our permanent identity in God. Only our spiritual identity as the child of God enables us to eat of that meat the world knows not of.

It is not by virtue of being a good human being that any of us can claim that we are "joint-heirs with Christ" because good humanhood is as far from heaven as bad humanhood. The scribes and the Pharisees were the very best of the Hebrews: the most religious, the greatest worshipers of the one God, the greatest supporters of the temple. Being good was an obsession with them, and yet the Master told his followers that their goodness must transcend that of the scribes and the Pharisees. Humanly that would have been well-nigh impossible because they had already practically attained perfection.

Real goodness lies in the ability to realize that the kingdom of God is ours, not by virtue of our goodness, but by virtue of our spiritual identity. This means being courageous enough to throw aside all thought of our badness past or present, and in the same breath to throw aside our goodness as well—throw them both out and take no credit unto ourselves for the good and no condemnation for the evil, but claim for ourselves only our spiritual identity in God. In this relationship with God we shall find that we are one with God, we are joint-heirs with God to all the heavenly riches, but as long as we think that our evil ways are keeping us from those riches or that our good is bringing us closer to them, we are missing the way.

The one who believes that some error, some temporary evil, or some mistake of omission or commission is separating him from God is just as far off the beam as the person who believes that his goodness is earning him God's grace. No one attains God's grace by goodness alone: God's grace is attained by the realization of spiritual identity; and in the recognition of our spiritual identity, we will be good in every spiritual way. How that good measures up with human goodness there is no way of knowing, but spiritual integrity can come only through our relationship to God, and not by virtue of any good qualities or because of any personal sacrifices or efforts.

Our human experience of the past and the present with its good and evil is the mortal dream, but within our Soul we are God-being; in our inner light, we are children of God; in the depths of our inner being, we are one with God; and we have "meat," which we may not even have earned or deserved, but we have it nevertheless by virtue of divine inheritance.

Many of us have received, or will receive, much that we know in our heart and soul we do not deserve. Far more will this be true in our spiritual experience when we find God's goodness pouring itself upon us faster than we can accept it and realize that nothing in our human life entitles us to this. It comes to us as the grace of God from which neither life nor death can separate us.

There is no place where we can go and be separate from God's care, God's jurisdiction, God's life, and God's law. Whether we live on one side of the veil or on the other is of no importance except to those few people who temporarily will miss our physical presence. But very soon, when that sense of absence is healed, nothing is changed, no one has lost anything, no one has been hurt, for in God, life and death are the same. They are mortal appearances, human illusions. To understand that both are of the same substance, the fabric of nothingness, and that there is no difference between life and death brings about an understanding of the meaning of immortality.

Immortality has nothing to do with life or death, for life and death are but illusory pictures, whereas immortality is the spiritually real, eternality is the spiritually real, incorporeality is the spiritually real. Life and death are two phases of human illusion just as are disease and health, poverty and wealth, sin and purity.

On the spiritual path we have to overcome both the evil and the good, and while it is true that in our first stage we do try to change ill health into good health, as we advance on this Path we realize that we have to rise above good health just as we rise above poor health into the realm and the realization and the consciousness of God's presence as Spirit. To the illumined consciousness, darkness and light are one.

CHAPTER XXVIII

THE TREE OF LIFE

To understand the nature of the mystical way of life, and to understand it fully, we must first of all understand the underlying conflict that exists among human beings, the struggle between all men on the face of the earth. Even between husbands and wives, parents and children, there is conflict, and the conflict is always a battle for the supremacy of the ego. Each one wants to be something of himself, and that something enters into conflict with the something of the other self.

So it is that throughout the human scene there has always been conflict. True, there is an appearance of peace, but as long as each one has a self of his own, he will be catering to that ego, trying to manifest, express, or benefit it.

This poses the question: Is it possible for human beings to live together harmoniously, or must they live in constant warfare of one nature or another? None of the efforts made to bring about peace on earth and good will among men has ever been successful for any length of time, largely because these efforts have been based on attempting to unite people humanly, when for the most part they have no common interest.

Some contend that in union there is strength, but this is a fallacy.

Ever since time began, tribes have been uniting, countries have been uniting, and churches have been uniting, but so far no such union has brought about permanent strength. It lasts for a while, then some other combination arises and falls to make way for still another combination. There is no strength in any union founded by human beings, nor has one ever proved to be enduring.

The only strength there is, is in spiritual union, but that in itself is a paradox. There cannot really be a spiritual union because there are not two to unite. There is only one Self, and as long as I recognize that the Selfhood of me is the Selfhood of you, I cannot be antagonistic toward you, but neither can I unite with you because there are not two of us: there is only One. There may be many forms, but back of the forms there is the One.

True peace can be established between us only when there is a subjugating of the ego in the realization that there is but one Ego, but one Self, and God is that Ego, that Self, and God constitutes the Self of every individual. Now instead of being in conflict with one another, we are united.

There may be a hundred papayas on one tree, but there is only one life, one tree, and anything that injures the tree ultimately injures all parts of the tree. The life of the tree constitutes the life of every branch, and of every piece of fruit on it. If each papaya felt that it had a life, a dignity, and an identity of its own, there would soon be a struggle. Only because of the oneness of the fruit with the tree can the tree, branches, and fruit all abide together harmoniously.

Now for a moment try to visualize a branch of a tree that is cut off, set off by itself, having no relationship with the tree whatsoever, and you will understand what is meant by twoness. Moreover, were it possible for any one part of the tree to have an ego, it would also be possible for a branch to become envious of all the good that is on the tree and want some of it, or the tree, seeing the glory of the branch, might want to subdue or possess it.

But look again and see that branch back on its tree: now there is one tree and one life, and the life of the tree is the life of every branch of the tree. There is no union there because there are not two: there is just one. There can be dozens of branches, but there is only one life, one intelligence, one source of supply—just one—and therefore, no single branch of a tree could ever be in conflict with any other branch of that tree.

As we understand this about a tree, soon we shall also be able to understand and realize that there is a Tree of Life, a central source of Life, and that we are all parts of that Life. We are not separate branches, as we appear to be, but we are bound together by an invisible tie, which is Life Itself, the central theme of being. Life is the Tree of which we are all branches, and we all derive our life, intelligence, love, care, and protection from the same Source.

Let us return once more to the branch that has been cut off from the tree, a branch that at this moment is laden with fruit. Imagine how proud that branch of the tree might be of its wonderful fruit, and how it might think, "What a glorious thing I am! I am so beautiful! I have such exquisite flowers! I can bear such luscious fruit!" Then imagine what might happen to all this fruitage in just a few days when, because the branch has been severed from the tree, life is no longer feeding that branch, and when life no longer feeds it, there is nothing left for it to do but to wither, and naturally there will be no more flowers and no more fruit of which to be proud.

This is similar to what happens to a person when he believes that he is intelligent, good, strong, wealthy, healthy, or moral. Think what happens to this person when one of these days, wandering around as a separate branch, he begins to feel himself withering up inside, and hears his friends say, "Oh, that's natural! You're getting old." But it is not natural at all from the spiritual standpoint. It is natural only because he has been feeding his ego, and believing that he, of himself, is something, when the truth is that he is something only because he is one with the Tree of Life.

Those who are living the ego-life are fighting or competing with one another, trying to supersede or be better than another, richer or more beautiful, living a life of friction because there is always a sense of twoness. Wherever and whenever there is twoness, there is bound to be friction because one person is always hitting up against the other. But all this friction disappears, all competition and all opposition disappear, in the realization of oneness.

When the conviction of oneness is realized, we perceive that each branch derives its good from its Source, and therefore there is no need for one branch to compete or fight with another branch, to try to get the better of, or overcome, another, because each branch then realizes what John Burroughs so beautifully expresses in his poem "Waiting": "My own shall come to me." Why will it come? Because it is coming to us from our Source, not from another branch, not from somebody else, and not from going out into the world trying to get it. This removes any desire or compulsion to take anything away from anyone else, or to draw anything to us from any outside source. "My own shall come to me"—mine, not yours.

Our own will come to us from the Source because we are branches of the Tree of Life, and we are fed by the life of that Tree, which finds a way to draw to us out of the Ground whatever our particular nature requires. The function of a branch is to be still and know that it is not merely a branch but part of a tree. When we look at a tree from afar, we do not dissect it and point out that here is the trunk of a tree, and there is a leaf. No, we see the tree as a whole, constituted of trunk, branches, leaves, and fruit. So is the Tree of Life constituted of you and me, and all the other you's and me's in the world, and even though our particular function may be that of a branch, a part of the tree, nevertheless, we are the Tree, Itself.

As long as we are united with the Tree, whatever it is that is functioning the life of the Tree is supplying us with our wisdom, love, guidance, direction, activity, remuneration, recognition, and reward, with whatever it is that is to become a part of our life.

The ego-man, the man of earth, is always asserting himself in the world: discussing, arguing, striving, competing, fighting. The contemplative, the man of God, may be out in the world doing whatever his work may be, but mentally and spiritually he is at home within his own being.

The contemplative does not withdraw from an active life; in fact, he may become increasingly active. He would undoubtedly be better qualified to be the president of a corporation than an ego-man, because the ego-man could accomplish only what his own mental power could encompass, but the contemplative would draw his wisdom from an inner Source to which the ego-man would have no access.

The contemplative knows that the branch cannot dictate to the tree, and that the branch need not tell the tree what it needs, or when it needs it. The branch knows that it has to be still and let the tree manifest its own glory, and any glory the tree manifests will be showered upon, and shared with, the branches, and that will include all that the branch may need. The only function of a branch is to be still and let, and in due time the life of the tree will provide the branch with all that it needs; and then when the branch is full of flowers and fruit, instead of taking pride in it, the branch will be humble and remember that it is but showing forth the glory of the tree, and that of its own self it did not, and could not, create this beauty, this fruit, or this wealth.

As good begins to unfold in our experience, whether it is peace, harmony, health, or abundance—whatever it may be—we have to develop that deep humility which enables us to recognize that this is the showing forth of God's glory, God showing Himself forth as our health, our life, and our supply; and in the recognition of this, we are contemplating God's grace, His love, omnipresence, and omnipotence. In dwelling in that contemplative state we are permitting the law of life to function in our mind, being, body, and business. Furthermore, the flow is normal because it is not cluttered up or cut off by an ego trying to boast or preen itself, and give credit to itself.

It is so easy to think that we can be of benefit to one another. This is the natural belief of the natural man, the ego-man. One branch cannot really benefit another branch, however, because whatever benefit may come to you or to me through each other is really only the Life Itself using us as Its instrument. The blessings that come into our experience from any direction are really God Itself flowing to us. It is true, of course, that as servants of the most High we also serve each other, but we serve only as instruments of God.

The truth that enables us to serve each other is knowing that I have nothing of my own to give you, and you have nothing of your own to give me: we derive our good from the same Source because we are one—one Tree. We are the manifestation of one Tree of Life and, by an invisible bond, we are all branches of that one Tree.

The person who knows this is beginning to purge himself of ego because he does not see himself as the source of someone else's good: he is thinking only in terms of one, not of two. Where there are two, there will eventually be friction, even when temporarily one is doing good for another.

The antidote for all friction is a realization of oneness. We must keep consciously before us a picture of the Tree of Life, and we must see ourselves as branches of that Tree, each growing from the center to the circumference, with no dependence upon one another, yet with a co-operativeness because we are parts of one complete whole.

In the mystical life, a person lives constantly and consciously as out from the Center, in the realization of oneness, and with every temptation to see twoness, opposition, or competition, he inwardly smiles in the realization: "Be not afraid, it is I. There is only one of us here, not two. There is not a 'me' and danger, there is not a 'me' and competition, there is not a 'me' and an enemy—that is twoness."

The way of the mystic is not a struggling to overcome enemies and a striving to make friends. The mystic knows, "It is I; It is I— this Tree is all there is. Even if I am seeing a thousand different branches, it is one Tree. 'It is I; be not afraid.' There is one Tree of Life, and we are all one in that Tree, and of that Tree."

The mystic has had long months, and sometimes even years, of being faced with outward temptations to believe in twoness, to believe that there is a "me" and another, and he has overcome such temptations by the ability to look around and realize that, while there may seem to be a dozen different persons, actually they are all one Tree, all parts of the Tree of Life, and therefore, whatever is good for one is good for the others. This is the Master's teaching of "Love thy neighbor as thyself," and it is only when we are seeing our neighbor as a part of this Tree of Life that we are loving him as ourselves: we are seeing him fed from within, sustained, strengthened, healed, and resurrected from within, needing no outside aid.

In living this life the mystic becomes a blessing without consciously desiring or attempting to be. All those who come into his presence feel something emanating from his consciousness. And what is it that they feel? Not any desire to do good: just the ability to live at the Center in this contemplation of oneness.

The ego-man is always desiring something out here; he is always getting something, doing something, achieving something, and that inner and outer resultant turmoil can be felt. The mystic is always living at the center of his being. Regardless of what work he is performing, he is not reaching out to attain or to compete, he is not striving to get anything from anyone: he is at rest, and that rest is felt by everyone who touches his consciousness, that is, everyone of a sensitive nature.

Whenever competition, opposition, or friction of any kind comes into our experience, we retire to that center of our being and by realizing that we are not two, but one, we again establish the order of divine harmony. As long as we can translate an appearance of twoness into the picture of the Tree of Life, we are the light of the world, and a blessing to it.

The principle which would unite people and ensure harmonious and fruitful relationships in the family, the community, and eventually the state, the nation, and all the nations of the world is conscious oneness with God.

When a person carries this relationship of oneness with God into his business or professional life, he increasingly draws unto himself those who more nearly represent his state of consciousness. The key to a fulfilled life, as well as the key to success, is in oneness with God. Only in our relationship of oneness with the Father can we have a permanent bond at any and every level of human existence—on the level of friendship, the marital, the social, and business levels. We can be one through our oneness with God, and in that oneness joy flows, a joy at every level.

It is only in oneness with God that peoples of all the world are united in the household of God: Americans, English, Chinese, Japanese, Africans. In that oneness we are of the same household: our relationship with God, our fellowship in the spirit, and our communion with God unite us in communion with one another.

One day we shall be able to prove that when a person makes God-contact the first order of business on his agenda, he will draw to himself in marriage someone interested in the spiritual way of life, someone searching for God, someone who is also seeking to attain conscious union with God, and that common interest will be the bond that will enable them to enjoy a marriage, fruitful in every respect. There are so many factors involved in marriage: companionship, parenthood, social and community responsibilities, and financial arrangements; but when there is this spiritual rapport, all phases of the relationship fall into their proper place. Without this spiritual bond even the best of marriages has little or nothing in it but a human relationship which is sometimes pleasant, and oftentimes very unpleasant.

It is not possible for two or more people to live together in God and lie to one another, cheat or defraud one another—it cannot be done. A person would wreck his mind and body who attempted thus to live contrary to the way of God or the will of God, trying to bring his human will, human desires, and human tricks into a spiritual way of life. Whoever attempted to deviate from spiritual integrity would soon be uncovered and be removed. No treachery or devious practices can remain covered up. Nothing is hidden from God. There is only one reason that dishonesty in human relations continues, only one reason: human beings do not knowingly or willingly expose their conduct to the light of God. They are clever enough to stay away from God, and for a time they may succeed in their wickedness, but when they bring themselves close to God, they find that they cannot deviate from spiritual integrity.

Nothing "that defileth . . . or maketh a lie" can enter the consciousness of those who are united in the family and household of God. When we understand that we are one with the Father and that we are the temple of God, is it not clear that sooner or later we will be compelled to live up to that estimate of ourselves? The moment that we can begin to catch that vision, we cannot then violate our integrity, nor can we violate our relationships with others, especially when we realize that inasmuch as we are the temple of God, so is everyone else.

To recognize others as well as ourselves as the very temple of God is a step toward the fulfilling of the Commandments to love God supremely and our neighbor as ourselves. The truth is that humanly nobody can do that. We can try, but we are on the Way only when the first instinct to want to know God aright comes to us, an inner desire to discover the nature of "My kingdom" and "My peace." Then our relationship to God and man changes: love enters in, not your love or mine: it is the love of God that has entered into whatever part of our consciousness we have opened to its flow, and that love of God becomes the love for God and for man.

We give evidence of our love for God in our love for our neighbor. There is no God hanging up in space—not in the space in this room or above the room, and not in the space above the ground, or the space above the sky. The only God there is, is incarnated in our Soul, and in the Soul of every individual.

The only way to love God is to love one another, but not just those others in our immediate environment. That would be such a restrictive sense of love that it would be selfishness rather than love. If this love that we feel for one another is true love, it makes us also want to help people who are in distress, people of any nation, any color, or any creed.

If this love that has entered our heart does not give us an interest in all of the unfortunates of the world, we can be assured that it is not the love of God, and we have deceived ourselves. We love one another only because we have opened ourselves to God and have thereby discovered the God in me and the God in you, and found It to be the same God, the same Life, and the same Love. Even though depressed and despised peoples of the world may not yet know their identity, we do; and moreover, we know that one of these days they will awaken to their true identity, just as those persons whose material needs are being met so abundantly that they feel no need of God will someday awaken to their spiritual identity.

There can be peace on earth, peace between nations and races, peace in our communities, peace in our homes, but this peace will come on a permanent basis only when it comes because of some measure of realization of our relationship to God. We ourselves must first attain that realization.

As we attain even a degree of realization that God has incarnated

Himself as our very being, that we are the temple of God and God dwells in us, we begin to draw unto ourselves from out of the world those who are traveling in the same direction, those whose goal is to dwell in the household of God, the Temple not made with hands. The invisible bond with which we are bound together is our conscious union with God, and because of our realized oneness, we draw to ourselves out of the world all those with any measure of love for God.

CHAPTER XXIX

BEYOND TIME AND SPACE

As human beings we live in the past, the present, and the future. The past has been, and there is nothing more we can do about it; the future has not come, and there is nothing that a human being can do except wait to see what the future is going to do to him.

On the spiritual path our whole attitude toward the past and the future is changed because we realize that we are building our future now. Whatever fills our consciousness this minute is the seed we are sowing, and it determines the type of fruitage we will have. If we are sowing to the flesh, we will reap a future of corruption; whereas, if we sow to the Spirit, we will reap in the future, life everlasting.

In the absolute sense there is no future: the future is only a continuation of the present; it is an extension in time and space of the present; and it is safe to say that our future will be this present, whatever this present is, extended into time and space.

Since life is consciousness, the seeds that we sow in our consciousness at any and every moment of the day will determine the nature of the crops that we will reap in that extension of the present which is called the future. There is no future separate and apart from this minute: the future is only this minute extending itself, and the nature of that future must be the nature of this minute extending itself. So, if we abide in the Word and let the Word abide in us *now,* we will reap richly, spiritually, divinely, and harmoniously.

Man is continually sowing the seeds of his own future. Each minute of his life he is building tomorrow, and next year, and the year following, and even ensuring that there will be these years to come. We build our life in consciousness by the nature of that which occupies our thoughts. As we live this minute, this minute extends itself forward into time and space, carrying with it the quality with which we have imbued this minute.

If constantly and consciously we are realizing that God is Spirit, and God is law, and therefore that law is spiritual, and if we are governed by spiritual law, that becomes the law, not only to this present moment, but this present moment goes on extending itself in time and space. All there is to time and space is our consciousness extending itself. If our consciousness ever stopped functioning, time and space would no longer exist for us.

Time plays no part in the functioning of God. There is only now in the spiritual kingdom, there is only this moment, this continuing moment. It is because of this continuing moment that everything that happens in the future will happen. If next month all the leaves on the trees in the park will have turned brown, yellow, or red, it is only because of the process going on in the tree this minute. When the leaves drop off the trees in the autumn, it is because of what took place in the tree prior to that time. What occurs this minute determines what conditions will be an hour from now, a day or a week from now. God is functioning this minute, and it is because of this minute that something occurs when it becomes "this minute" a minute from now.

Whatever activity of the Spirit is going on now determines the activity of the universe a second from now. God cannot inaugurate an action. God cannot make two times two four now, and if He wanted to do so, He could not make it five either. What two times two is has been determined from the beginning of time.

God *is,* and the only time God is, is now. God is "is-ing" now, and this "is-ing" continues as a continuity of the *now.* It is always *now* in God's kingdom: it is never fifteen minutes ago or fifteen minutes from now.

We are living a godless life every moment that we waste time living in the past. There is nothing God can do about the past because God is not there: God is here, and God is now. The place whereon we stand is holy ground—now. If anything is to take place in what we call the future, it has to be as a continuing of the presence of the God of now. The only way to bring ourselves under God's law is to give up both the past and the future and align ourselves with God through the realization of Omnipresence, Omniaction, Omnibeing, all here *now*.

This is living the life of the-place-whereon-I-stand-is-holy-ground. If at any time our lack of understanding of that has resulted in our being in prison, in a hospital, in sin, in disease, or in poverty, then the remedy is to begin this second where we are, get up-to-date with God, and realize Omnipresence.

We know nothing about tomorrow, nor can we have the faintest idea of what will take place tomorrow. If we think we know, we are limiting our tomorrow to what we know about yesterday and today; and if we do that, we are not leaving ourselves open for a God-experience.

God does not operate tomorrow. The tomorrow-operation of God is dependent on the now-operation of God because God is functioning only in this split second, and in every continuing split second. Even God cannot take a rosebud and in a few minutes turn it into a full-blown rose. God functions now. We, then, being a part of the functioning of the now, unfold in accordance with the nature of our being, but we cannot do this without God. We cannot get God to do it yesterday, and we cannot get God to do it tomorrow. The tomorrowness of God is due solely to the nowness of God. Now, God is God, and God is an eternal God, functioning eternally in the now, never in the past and never in the future. When we are living in the future, we are living as godless a life as if we were living in the past.

If we are leading the mystical life, however, we will have a period of thanksgiving when we retire at night, thanking God for the way He has managed this universe the past twenty-four hours, and giving Him a little pat on the back because the sun and the moon came up on time, the rain came in due season, and the sunshine; the tides came in and the tides went out on time. He deserves a little credit for such accuracy and balance, and with that as a basis, we can look forward with confidence to tomorrow. Undoubtedly, tomorrow He will take care of all this, too, so that tonight we can go to sleep and trust it to Him.

And when we wake up in the morning, we will not again attempt to take over all the responsibility for this universe but we will remember, "God, You did all right last night without my help. I think I'll trust You with today."

The mystic does not sit around worrying about what is going to happen to the world: the mystic beholds life and watches God at work. If he wants to see the sun rise, he gets up early, but then realizes that he is watching an activity of the Principle that governs this universe.

As we become beholders and watch each hour unfold to see what God does with it, we overcome the egotistic belief that this is our world and that we are responsible for it. We do not fear "man, whose breath is in his nostrils," man who has forged the weapons of this world; but we awaken in the morning with the same confidence with which we went to sleep at night, leaving this world in His care. And we leave the day in His care, too, and learn to stand a little bit to the right of ourselves, watching how beautifully God runs this universe, and how He provides in advance for every need. This is a glorious universe when we behold God at work, God in action.

This is being a witness. A witness is not an active participant: a witness is one who bears witness, who sees and beholds. That is what we are: God's witnesses. At first this principle is difficult to practice. It takes time to become accustomed to trusting God with our days with the same degree of confidence that we trust our nights to Him. Some of us would not trust Him with the night, except that we are too tired to stay awake!

Those of us who do sit up much of the night meditating and communing are not doing so for the purpose of helping God. We meditate because we like to behold God at work even in the middle of the night, and He does as many miraculous things then as He does in the day.

"Now is the day of salvation." Now is the only time, and now is the perfect time. Now *I* am. "Beloved, now are we the sons of God." When? Not tomorrow, not when we are dead—now! *Now* do we live and move and have our being in Christ-consciousness.

All life is predicated on now. As long as we are living on the human level of life, the law of as-ye-sow-so-shall-ye-reap will operate in our experience; and that means that as we sow *now*, so will we reap. The nature of our sowing determines the nature of our reaping, but the reaping in the future cannot be any more harmonious than the sowing that we do in the now. The spiritual fruitage of tomorrow is the product of the spiritual sowing of now, and if we do not sow spiritually now, there will be no spiritual fruitage later. All karma can be erased in any moment because the results of karma can last only while the seeds of karma are operating. As soon as a person moves out of that material consciousness where he sowed materially, there is no more material reaping because he is not there: he has "died."

In the moment that we "die" to the past, we are reborn in this nowness, and in our rebirth in the Spirit, we carry with us nothing of the past, not any more than the butterfly carries with it anything of the worm. After the worm has spun its cocoon and has had a long period of quiet, separate and apart from the outside world, it dies, and the butterfly is born, but that butterfly has no remembrance of its worm-state.

Any moment in which we have the conscious realization of the presence of God, we have "died" to our materialism. The birth of the Christ has taken place. Twenty times a day it can take place in meditation, and each time it does, some part of the human past that has continued to intrude is wiped out.

It is necessary to have periods in which we consciously live as though we were looking right down a long straight line of now, seeing nothing of the past, being unconcerned about the future, and living now in conscious oneness with the Father.

When in our silence this oneness has been confirmed in us, God is working with us, and we can go ahead. If we are called upon to make plans for next week or next year, we can make them, or even for ten years ahead, if after our meditation we are given any plans. Such planning does not make this an act of the future: it makes it an act of the present extending itself forward.

When it is said that we do not make plans for the future, that is true in one sense, but not in another. For example, when an awareness comes that there should be class and lecture work in various parts of the world, this idea is presenting itself to me in some given present moment. Although this involves the future, the idea came in the present, and the carrying out of it can be considered a continuation of the present, and I can then go ahead with plans of a human nature which include the necessary arrangements. In that sense we do plan for the future, but these plans are only the product of God working with us now, and revealing to us that there should be a class here or there at a particular time. As soon as that conviction comes, then we make all the plans, but that is not human planning: that is merely taking the human footsteps following the divine plan that has been revealed to us.

Worrying about the past, being concerned or having a guilt complex about it, is a waste of time because there is no God in the past, and if God is not in the past, we might as well remove ourselves from it, too. Moreover, there is no need for undue concern about the future, except insofar as plans for the future are the natural result of ideas that are given to us in the present as to what to do about the future.

As this principle of nowness is grasped, every moment of life becomes a vital and important one. No yesterdays can ever be important after we have learned this lesson. Even if we achieved some great thing yesterday, we cannot rest back satisfied with that accomplishment because we are not going to achieve anything in the future except as a product of what we do today. It is today that we are building our future. The past is past, and there is nothing we can do about it. But there is a great deal we can do about the immediate present which governs all that we call the future.

A spiritual realization now produces harmony that can make itself evident tomorrow or next year; it can set in motion forces that may bring about tangible effects a year from now. The realized truth of this instant is preparing the way for our next incarnation and determining at what level it will be. If we are satisfied with whatever we have achieved during our years here, if we are not concerned with anything beyond this lifetime, or if we are convinced that we live only for this earth-span, there is no need to pay attention to any of this.

If, however, our study of spiritual wisdom, our meditation, and our contemplation have convinced us that life did not begin at birth and that it will not end at what is called death, we must of necessity be as much concerned for our life a hundred years from now as we are for our life next year. It is for this reason that we have to come consciously to a realization of the nowness of life because we cannot even mold next year, except on the basis of what we are molding in this moment of conscious awareness.

Life is a continuing experience; consciousness is a continuing experience; and what we are conscious of now determines the nature, state, and degree of our consciousness in all the tomorrows of which we may ever dream. We never live in any time other than now; we have never lived other than at this moment. Every moment of our life has been a "this moment." We cannot live behind it, and we cannot live ahead of it: we must live out from it. When we realize that the depths of our consciousness and the heights of our spiritual attainment are the measure of our peace as we rest and sleep tonight and the measure of our health and harmony tomorrow, then ours is the responsibility for living every single moment in the consciousness of *now*, and the consciousness of that *now* determines all the future "nows."

The harmony of this month is the product of the depth of our spiritual vision of last year, of our hours, days, weeks, and months of study, meditation, and preparation. Every moment of last year went into whatever degree of harmony we are experiencing this year. So it will be unto eternity—not only throughout this lifetime, but throughout all the lifetimes to come.

It was only because the Master had demonstrated life to be eternal and immortal that he was visible to his disciples after the Crucifixion. His life after the Crucifixion was the product of every moment of his life on earth. Whatever he had attained on earth he carried with him. The great lesson of the Resurrection, as far as we are concerned, is that it demonstrated that life goes on beyond the grave.

The question is: What is the nature of that life beyond the grave?

To the world, this is a serious problem, and one for which it has no answer. No one is certain what form life will take on the next plane of experience, whether it will be lived on Cloud Nine, or whether it will alternate between heaven and hell. Although the world as a whole has not yet arrived at any understanding of that, mysticism reveals that our life after the transition will be the result of our life before the transition, and that every bit of spiritual awareness that we embody on earth is the degree of spiritual awareness with which we will begin our new experience.

A high school graduate with an A and B record needs no fortune-teller to predict what his scholastic achievement in college will be. It is very likely to be of a high order because the knowledge and study habits gained in his high school years will serve as the foundation upon which to build greater achievements. So it is that the degree of our attained spiritual awareness is the degree that carries over with us this year, next year, the year after, and eventually beyond the point of transition.

We can accept and prove this only if we can realize that, because of our study and meditation in the preceding years, we at this moment exist at a certain degree of realized consciousness. Because of our willingness to give up some of our material pleasures and profits for the development of our Soul—keeping our thought stayed on God and dwelling in the secret place of the most High—there has been at least some measure of unfoldment of our consciousness. And that unfoldment is responsible for whatever degree of harmony, peace, happiness, satisfaction, and abundance we are now expressing and enjoying. By the grace of God we have given ourselves to the attainment of further spiritual light, and we are now in a state of consciousness showing forth some spiritual fruitage.

So it will always be. The health, the success, and the fruitage that will come to us this year or the year after can be measured by the degree of our attention to our spiritual development. How foolish it would be to feel that all we are doing is making life a little more comfortable for ten, twenty, or thirty years, that all this ends at the grave, smack up against a tombstone. But that is what we will bring to ourselves if we accept that in our thought.

Now, now, now are we the children of God, not yesterday or tomorrow, only now! *Now,* "I and my Father are one," and this now that we are living is a continuing experience because whatever we are now we are infinitely and eternally, and if we are one with the Father now, and if all that the Father has is ours now, we have only to live in this now.

According to the clock, it may have been ten minutes ago when we first began considering this whole subject of "now," but are we living ten minutes ago, or are we living now? And is not that *now* of ten minutes ago the continuing now unto this moment, and are we not higher in consciousness now than we were ten minutes ago? Ten minutes of now-living in the Spirit must bring forth a deeper, richer consciousness, and yet, if that living in the consciousness had not been started in the now of ten minutes ago, where would we be now, ten minutes later? We would be back where we were ten minutes ago, but we are not. We have more truth, more awareness, more conscious alertness, and that only because we started with what we had in the house ten minutes ago, and we have built on that.

What have we built on? Now! Now! The conscious remembrance of what we are now, of who we are now, the conscious remembrance of the nature of life, and of law, and of Spirit *now*.

It is this realization of the nature of consciousness, the realization that consciousness is conscious only now, that helps us in every department of our life. As we look out at the trees in the park or in our garden, we can see that they are living now. They cannot live yesterday, and if there is to be a tomorrow for them, there has to be a continuing now. There will be no tomorrow for those trees unless it is that of a continuing now. So there is no after-life for anything or anyone except as that after-life is a continuation of now.

For I am persuaded, that neither death, nor life, nor angels, nor principalities, nor powers, nor things present, nor things to come,
Nor height, nor depth, nor any other creature, shall be able to separate us from the love of God, which is in Christ Jesus our Lord.

ROMANS 8:38, 39

Neither life nor death can separate us from the consciousness of living now, and that is the only moment we should want to live.

Now is a continuing experience beyond the confines of the flesh. Life is expressing Itself now. That takes away the words "I," "you," "he," and "she" and enables us to move out of finiteness and mortality into Infinity and Eternality. When we use these personal pronouns, whether consciously, unconsciously, or subconsciously, our thought goes back to the space between the cradle and the grave, to birth days and death days. We are attached to that appearance—that finite appearance—but if we live in the realization that just as Consciousness is expressing Itself, so Life is expressing and living Itself, we have gone beyond the finite form, and are in Infinity and Eternality.

As long as we are thinking of our life, our body, and our affairs, and how to change or improve them, we are in the parenthesis, in finiteness and in limitation. But the moment we can see the whole circle, we are not confining Life to the parenthesis. We may be witnessing It at the point of this particular parenthesis, but at least we are witnessing the Life that has no beginning and will have no ending, and we are thereby erasing the parenthesis.

No spiritual truth is true about life as lived in the parenthesis, so we have to go beyond the parenthesis and realize that Consciousness is now revealing Itself as form. If we think of form as the Life, however, we are in the parenthesis, but if we see form as Life expressing Itself, It must go on and on forever even if It has to create new forms every hour.

If you and I believe that we are expressing love, we are holding ourselves inside the parenthesis. If, on the other hand, we see that Love is expressing Itself, Life is manifesting and forming Itself, and Consciousness is unfolding and disclosing Itself in infinite form and variety, we are lifted out of the parenthesis and moved into Eternity. Eternity never ends. Eternity has no past; Eternity has no future; Eternity is a continuous now.

Through meditation we can reach back into that Eternity because in meditation we are opening ourselves to Infinity, watching for It to express Itself, watching for Consciousness to appear as form, whatever the form may be at the moment. When we are in meditation, we are inside of the parenthesis but reaching outside, reaching way back into Consciousness so that there may be more of Consciousness, more of Life, Love, and Truth expressed in what appears to be the parenthesis, but which is rapidly breaking the bounds of the parenthesis. We are sitting in what appears to be finiteness, reaching back into Infinity and Eternity. That Eternity is always functioning now, it is always now that we are reaching back into Eternity, and this makes for a continuity of now.

As we gain the true concept of what now means and as we live in this now, then all of a sudden we awaken to realize that what we have been trying to do is to live three lives at one time—past, present, and future. We have been thinking of the good of the past and thinking of getting more good in the present and the future. All this has proved to be merely a way of separating ourselves from God. But *now* is the only time when we are the sons of God; now is the *only* time when *I* is with us, and that *I* will never leave us, nor forsake us. *I* is the bread of life *now*.

It all comes back to nowness, living in the now, and not trying to hug to ourselves the tatters of what we wore yesterday. If we can give up our yesterdays and our tomorrows for a spiritual experience that we can have in meditation now, and then continue living in the realization that the grace of God is functioning now, we become the leaven, until all of human consciousness begins a process of being lifted out of the parenthesis.

CHAPTER XXX

GOD MADE THIS WORLD FOR MEN AND WOMEN

Man is a prisoner of his mind. He is locked up inside his mind just as a little chick is locked up inside the egg. If it could look around inside the shell, it would see only darkness; it might even feel a sense of hunger and find no food there, and certainly, above all things, no companionship. In this lone, tightly locked up shell, that little chick must wonder what it has to live for. There is nothing for it to be happy about, but on the other hand, there is also nothing to be unhappy about: it has never known the world so it does not know what it is missing. All it knows is what it is experiencing while locked up inside the shell, and yet it does not even know that it is locked up inside its shell.

As far as the chick is concerned, it might stay on there forever, living in that darkness. It might even find enough food in the shell to keep it alive. It would not really be living: it would be existing, and of itself it could no nothing about it. There it is, and it looks as if there it is doomed to be. But fortunately for these little chicks, there is something beyond themselves, there is something that causes a chick to peck at the shell, and to keep pecking and pecking at it until it breaks a hole in it and sees some light.

Imagine what goes on in a little chick's mind when it begins to catch a ray of light from outside, and realizes that there is something out there that it has not seen, something it has not felt, some place it has not been. It keeps pecking away, and pecking away. It knows nothing about an outside world; it has no desire to get out; and probably left to itself, it would be satisfied with the comfort of the shell in which it is enfolded; but there is a something that eventually compels the chick to break open that shell and come outside, and find a great big world in which to go looking for food, and other chicks with which to play.

In the first six hours that that chick is out of the shell, it will find more new and interesting things than would a child at the foot of a Christmas tree on Christmas Day. It is now no longer restricted, no longer bound, but is able to look out into the world and see, hear, feel, and experience countless things in a great new world.

Is not the force of nature that pushes the chick out of its shell the same force that urges and pushes the unborn child forward and out of its mother's womb? It, too, knows nothing of the great outside world, and all it learns from the moment of birth is gained from its parents, teachers, environment, and experience. Knowledge from these sources comes through conditioned minds, and enters a mind conditioned by these factors. All that most people know about what is going on in this world is known through the limitations of a conditioned mind. They are living a restricted and limited life: they do not know the limitless possibilities of their own being. They are living in a shell that we call the skull, thinking only their own thoughts, believing only their own concepts, and accepting their own limitations.

It is a stultifying world in which to live, this world of one's mind, because that mind knows nothing beyond its own limitations. It knows nothing except what it has experienced, or what somebody else who may have a very limited concept of the world has told it, and so it accepts every kind of belief that is given to it, every law of limitation, finally settling down on a little plot of ground about thirty by sixty and calling it home, considering itself lucky even to have that much.

Most persons are on a treadmill: they eat, drink, and sleep; they have families; they are living a life of limitation, locked up in their minds. In a few, something stirs inside the mind and makes them wonder: Is there something beyond this that I know? Is there something beyond this that I am seeing with my eyes, or hearing with my ears, or thinking with my mind?

Let us take the blinkers off our eyes and really begin to see the trees, plants, and other forms of life on this planet, picture the vastness of the ocean stretching out to the horizon, look up at some of the towering mountains of this world, and see the world beyond the mountains, beyond the seas, and watch the moon shining on the ocean with its cool beauty, lighting up the mountains, showing us something of the vastness of the Infinite; observe the millions of stars up in the sky, each one a world, each one telling its own story of light, of fire, of its reason for being where it is, and of that which caused it to be. Why are they there? What are they doing there? What purpose do they serve?

Suppose that there were no men or women on earth? To what purpose would all of this be? To what purpose would there be a sun, a moon, and stars; those gigantic trees of all kinds; plants, flowers, vegetables, fruits; diamonds in the ground and pearls in the sea; if there were not men and women, if there were not what we know as human life on earth, which is not human life at all but divine?

Once we begin to peck our way through the shell of the human mind and look outside, we find that all of this glory is there for you and for me. God has created an illimitable universe, not only for birds to fly in the atmosphere and fish to swim in the water, but that man should travel, own, and enjoy it—not own it in a sense of having title to a little piece of land, but own it in the sense of being a part of its beauty and magnificence. If we think in terms of owning even a square mile of land, we must see how small that is in comparison to the vastness of the world. But when we can look down on the panorama that stretches out before us and realize that God made this for our enjoyment, the wonder of this universe surges through us.

Nobody can buy an ocean, and nobody can buy a large enough piece of land to feel that he possesses very much of this earth. If only we lift the restrictions imposed upon us by the mind, and, instead of seeing our own man-made limitations, mind-made limitations, come out of this ironclad skull and live, not exist by circumscribing our lives to eating three meals a day, having a place to sleep, or a family to enjoy, we will begin to see that a universe such as we have here must have been created by nothing less than what we call God.

To create a universe such as this must have taken the wisdom of an infinite Intelligence, of a divine Love—a great love—but a love for what or whom? It must have been a love for us that all this has been given us to enjoy, not to own or possess, but to enjoy, to be grateful that there is a God, a Something, a Spirit that has created this great universe and then set us down in it.

If we compress ourselves inside our skull, we have no more vision than the chick that is inside its shell. That is the limit of its world, and this skull will be the limit of our world if we permit the petty little thoughts that crowd in upon us, the little room, the little town, or the big city where we live to shut out the grandeur round about us. If we let these "little foxes . . . spoil the vines," we are unable to open our minds to an awareness of the divine qualities that exist throughout this world, the qualities that exist as the love of men and women, not only family love, but the love that is the cement of relationships on a world-wide scale, and on a personal as well as an impersonal scale. It is a love that is not limited to the few people who are around us: it is a sharing of the love of people throughout the world.

How can we be aware of the people in this world? There is only one way. We have to peck that shell open; we have to break through the limitations of this mind that tries to tell us that there are only the people and the territory around us, and we have to open our vision until we are aware of the sun, moon, and stars, the oceans and mountains, and then before we know it, as our vision grows wider and wider and wider, we discover that there are lands and countries across the sea filled with people. We may not have seen them with our eyes, but when we stop this limited thinking, based only on what we know, we open ourselves to what God knows, the God that placed us here and that placed all of this here for us; and the God within us reveals that there is something beyond our immediate environment: there are people beyond, there are joys, glories, and experiences beyond this present one.

It is not necessary to travel the world to experience this expansion of consciousness. Once we have opened our consciousness to the tremendous universe about us, it begins to come to us. It comes in books, in visitors, in new experiences; and it comes in interior revelations. We would never have to leave our own environment, and yet this whole universe could be brought right to our doorsteps. In one way or another, we can enjoy art, literature, sciences, inventions, and discoveries, as well as people because there are always people traveling from country to country so that the joy of meeting them would be ours—but only if we have broken through the limitations of the mind so that we are not anchored to this finite sense that tells us we are restricted to the room in which we are sitting.

If it could consciously think, the chick would call the shell in which it lives its world, but then, when it is out, roaming around its barnyard, it unconsciously goes a step further and thinks that this new environment is its world. That may forever be the limit of the world of the chick, but to us it is not. We are never confined to time or space because we are not locked up in our skull: we are not even locked up in our body. There is something that acts as a force to drive us to look out, to look up, to look around. We would not do it but something within us is nudging, pushing, and compelling us to look around until we become aware of this immensity all around us, of the beauty, harmony, joy, and companionship, of the past, the present, and the future.

Simultaneously with this increased awareness comes introspection leading to Soul-searching questions: Why am I on earth? Am I really living, or am I only existing from one day to another? Is my life just a round of going from home to office, or from home to the market place? Does my life consist of going from one meal to the next, from one night's sleep to the next? Am I really living? Am I a part of this world? Was this world meant for me? Was I born to live in a tiny corner of the world, or was this whole world created and given to me? Is not the earth mine? Are not the heavens mine? Are we less than Abraham? And did not God say to him, "For all the land which thou seest, to thee will I give it, and to thy seed for ever"?

The higher we climb in an airplane, the further we see; the higher we rise in consciousness, the wider and broader will be our vision. Soon we will realize that we are not here. We are not here even on this limited piece of ground. We have broken through the limitations of the skull; we are no longer tied up inside of a skull bone; we are not even limited to this body: we are I.

Now, as we look up and see ten thousand square miles of sky, ten thousand square miles of ocean, and the people of all nations, of every quality and quantity, all of a sudden we find that we are I. We are out of the shell, out of the skull on a mountaintop of vision, and we hear: "All that you can see is yours." See? Not with our eyes! All that we can apprehend, all that we can comprehend, all that we can discern. Anything that we can envision is ours!

This world was created for us. The whole earth, the times and the tides, are ours. We are heirs to this universe, joint-heirs. We do not want title to it, any more than we want title to a two-million-dollar painting. It is enough to be given the privilege of going into an art museum, filling our Souls, our eyes, and our minds with its beauty, and then in the quietness of our homes, reliving the wonder of that painting. Our enjoyment of it may be far greater than that of the man who paid his two million dollars for it, for he may be too much aware of its dollar value and his sense of possession. In that sense of possession he is locked up in his pocketbook. To be confined to a pocketbook—even a big one—is a dark place to be locked up in, a strong prison.

But what freedom comes when this that is within us forces us to go higher and higher in vision, breaking bit by bit out of the skull, and more and more realizing the nature of our true identity as I, the offspring of God, the heir of God, joint-heir! There are no limitations then to our inheritance, no limitations to our vision, no limitations to what we can possess. The whole earth is ours, and the sun, the moon, and the stars. How much more could we have if we had legal title to them? We would still have to leave them where they are for everybody who did not have title to them to enjoy.

This that pushes the chick out of the shell, this is pushing us out of the shell, out of this limited skull, forcing us to push those skull bones away so that we can be free, and be the *I* that we are. When we do this, we realize that wherever we look we are meeting our brothers and sisters, wherever we look we are seeing our mother and father or our children—everywhere, everywhere. Even the birds, the dogs, and the cats come running up to show that they sense that they have been recognized by their brother, and they, too, see their brother and know as they are known. The vision through which we see is the vision that is given back to us.

There is no limitation, and now we know that there is not even the limitation of time. We are not even limited to the century in which we live. There, too, is another example of how being locked up in those skull bones makes us believe that our life is being lived only in this twentieth century. That is such a small part of our life. Our life really encompasses all the past and the present, and all of the future that we can climb high enough to envision. If only we climb high enough in our spiritual vision, we can know this whole world for generations to come. It is all here to be seen; it is all here to be experienced.

Nothing new is going to be created tomorrow, not a thing; all that was is now, all that ever will be is now; but we have to ascend to the mountaintop of vision to behold it, and we arrive at that mountaintop when we have broken through all limitations and know, "I am *I*, the son of God, heir of God, joint-heir to all the heavenly riches." Then we walk out on the street, by the sea, up the mountain, or go flying through the air with no sense of personal possession, just a sense of enjoyment of all there is because it is free.

In the early years of my work, a very prosperous and successful businessman came to me for help. He was an extremely busy man and claimed that he had no time or money for any kind of relaxation or recreation. Morning, noon, and night were spent taking care of his possessions. As he studied with me, I would say to him, "Let's take this weekend off."

"Oh no, I can't do that. No, I have to take care of my business."

"Oh, come, let's enjoy ourselves for a few hours!"

"No, no; I have appointments."

"What are you going to do with all this money? After all, at the rate you are going, you will probably drop dead before you get a vacation to spend it on." So it was that out of the Spirit it came, "Let's look around here, and see if we can't find some things to enjoy that don't cost any money. Let's go over to Central Park, stand around the lakes, and watch the children with their little boats, and the birds in the bird sanctuary."

So we went to Central Park; another time we sunned ourselves on a roof garden; and yet another time we attended a concert. It was not long before he began to say, "You know, the best things in life really are free." And they are, if we can free ourselves. The world is free, but we are not free.

It is because we are not free that we bind everything with a price tag. Originally, the most worthwhile things in life never had price tags on them: it is we who placed these on them. God has never put a price tag on time, space, or place. God has never put a price on mountains, lakes, or oceans, and it is only when we are locked up in this skull that we are bound by the limitations that the human mind has placed on such things.

Come out, break through the limitations of your mind, and do not believe the signs that you see. Work more with yourself; realize who you are. There is no more rewarding experience than to take a day off for walking where you can see mountains, lakes, or the sea, and if you do not live where these are, you can always look up at the sun, moon, and stars, at the flowers and trees. All of this was made for the upliftment of our Soul, for the fulfillment of our lives. They were given to us so that we might have beauty in our lives, not the kind we must pay for, but the beauty that is already present by virtue of the fact that God made it before He made man, and then He made man to enjoy it. God placed food in the ground and trees in the earth; He formed the mountains, the lakes, the seas, the rivers and streams, and He did it for us; but it is we who put the beauty and the value into these. Everything in this universe is translated into its true worth by our inner awareness.

Men and women are prisoners of their minds, and they see only the limitations of their own thinking until they begin to break through its barrier and look out at this world, and in observing the grandeur of the universe, then realize, "It is all here for me. See what God has done for me, to give me this universe to live in and all this beauty to enjoy."

Parents work a lifetime accumulating an estate so that they can have the joy of leaving a munificent legacy to their children. How much greater God's love must be that He has stored up the secrets of mathematics, science, art, literature, music, and all the great wisdoms of the world for us, His sons and daughters! Why then do we go around bemoaning our fate, fearing some insignificant little event or condition, with the great fear of death lurking always in the background, as if death could make any difference in our relationship with God? Neither life nor death can separate us from the love of God; neither life nor death can take from us that which God has stored up for us—and God has stored up this whole universe.

Is it not sinful to believe that God stored it up for some particular person, family, country, or race? Would we not have to be locked up within the confines of a skull to believe that what God has done is for some one person or group of persons? It is not for some special person or group: it is for everybody capable of accepting it, when he can break through this limitation and realize: "I am I; I am the offspring of God; I call no man on earth my father. There is but One, He that created me in His own image and likeness and made me heir to His whole creation."

If we keep living within the confines of our mind, we are like the chick in the shell, and will never be able to encompass the limitless heritage that Abraham was given: "Look, look out! As far as your eyes can see, I am giving to you." How far can our eyes see, not our physical eyes, but the eyes that look out from the mountaintop of spiritual vision? How high can we rise in consciousness to realize we are not another kind of chick in a shell, not a man locked up in a skull? Let us break open that shell, stop thinking in terms of finite personalities, come out, and realize, "I am I."

When we are on this mount of vision, we can look down and see into the mind, see the nasty little scrawny things that make us do the things we do—the limiting things, the evil, selfish, and jealous things. We see these dark places in our mind, and longingly wish, "Oh, if I could only break open that shell and come out and realize that I am I, and that there is no reason for me to act this way, no reason to do this because I am an heir of God." Then when we have grown sufficiently beyond and above our little "I"-self, we can look out and not be jealous of another's success, but rejoice that another soul has opened itself to the vision of its true identity, and come into its heritage.

Only from the spiritual heights can we see that the earth is not matter, and that it cannot be divided up into building lots. It makes no difference if we are on a small island or a great big continent, we are subject to limitation as long as we are living in that skull bone called "me." There are persons who are gloriously free, persons who have never traveled beyond their small community, but through their vision they have brought the wealth of the world and the people of the world to them.

We do not live in time or space: we live in consciousness. We can live as big as our consciousness can be, or as small as what can be compressed between the bones of the skull, as if all that is taking place in there is the world. The less time we spend in our limited sense of mind, the better off we will be.

When we go into meditation, we are not living in the mind with our thoughts: we are living in a receptivity to Infinity. That is why we do not think our own thoughts in meditation; that is why we do not restrict ourselves to what we know; we do not just declare what we think, or believe, or what our concept is. When we turn within in meditation, it is to realize that the kingdom of God, the Kingdom of this whole universe, is within. So our chest expands to include the whole of God's universe, and now we can look into that silence and darkness and experience His whole wisdom coming to us, His whole love, His whole life, His whole companionship flowing forth, because now our consciousness is as big as the universe: it is holding the whole universe inside of it.

If we think in terms of our education or lack of it, we are bound up in finiteness because no one person could store up enough knowledge out of books so that it would be equal to one grain of God's wisdom. We have to go beyond all that we know or think we know, all that we have learned or think we have learned. We have to go beyond that to the infinite Unknown, and until we reach into the infinite Unknown, we do not have the limitlessness of God's kingdom. The wisdom of God can reveal itself to any individual in the world today just as it did to those ancients to whom the laws of mathematics and engineering were first revealed, the laws that made possible the pyramids, the great temples, and Caesar's roads that are still being used in Italy and in England, roads that have stood for thousands of years.

The architectural wonders of a bygone world that are unequaled and still stand as marvels today were possible to men because they had access to the Wisdom behind the wisdom of man. The only way in which they could have accomplished these miraculous things was to go back in consciousness into the infinite Unknown, and let It declare Itself. Just as the great music, art, literature, and science must come through contact with the Source, so must the secrets of the universe that are being unlocked to us today be tapped through contact with that same Source.

Why are these great things being revealed to us today? Are they not being revealed because man is an heir of God and entitled to all that the Father has—all the joy, all the abundance, all the infinity, all the life, all the love, and all the wisdom? Man is entitled to every bit of it, and it is being revealed unto him for his use, his joy, his beauty, that his life may be one of Grace and peace. When this is understood, we can then take the next step and realize, "I am that man; I am that being for whom all of this has been created."

To each of us will come whatever fulfills his nature. To me, the principles of mathematics and science will not come because that would not fulfill my particular nature. To me come the secrets of the spiritual universe and of the Soul of men who have lived throughout all the ages because that fulfills me. In that, I find my joy and my companionship; in that, I can tabernacle. But then there are others to whom will come the mathematics, the chemistry, the arts and sciences because these will fulfill their nature.

God is infinite, and we are infinite in being. There is an infinity of nature on earth, and each one of us has some part in that nature as which we are to be fulfilled. It is all here for us, and we are so great in God's eyes that He has stored it up for us, that we may know infinite and boundless good.

When I consider thy heavens, the work of thy fingers, the moon and the stars, which thou hast ordained;
What is man, that thou art mindful of him? and the son of man, that thou visitest him?
For thou hast made him a little lower than the angels, and hast crowned him with glory and honour.
Thou madest him to have dominion over the works of thy hands; thou hast put all things under his feet. . . .   PSALM 8:3-6

The greatest thing on earth is men and women. In them we find fulfillment; in them we find God's Soul, full of life, full of love, full of joy, full of peace. We can enjoy the magnificence of this universe—its mountains, lakes, oceans, stars, sun, and moon; we can enjoy good food, comfortable homes, and wholesome recreation, but none of these constitutes our real joy. We know real joy only in men and women because in them we find the whole of God revealed. The whole of God is stored up in us, and all this world is really an instrument, a playground of joy, a place of inspiration made for our fulfillment.

CHAPTER XXXI

"THERE REMAINETH A REST"

Of old it was taught that there should be one day of Sabbath each week, a day devoted to worshiping God and living in His word. In order to be immersed in the Spirit, this Sabbath was to be kept entirely free of all worldly cares and worries.

The mystical meaning of Sabbath is a resting from power. All through the year and throughout our entire life, we resort to material and mental forces and powers, and the period in which we rest from the use of these forces, thereby experiencing the spiritual Presence, is in reality the only Sabbath there is.

Ideally, there should be at least one entire day in the week set aside for such rest, but because of family duties and professional responsibilities that is often well-nigh impossible. Everyone can have a Sabbath during the day or night, however, even if it is only in ten-, fifteen-, or twenty-minute periods. Then, when an occasional day comes along completely free, there is the opportunity of living with the Bible and other spiritual writings, living in meditation, and thus experiencing a full and complete day of spiritual refreshment.

A Sabbath is only truly a Sabbath if we do not permit the human world to come into that period. We must have one purpose alone: to seek the realization of His presence, His power, and His grace.

When we emerge from these periods, usually we find that the "things" are added unto us: whatever knowledge we need to carry on our business, whatever physical strength or moral support.

In The Infinite Way no provision is made for specific Sabbath periods such as any one day of the week or any one hour of the day, nor for rest homes, churches, monasteries, or retreats. In the light of spiritual revelation the Sabbath is not so much a specific day of the week as it is a specific state of consciousness. Any day of the week—Saturday, Sunday, Monday—any day can be a Sabbath. This very hour can be our spiritual Sabbath, and again tomorrow morning at six o'clock, if we understand that the Sabbath means a period of rest from our physical labors, material resources, human faith, and more especially a rest from temporal power.

The true Sabbath is a resting from any power which we know or can understand, and in that resting period something takes possession of us and renews us. There is no indication anywhere in Scripture that on this Sabbath we must sacrifice our thinking capacity, our thoughts, or our actions. It is not said that we shall not think thoughts, only that we shall not "take thought" for what we shall eat, or what we shall drink, or wherewithal we shall be clothed: it is pointed out only that there should be spiritual renewal.

As a matter of fact, even to fast from food for a period makes of our particular Sabbath a period of renewal. The holiest Sabbath periods are the days of fasting: fasting from the pleasures of the senses, even fasting from the necessities such as eating and sleeping, and from those things upon which normally we place reliance. "In quietness and in confidence shall be your strength"—in quietness and in confidence is the source of strength, in quietness and in confidence is the period of spiritual renewal because it is a denial of sense.

Jesus did not teach that we should not eat bread: he said that we should not live by bread alone. Jesus did not deny to anyone the eating of meat: he said, "I have meat to eat that ye know not of." He did not deny to anyone the partaking of bread, water, or wine: he said, "I am the bread of life."

Those on the mystical path do not deny the human body: they

bring spiritual refreshment to it. They bring a food to the body which is not a material food, but a spiritual food which produces spiritual energy. That spiritual food is obtained through fasting from material food and physical activity, even from mental food and mental activity, during which period the transcendental Presence permeates mind and body, renewing them, so that a person then finds himself with greater mental capacities and greater physical capacities than he has heretofore known.

In The Infinite Way there is no denial of the mind or of the body. Rather do we let the mind and the body become imbued with the Spirit; we let the mind and the body be fed, clothed, and housed by the Spirit; we let the Spirit be the resurrection to both mind and body; we let the lost years of the locust be restored to us—those years of our spiritual barrenness, years in which we were only physical and mental beings—in order that our ancient, true Selfhood may be revealed. This can be done only through the Spirit, and the Spirit can be entertained only through silence, in quietness, confidence, and assurance, and in a resting from the physical and the mental activities of daily experience.

Resting from worry and fear; resting from knowing, doing, thinking, and taking thought; resting in stillness, peacefulness, assurance, and confidence does not mean that we have to play God. Our only function is to be still, to be quiet and at peace. Nothing is expected of us, for I, the Spirit of God in us, will perform that which is given us to do.

If we give the first fruits of our time, the first few minutes of every hour, to God, sooner or later we shall learn that we can earn our living in a shorter number of working hours than heretofore seemed necessary. So it is that we do not need to use sixty minutes of every hour: we can accomplish more work in fifty-four, -five, -six, or -seven minutes than we ever did before in the full sixty minutes, if those other minutes are reserved for quiet and spiritual renewal. Everyone who has ever lived the spiritual life has discovered that when he has given himself wholly to God and dedicated his work to God, the quantity of his work is greater and the quality better.

The bibles of the world are replete with accounts of religious men and women who have at some time or other laid down their personal sense of life and dedicated themselves to God. They have not gone hungry, homeless, or friendless, but rather have they prospered.

The Old Testament prophets experienced intervals of spiritual refreshment for as long as forty days and forty nights. It was also the custom of the Master to go apart for many hours and have a Sabbath, a freedom even from ministering to his disciples, and spend them in an inner contemplation of the spiritual universe. There were times when he went apart for days and fasted from his labors, fasted even from acts of benevolence, and lived wholly and completely in the Spirit.

In monasteries and wisdom schools the idea of the Sabbath reached a high point of development. Those entering such schools or monasteries were required to give up all their worldly interests, desires, and possessions in order to devote themselves to a lifetime of resting in the atmosphere of God and making themselves subject unto God.

Living in and through God is what we are all striving for, but the one great fault to be found with a complete withdrawal from the world is that once the normal, human activities of life are separated from the spiritual life we are likely to think that the world of the Spirit has no relationship whatsoever to daily life. Under such a system the spiritual life is set apart, and in the end rendered valueless because unless the Word becomes flesh, that is, unless the atmosphere of God can be made a part of daily living—not something set apart for those people who desire to retire from human life— unless the atmosphere of God can really come to embrace the human universe and have a part in its functioning, It does not fulfill Itself.

All periods of turning from our customary reliances and hopes, from our recurring fears and doubts, to an inner stillness in which there is no power—no power that we know, no power that we can understand, and no power that we can use—are Sabbaths.

For the laborer in the field, the worker in the factory, or the office worker, the Sabbath may be the one day in the week which he can dedicate to God, but eventually all of us must learn to seize upon short periods of stillness and quietness while about our labors, so that out of every block of time there will be one, two, or three minutes for inner devotion, a time set aside for the eating of spiritual bread and spiritual meat. "Labor not for the meat which perisheth" is only another way of saying, "Rest and relax from your labors for this brief moment."

Spiritual work, or laboring "not for the meat which perisheth," is a resting from mental activities as well as a resting from physical activities because spiritual power is not generated by what we know with our minds. What we know intellectually leads us to the place where we are released from doing and from knowing into that moment of listening, and then being filled from within.

If we have such Sabbath periods and are able to abide in the presence of the Lord and be absent from the body, the body of our home or the body of our work, be absent from this world and be present in the consciousness and Spirit of God, we shall discover that when we return to our labors, we carry with us the atmosphere of God. By casting our burdens upon the Lord, our labors become lighter and our burdens less. His yoke is easy, and when we take upon ourselves this yoke of God, it carries the weight of the labor and frees us to perform whatever we have to do without worry, without fear, and without any feeling of heaviness, any drag, or any weariness.

Our periods of meditation are really our Sabbath periods of inner spiritual refreshment and renewal. When they are observed regularly, there is no need to set aside one whole day in a week because our Sabbath is being observed throughout every day of every week. Usually, when we begin with one period of ten or fifteen minutes of Sabbath each day or night, that time becomes so important that we find it necessary to have three or four such periods. We feel a greater hunger for these ten- or fifteen-minute intervals of Sabbath than we will ever feel for food.

The possibility of having a whole day or a weekend once in a while, in addition to those periods of meditation, is really worth thinking about because only those who have had the experience of living for an entire twenty-four hours in nothing but spiritual literature, meditation, and Scripture can appreciate what a difference this Sabbath can make in one's experience. Being able to live in a piece of beautiful poetry, more especially of a spiritual nature, or in some thought-provoking bit of prose brings us into that same holy atmosphere in which these writers were living when those gems came through.

All mystics and the founders of the great world religions have had periods when they were completely in the Spirit, and in those moments they received the highest and most spiritual impartations, many of which comprise a great part of the scriptures of the world, whether Hebrew, Christian, Hindu, Buddhist, or Moslem.

There are degrees of awareness of spiritual consciousness. *Consciousness* Itself is always at the standpoint of absolute perfect Being, but *we* are not always in a state of absolute awareness. When we are abiding in the impartations of truth which have come through the great spiritual lights of the world, however, and particularly in those hours when we have gone apart from the world, we are living in the consciousness of those who brought them forth, and then we actually feel ourselves in the very presence of God just as those great seers did when they were receiving these impartations.

The object of a Sabbath is to lay aside the world, that world which Jesus said he had overcome. We, too, are to overcome it, even if we overcome it for but fifteen minutes or an hour. Whether we give one hour a day, fifteen minutes, or whether we take a full Sabbatical day or occasionally a full Sabbatical weekend, we become so filled with the Spirit that like spring, it is bursting out all over. Then we come down from the mountain into the valley, as Jesus did, and heal the sick, comfort the comfortless, feed the hungry, and help to lighten the burdens of the world, sharing with others some of the Spirit that has been given to us in our Sabbatical period.

The day will come when every person will have free access to the Spirit and the presence of God, and every person will be able to walk into that holy sanctuary, the Shekinah, and there tabernacle with God in meditation and contemplation.

Father, I am here with Thee for only one purpose: I must know what Thou art, who Thou art, where Thou art, and why Thou art. I must even find out if Thou art, attain some awareness, some con-

sciousness, that Thou dost exist, and that Thou dost really exist within me. I must find some way of linking up Thy Spirit with my individual life.

I hunger and thirst to know Thee. I must tabernacle with Thee, commune with something within myself that is greater than my human self, something greater than my human capacity or my human goodness or human evil, tabernacle with something in me that is divine. If there were not something divine in me, or about me, I could not be alive and I must know what this something is.

O Lord, how long can I go on living without knowing Thy presence within me? How long can this go on? Am I to live here threescore years and ten, twenty, or thirty, and at the end feel that I have contributed nothing to this world, nothing to Thy kingdom, nothing to Thy people? Why am I on earth? Am I to live a wasted life with nothing to show for it at the end but just a living?

I would do Thy will if I but knew Thy will; I would live the spiritual life if I knew how to live it. Now, here in the inner sanctuary of my own being, cut off from the world, Father, reveal Thyself. Reveal Thy will, Thy way, Thy kingdom; reveal Thy purpose to me.

As we continue with this kind of meditation, eventually an answer will come from within. There will be a period of release, and we will feel a quietness and confidence and a complete freedom from this world. Then we can go back to our life again because we have had our interval of spiritual renewal and peace.

One day we come to what is the grandest experience that can take place in a human life: we lose all desire except the one desire— consciously to know God. Now as we go into our meditation, we have overcome the world. It is almost like feeling a hand on top of our head in a benediction as we pray:

Let Thy grace be my sufficiency. I ask not for persons, things, or conditions: I ask only that I may honestly be able to say that Thy grace is my sufficiency, whatever form it may take. Just let me know Thy grace, know and fulfill Thy will, sit at Thy feet, tabernacle with

*Thee, and feel that Thy life is my life. Let me only know that
wherever I am, Thou art; and that wherever Thou art, I am.*

*I am at the state of unknowing. Let Thy wisdom be expressed
through me; let Thy wisdom be my wisdom. Supply the wisdom,
the energy, and the Grace that I may always feel my own nothingness, and yet feel an eternal and ever-present perfection and completeness through Thy grace and Thy wisdom. I have no work to do
but that which Thou givest me, and I have no wisdom with which
to do it but Thy wisdom, and no power with which to perform it
but Thy power. Let me always abide in Thee.*

We are not surrendering ourselves to God's will unless we make a
conscious surrender of ourselves to that Will by disclaiming any will
of our own:

*I have no will and no desire of my own. Fill me with all that Thou
art. Fill me with Thy wisdom, Thy might, Thy justice, that I may
have nothing of myself and be nothing of myself, but be the All that
Thou art.*

What a Sabbath that is! What a fasting that is from the world,
the things of the world and the people of the world, and how it
spiritually fills, renews, and rejuvenates us! After that we can come
down from the mountain into the valley, mingle with and help meet
the needs of those who are drawn to us, not because of any virtue
in us but by virtue of the grace of God which now fills us.

We are in the presence of God any time that we can close our
eyes to this world and retire into our inner sanctuary. If we have
these periods of Sabbath, we shall find that as we go out into this
world we will be a light unto those who are still in the darkness,
worrying only about this world, a light to those who have not
learned to tabernacle with God.

CHAPTER XXXII

ADDRESS THE WORLD SILENTLY WITH PEACE

More and more, as we follow the mystical path, we become spiritual centers, and out from us is projected spiritual light and wisdom, the spiritual Presence and Power. Sometimes it is hard for beginners to grasp the idea that no one attains spiritual wisdom or spiritual light for his own sake, or for any personal benefit that may come to him. Whenever spiritual light comes to a person, he is called upon for that light, and from those who have the most, of them is the most expected.

It is almost unthinkable that Moses could have gone away to live the rest of his life by himself after he had received his illumination on the mountain. How could Elijah, Elisha, Isaiah, Jesus, John, and Paul have hidden their spiritual light under a bushel basket, or gone away to a cave somewhere or a mountain retreat, and lived this spiritual life unto themselves?

This is true also of those who are lesser lights. Every grain of spiritual light that we attain is meant, not for ourselves, but that it may be used for the benefit of human consciousness in general, until human consciousness is entirely dissolved, and nothing remains but that mind which was also in Christ Jesus. It might seem that the

light an individual receives dissolves some of the grosser consciousness of his own being, but that is not true, because no one, of himself, has any mortal consciousness. All the mortal consciousness there
is, is the universal sense of separation from God, which is a universal
hypnotism.

Every bit of light that any person receives, therefore, dissolves
some measure of that human, mortal, or carnal mind, some measure
of the vast human illusion of which material sense consists. This dis-
solution of material sense can be observed in our own experience or
in that of our family as these spiritual principles solve some problem
for us or remove some undesirable trait or negative experience.

As we take each principle of truth and apply it to the working
out of some personal problem, and as we attain enough light so that
the particular problem is met, we will find that thereafter we will be
called upon, day after day, to share our understanding and to apply
the wisdom given us to the problems of others. We may wonder how
our friends know that we have this light, and humanly they do not
know: it is only that spiritually they have discerned the direction
toward which they can turn for help.

The demands made upon us will become greater and greater, as
our spiritual light and wisdom increase, until eventually we discover
that we are not only more aware of the problems of the world, but
we are also beginning to apply our understanding of truth to them.
Then we will observe how quickly the light that we have received is
beginning to dispel the darkness of the wider circle of humanity.

In our early experience there are practitioners and teachers to
whom we can turn, and they usually solve most of our problems
for us. This is but a temporary relationship because the time comes
when we begin to meet our own problems through our own understanding, and turn to someone for help only when we are faced with
a problem that does not yield to our present understanding. Then,
of course, we have every right to seek the help of those who have
attained some deeper realization of truth, and who have gone a step
further on the Path. As we continue, however, we find ourselves asking less and less help of others, more and more able to solve our
own problems, and also able to help those in our immediate environ-

ment, and eventually we begin to work spiritually with the problems of the world.

All the help that we can ever be to anyone, any group, or to the world is in direct proportion to our understanding of the spiritual principles with which we are working, and to the degree of spiritual consciousness we have attained. Ours is the responsibility to study, to meditate, and to do all that is necessary to bring greater light to our individual consciousness, not for our own sake alone, but that this light which touches our consciousness may flow forth to the world and benefit it, that we may become a center from which goes out this light of healing, regeneration, blessing, peace, comfort, and especially forgiving.

How few of us realize the importance of the forgiving consciousness! Does not everyone carry with him the memory of some sin of omission or commission which, if he could, he would recall or undo? Do we not all have at least some small feeling of guilt? Are we not always hoping for our own forgiveness and trying to forgive ourselves, and often finding that very hard to do? That is why it is so necessary that each one of us develops the forgivingness side of his consciousness, so that everyone who comes to us may feel a complete absence of judgment, criticism, or condemnation.

We do not go about telling anyone that we do not condemn him. We would hardly say to another, "I know that underneath, you are as much of a sinner as I am." We do not express this audibly: we know it, and we know that just as we wish to be relieved of our sins of omission and commission, so do we know that everyone else does. Above all other things, it behooves us to develop within ourselves a consciousness that inwardly, silently, and sacredly—not outwardly in speech—can say to our relatives and neighbors, "There is no judgment upon you; there is no memory of the past: there is only the understanding of this moment." This was the attitude shown forth by the Master when he forgave the woman taken in adultery, and when he said to the thief on the cross, "Today shalt thou be with me in paradise."

Sin has a far deeper meaning than the commonly accepted concept of it. Sin is not only lying, stealing, cheating, bearing false witness, committing adultery and murder; sin also includes those minor ignorances into which we were all born: the human judgments and inhibitions, the human fears and superstitions. The forgiving consciousness dissolves all of this.

Anyone who can realize that the errors of his life have all been brought about by ignorance, superstition, and fear can easily develop a forgiving consciousness. That kind of a consciousness is a healing consciousness because it understands the nature of the universal fears, superstitions, and ignorance. It lives always in that atmosphere of releasing everyone from his hidden fears and hidden sins, whether of omission or commission, all of which are not personal, but the result of a universal sense of condemnation.

For what I would, that do I not; but what I hate, that do I.
ROMANS 7:15

In this statement Paul recognized that there was nothing personal about sin. Sin becomes a part of our experience only because it is a part of the universal ignorance of human consciousness; and then in some weak moment we indulge the very things that later we regret, most of them minor, but occasionally something of a major nature. What a blessing it is, when faced with a sense of guilt, to come into the presence of a person whose mind is not filled with criticism, judgment, and condemnation, but who understands, forgives and forgives, and whose gentleness is such that no thought enters his mind of any harsh nature!

This is having that mind which was in Christ Jesus, and as we rise to that state of consciousness, everyone who comes within range of our consciousness feels what the world calls love. Forgiveness is an attribute of love; understanding is an attribute of love; and above all, understanding the universal nature of the evils of the world is love. To understand is to forgive; to forgive is to love our neighbor as ourselves.

When we understand the impersonal, universal nature of evil, we will understand the spiritual nature of individual being, and why, in spite of those things that outwardly appear to be our faults, we are forever and always the temple of God. We will understand why it is that these faults are not ours, but the universal hypnotism, and that our real nature is a center from which emanates God's grace and God's love, a very center of peace and harmony. This inner peace can come to us only when we have released mankind from its faults, our neighbor from responsibility for his past, and our friends and relatives from our condemnation: "Go thy way in peace. Thou, too, art the child of God; thou, too, art the temple of the living God."

On every hand mankind is gripped by fear in the face of nerve-shattering world conditions, and those of us who have been able, even in a measure, to see the unreal nature of the evil rampant in the world have not only the responsibility of releasing people from their fears, but, in releasing them from their fears, preventing the greater tragedy that their fears may bring upon them. People do not fear because they are cowards: they fear because they are gripped by a universal hypnotism that makes them act in ways foreign to their own nature. It is mass hysteria, having its foundation in ignorance.

All world affairs eventually will be subject unto the influence of the Divine through the prayer that God's grace is sufficient unto this world. We do not pray to God for victory or that our enemies may be destroyed. We abide in the will and the way of God. We do not make the mistake of trying to channel God to do our will: we pray that the Spirit of God flow through us and bring justice to earth, not in accord with our concept of it, but in accord with the divine idea of justice; we tune in to God in the realization that if we make this contact and God is on the scene, there will be equity, mercy, harmony, peace, and all the divine qualities made manifest equally everywhere. We do not let the conditioned mind determine what we hope God will do, or how He will do it: we approach God with an unconditioned mind:

Thy grace is my sufficiency. Thy grace is the sufficiency unto this universe. Let It take form as It will.

The Word becomes flesh. All that concerns us is to hear the Word, and then let that Word become flesh, not outlining what form It should take. Let us never go to God with any thought of victory over anything or anyone. Victory always implies a right and a wrong; it means a winner and a loser, and there cannot be winners in God, nor can there be losers. There cannot be a right in God or a wrong in God: there can be only Spirit, spiritual Grace, and spiritual harmony, and this not in accord with man's opinion.

The questions knocking at the consciousness of all those who, to a degree, are living in the circle of eternity, and who are thereby living according to the two great Commandments, are: How can we express our love for our fellow man in a concrete way? How can we help to allay these fears and quiet this mass hysteria?

First, and above all things, we must withhold judgment and understand that people are not responsible for their fears: they are victims of a mass hypnotism. After we have done that, we can turn to the specific truth of Scripture which reveals that God is the life of man, the life of the universe, eternal and immortal life. Whatever life we have, then, is the life that was given us of God, and it must be God's life that is our life—divine, spiritual, immortal, and eternal Life. Do we, therefore, have any other life but that which was given to us of God, our Father?

What a release from all fear would come to us once we could realize that God constitutes our life eternal, that the Father's life is our only life, that we have no life of our own to lose, that we have never had any life but the life of God, that the very Spirit of God dwells in our being, even in our body, and that our body is the temple of the living God!

Disease has no power of survival in our body once we are able to discern that we have no life of our own. God constitutes the very breath of our being, the very life of our being. The belief of age and limitation has no power when we see that our life did not come into being fifty, sixty, or seventy years ago, but that the life that came into expression then is the immortal life that came forth from the Fountain of Life. God breathed into us His life—not your life or mine, but His life—and His life is my life and your life, and His life is immortal life and eternal life, and you and I are the temple of that Life:

Thank You, Father. I had no life of my own to begin with, and I

*have no life of my own that can come to an end. The life that I have
been given is Your life, the life of the spiritual son of God.*

As we abide in that Word and let that Word abide in us, as we
consciously entertain this truth, we become aware of the effect that
it has on our mind and body. To understand that the life of God is
animating us is to "die" to the belief that we have a life of our own,
and that it even has an age attached to it.

It will not be long before we feel the magical effects of this truth
in our mind and in our body, and as we continue to dwell in the
Word, quickly we will begin to realize that this is a universal truth.
Silently and secretly, we shall find ourselves looking at every member of our household and rejoicing in the truth: "I know thee now
who thou art. The life of God is your life; the Christ-life is your
life"; and soon there will be changes in the mind and in the body
of everyone around us.

Now we are becoming the center from which this light is flowing,
the center through which forgiveness, understanding, and truth will
begin to pour. Then, as we read or learn of this mass hysteria, whether
it is some epidemic going its rounds or whether it is long-range mis-
siles or bomb-proof shelters—whatever it may be—we will be so at
peace within ourselves that as we see our friends succumbing to this
hysteria, within ourselves we will say, "Thank God, I know that you
have life eternal, and whether you know it or not, I know that your
life is not in danger. I know that not even your body is in danger,
for your body is the temple of the living God." The peace that flows
out from us will be felt throughout the whole community, and as it
flows from community to community, the day will come when this
hysteria will end.

Peace must begin somewhere, and it must begin with one individual. Spiritual light has always entered consciousness through
one individual so permeated with truth that a dozen disciples here,
or a half dozen there, have caught hold of it, and then from them
come the fifty, the two hundred, and the two thousand. No one can
be the light of the world: he can be only the light that sparks the
light in others until it spreads around the world. So it is that we be-

come that one in our household, that one in our neighborhood, and, depending on the depth and degree of our own love, we can become the one to a whole nation or a group of nations. Why not? It always begins with one.

We can be that one; we can be that light in the measure of our understanding; but if we do not perceive that the God that is our life and the life of every individual is the same God that was the life of Jesus Christ, we can have no part in bringing peace to this troubled and fearful world.

Are not all death and destruction based on the belief that each one has a life of his own, a life that can terminate at some particular moment? But there is only one Life, one Father, one Creator, one creative Principle, and this One has breathed into us that Life which is eternal and immortal. How could any weapon destroy that Life? Once we can really see this, we become, not only the light unto our world, but the *life* unto our world. We resurrect our neighbor from the tomb of the belief that he has a life of his own and that it is in danger. We become the source of the peace that passes understanding; we become the source of forgiveness; we become the comforter,

None of us was born just for the purpose of living threescore years and ten, twenty, or thirty, accomplishing something for ourselves or for our families, and then dying. None of us was born to attain name or fame, except such as comes to us as a part of God's glory. We were all born to show forth God's glory, and the only reason we exist is to show forth God's life on earth, His eternal and immortal life. When we really know that, deep down inside, we are virtually addressing it to every member of our household, but if we are wise, we do this silently, sacredly, secretly.

The prayers that we pray in secret are the prayers that are answered openly. The truth that we address to another which has for its main purpose letting the world be made aware of how much truth we know is so much wasted truth. It is a waste to those to whom it is addressed and, furthermore, it deprives us of the benefit of it because we ourselves lose a little in giving it where it is not wanted.

There is only one time when truth should be voiced, and that is when truth goes out from a spiritual teacher to an open and receptive consciousness. Then it goes out in a circle and comes back because there is that spiritual bond between teacher and student. Teaching truth to the masses serves no purpose, but when seekers bring themselves to a spiritual message or teacher, they are receptive and responsive, and the message that comes through is a blessing to them and to the teacher. When we find someone eager to hear and to learn, then we share openly whatever we have learned: otherwise we pray silently, secretly, and sacredly, and these truths that we know within ourselves are received by those who could not receive them consciously, but who can receive them because of the spiritual bond that exists among all children of God.

Within ourselves we can know the truth about everyone in our household:

You are the child of God; you are the temple of the living God. God is your life, your Soul, your being, your mind; and even your body is the temple of the living God.

We know this truth silently and sacredly, voicing it audibly only to those who ask and seek it, those who welcome it.

Then, as we leave our household, we remember that in order to love our neighbor as ourselves, we must know this truth about every neighbor, friendly neighbor and enemy neighbor, nearby neighbor and neighbor ten thousand miles away:

You are the Christ, the son of the living God. The Christ-life is your immortal and eternal life. The life of the Father is the life of all mankind.

Such a realization may touch those in high places and in low places, in every kind of place, and may awaken them in the measure of their readiness.

Our responsibility in life is to be a center of light, to be the light of the world, and so to permeate ourselves with truth throughout our waking hours that it circulates in our consciousness even when we are asleep. Our spiritual being never sleeps, and anyone who reaches out to us finds this truth awaiting him, even while our physical senses are at rest. Our consciousness rests in action, but we spark it by the fact that our last thought at night is one of spiritual truth, a welcome to anyone in the world, anywhere, any time, to reach out to our consciousness to find the blessing of the truth we have known before we dropped off to sleep.

Every time that we consciously remember that the only life there is on earth is the life of God, we are helping to allay fear, we are helping to restore the peace that passes understanding. Until peace has been established in our innermost being, there will be no domestic or world peace. Only when peace shall have been established in the minds and hearts of mankind will peace be restored nationally and internationally.

At some period of each day, we must face out toward the world and remember:

Lo, I am with you always. I am the life divine; I am eternal life. I am with you always.

As we thus address our household, our neighborhood, and then go to the window and address the world, we will be the light of the world.

When the grace of God is received in your consciousness and mine, it is not a static and limited something embodied somewhere within our frame: it is a light that permeates us and flows out through us and from us; and inasmuch as there are no barriers to the activity of Spirit, this light which we have received as the result of our union with our Source flows out through the walls and windows of our homes into the world and becomes a leaven wherever an individual is raising his thought to God, regardless of what concept of God he may entertain. Whether he be in a hospital or in a prison, whether he be walking the earth free or be living in some nation where he is in slavery, if he is lifting his thought above human power, to whatever may be his concept of the Divine, the light which goes out from us and through us because of our meditation reaches that receptive

Soul, and in some measure lightens his burden, sometimes freeing him from sin, disease, and false appetites.

As we unite with the Source of life and *let* It have Its will, Its rule and reign on earth as it is in heaven, wherever there is a receptive thought, wherever there is an individual who may be saying, "Oh, God, God, God, help me! Is there something beyond the human?" that Soul will be touched by the Spirit of God that is upon us. We thereby unknowingly become transparencies through which this light flows to a world full of darkness, sin, ignorance, poverty, and bondage. To be the instrument through which God's grace may touch all human consciousness and enlighten and awaken it that all mankind may be free—this is living the mystical life.

CHAPTER XXXIII

THE INNER UNIVERSE

Every spiritual aspiration, every effort in the direction of God-realization, is a step forward out of the parenthesis into the full and complete circle of eternity. As we sow, so shall we reap, and if today we are sowing to the spiritual awareness of life, the parenthesis is becoming fainter and fainter. But if we are sowing only to physical comfort—health, wealth, and position—is it not inevitable that we will remain imprisoned in the parenthesis, reaping both material good and material evil?

Our primary concern, therefore, is with the sowing of this present moment, and that has nothing to do with anyone else. There is no one who can help and no one who can impede our spiritual progress. We determine to what extent we will dedicate ourselves to the spiritual path; we determine how seriously we will devote ourselves to this Way. If we are devoting ourselves to an inner spiritual practice, no one can interfere with it because no one knows that it is going on.

It makes no difference what violent objections to this way of life we may encounter in our home, in our business, school, or social life. Nobody knows what is going on in our mind because we are praying in secret; we are living in an interior world, an interior universe.

This is a secret life that we are living, this mystical life, and it does not serve any purpose to violate that secrecy by telling others about it, more especially those who have no interest in it.

In this moment we can leave our family outside—father, mother, sister, brother, husband, wife—leave all to enter the Christ-Spirit. Life is so completely individual that, for the time being, we can forget that there is anybody else in the world but ourselves. We can forget any obligation or duty we may have to others; we can forget our past, whether it is good, bad, or indifferent, and even if we are not fully able to do so, we can try to forget the future in the realization that we are creating our future: our tomorrows are determined by what we do today.

The Christ-Spirit is right here where you are and where I am. This presence of the Christ is in the midst of our own being. It is filling our consciousness. We do not have to reach out for It; we do not have to think: all we have to do is to be still, and let It talk to us from within our own being.

The kingdom of God is within us. Within our very own being is the kingdom of Love. If it is love that seems to be lacking in our experience, we do not look outside our own being for it, for even if we seem to find it, we will be disappointed. All we have to do to find love is to turn to this great spiritual realm that is within us, and there divine Love has Its abode.

Go within yourself, rest there, and acknowledge Its presence, pray that It reveal Itself to you, invite It to flow out from you, and then give action and expression to It by letting that love pour out to your friends and your enemies, to your nation's friends and your nation's enemies, to men of good will and men of evil will. Open your heart, embracing the whole world, and say to yourself, "Love, flow out: flow out to the saints to support them in their activity; flow out to the sinners to cleanse and purify them; flow out to the tyrants to soften and give them mercy and justice."

If you seem to lack wisdom, turn within, remembering that the nature of God is infinite intelligence, and infinite intelligence is in that kingdom of God within. If you need wisdom, pray that the wisdom already locked up within your being as the grace of God be made manifest to you in proportion to your need of it. Seek wisdom, but seek it within yourself. Pray for it. If your need at this moment is for guidance, turn within. Do not seek the guidance of "man, whose breath is in his nostrils." Turn to the one place where infinite intelligence and loving guidance await you, the kingdom of God.

Freedom—seek your freedom from within: do not seek your freedom in the externals. It makes no difference whether it is a government or a church that would shackle, whether it is a sick body, sin, or fear, turn within and you will find that freedom is a quality of God, and it, as every quality of God, is already locked up within you.

When you achieve the demonstration of freedom from within, you will experience it in the without; but be sure that when you invite freedom to come forth, you are also willing to give freedom to those you are holding in bondage. Even if you are holding them in bondage to the belief that they are human beings, give them their freedom. Recognize that nobody is a human being, but that God sits in the midst of every individual, past, present, and future, so-called living, so-called dead, and so-called unborn. You cannot have freedom unless you first give freedom. You cannot have love unless you first give love. You can have only what you are willing to give: what you hold on to you lose—that is a spiritual law.

You can never get supply spiritually or in any other way. Supply is an activity of God; supply is the gift of God; supply is that which is embodied and embraced within God, and God is in the midst of you. Therefore, an infinity of supply lies within you, but if you let your vision stray outside to the husband or wife who may seem to be the channel, to the position, the business, or the securities that may seem to be the avenue, you may be lost, for everyone on earth has found sometime or other that all outside reliances collapse.

Whether you think of supply in terms of a supply of love, of home and companionship, a supply of opportunity and recognition, a supply of money, compensation, or reward, the supply is within you and must flow out from you, and you must live your realization of its omnipresence by beginning with a penny, if necessary, and giving it to some impersonal purpose. Supply is omnipresent within you; supply will never leave you, nor forsake you. You can never go any place where supply is not. You carry it with you just as you carry your integrity, your loyalty, and your fidelity. You cannot leave it behind because supply is spiritual: it is your awareness of God in the midst of you to be proved by beginning at once to give, share, and express it.

If necessary, you have to give forgiveness: you have to sit down and search your thought and see what or whom there is on the face of the globe that you are holding in condemnation, criticism, or judgment, and forgive it or them. Forgive, forgive.

God is infinite being, and God is the infinity of your individual being. Demonstrate this, prove it. Begin, in whatever way is open to you at this second, to let God's grace flow out from you. Do not pray that God's grace come to you: open out a way to let God's grace flow from you.

There is a Presence within you that goes before you to "make the crooked places straight." Your realization of It releases It. There is a cement within you that cements your relationships with everybody in the whole world: your realization of that releases it.

This world is governed from within. This world, this outer world, is governed from within. No flower blooms except by virtue of an invisible activity. An invisible activity draws from the earth into the roots, and sends that which is drawn in up into the branches and out into the shoots that finally become the blossoms and the fruit.

There is an interior bond between you and God that makes it possible for God to send you where you will find whatever you need: the truth, the employment, the human relationships. The power is within you, and it is invisible.

What you behold in this world consists of effects, but there is not anything that you can behold that is not the result of an inner activity. You release this inner activity which goes out into the world invisibly and then produces visible fruitage. To abide in the Word is an invisible procedure. You cannot live in God externally; you cannot live in the Word externally: you must live in the Christ internally; you must let the Christ-word abide in you internally; and then you will bear fruit richly externally.

This world is invisible. The effects of it become visible—the fruitage and the harmonies—but the Cause, the Law, the Creator, the Activity, and the Substance are invisible. They are part of an invisible universe, and thanks be to God, that invisible universe is locked up within you. The Kingdom, the invisible Kingdom which is the source of the visible universe, is within you. You release the forces that bless you, and in your ignorance you release the forces that curse you. But the kingdom of God, the whole of God's creation, is within you.

This is an invisible world. Human beings live only on the exterior fringe of life, and that is why they find little or no satisfaction. In childhood they gain a momentary pleasure from their toys, and then they smash them: they are no longer useful, no longer satisfying, so they are broken, and another toy has to be found, and another and another. Then man finds a game, and then a business, and sometimes he finds a church, but nearly everything he finds is in the exterior world. He lives on the surface of it, and he gets a little pleasure out of it, a little joy, and perhaps a little profit, and then because it does not bring lasting satisfaction, he wants to break it up. Nothing in the exterior will ever satisfy, but when we learn to let the Invisible flow out and release Itself through us, It appears as fruitage of which we never tire.

The kingdom of God, the whole Source and Fount of this world, is within you, and it is this invisible world, so beautiful, so satisfying, and so complete, that appears as outer fruitage, as food, clothing, home, human relationships, marriage, or whatever it is that is needed. Then you never weary of it; you never tire of it: it is always joyous. You pass from glory to glory because, in this mystical life, you no longer hold on to form. You find joy in this city or that; you find companionship in this person or that; you find truth in this religion or that; you find peace in this church or that. You find them because you did not seek them in external forms, but released them from within your own being, and then they appeared outwardly as infinite, eternal, joyous, and satisfying forms.

This world within has been called a mystical world, and the life that flows from it, a monastic life. Many persons have misunderstood these terms, and they think of the mystic and the mystical as something mysterious, or of the monastic life as entering a monastery or a convent, bottling oneself up away from society, thereby avoiding labor and removing all temptation to sin. Is it not foolish? Some of the hardest workers in the world are in monasteries and convents, and if they did not lose their sense of sin before entering upon this life, they carried their sin with them right into the monastery and convent. You cannot bottle yourself up in any place where you will not find some measure of loneliness, sinfulness, lack and limitation—if these are in you.

The mystical life is the life you live when you recognize that the invisible Presence within you is the reality, and that It forms the joys of your outer experience. When you find the source and substance of your joy, prosperity, happiness, wisdom, and love within you, and then automatically find it developing into fruitage in the without, you are living the mystical life which often results in living the monastic life.

In the monastic life, you live within, where you find your completeness in God, and where you discover that you do not need anyone or anything because you have found Self-completeness in God. You draw to yourself worthwhile companions, understanding and loving relatives, capable and honest business associates, because the monastic life bears fruitage on the outer plane in harmony and all forms of good.

You are living the monastic life when you are in the business world, even if you are surrounded by a thousand people, because within, you are living as one with the Father. You are living the monastic life when you are married if you have found your Self-completeness within, and then share it with your companion without. You are not living the monastic life if you are dependent on parents, wife, husband, or children, and cannot find your peace without them. You have not found the monastic life if, out in the business world, you are placing your dependence on person, influence, power, or money.

The monastic life is a life of Self-completeness. You can lead the monastic life while living in the midst of a busy city or alone on a desert because you have found your Self-completeness within, and yet that Self-completeness you have discovered within, you share with others. That is the true monastic life.

You do not have to live separate and apart from your family or your business; you do not have to be separate and apart from this world. You can hold political office, and still lead the monastic life, if you have inner integrity, and bring to that political life the integrity of your inner life.

The greatest, the most satisfying, rewarding place in all of this world is within you. There you can tabernacle with the Spirit of God in you. And do not be surprised if in that temple within yourself you meet the saints and the sages of all times, for these saints and sages are only spiritual consciousness at different levels, and you must expect to meet spiritual consciousness within yourself at many levels. When you make your contact with God within, you find fulfillment, for it is by what takes place within that you establish your outer life, and the degree, intensity, quality, and quantity of the without.

Living in the interior world ensures a perfect balance to life. If you live wholly on the outer plane, everything with which you come in contact ultimately becomes just a toy that either breaks of its own weakness or that you yourself break. If, however, you live part of your time in this interior world, tabernacling in the kingdom of God, communing with the inner Presence, you will then find that that inner substance you have released will appear outwardly as a successful day, a protected day, a day in which you can bless those with whom you associate.

Of your own self you can bless nobody. You are of no value to anyone except in the measure of your contact with the Spirit within. As you draw on the kingdom of God within you, it has a way of satisfying all those who come to you. It becomes meat and drink, opportunity, supply, home, happiness, and joy.

The springs of water within bubble up into life eternal, and it is water you can draw without a bucket. How? By living an interior life, by realizing that the Substance of all form is within, and then by going in and being with It, praying with It, living with It, and releasing It.

You have meat that the world knows not of, but you must go within to find it, to share, experience, and release it. "I am the bread of life." Why struggle so hard for bread? Why fight for it, sometimes lie, cheat, and deceive for it? Why? You need not fight. All good is within you, but if you do not go within, if you do not learn to spend a little more time there, if you cannot find there a peace, a joy, it will not appear outwardly, and you will walk through this world, with nothing to give anyone.

If you have quantities of money and give of it, the world may hate you for it. If you forgive those who have wronged you and tell them so, they will hate you because they wronged you. You have nothing to give humanly—no one has, not even Jesus Christ himself had. But as you spend time with your Father within, God's grace within you can flow out, and you can share abundantly with all who are a part of your experience. God's grace is equal to any demand that can be made upon it. No demand upon you can be too great when you have divine Grace upon which to draw.

The interior world, the world within you, is the world of Reality. Externally, you find only forms, hollow forms, if you have not first gone within to make contact with the Father. The promise is, "I will never leave you, nor forsake you." What good is that to you if you do not go inside and meet that I? I is there in the midst of you; I is mighty in the midst of you. But what good is that to you if you will not go in and get acquainted with that I?

You must have periods day and night when you go within to meet God. But because for centuries He has been hidden under layers of humanhood, centuries in which man has been walking up and down the world, living on the edge, the outside of the world, living for the externals, the first few times you go within you may not meet Him. With patience, however, eventually you will.

There is probably a thick crust of self between you and the I that is within you. Be patient: knock, and it will be opened unto you; ask, and it will be given to you—but go within and knock, go within and ask, "Father, reveal Thyself." Learn to go within because the whole kingdom of Reality is locked up deep inside of you; the whole of the Christ is embodied within you. It is not walking the streets of Jerusalem, although I will say to you, that if you walk the streets of Jerusalem with sufficient humility, you will feel It there. You can walk the streets of Damascus and feel Paul walking right beside you.

In that great rush of mass humanity that today walks the street called Straight, where Paul walked, you can actually feel Paul's presence.

The Spirit of God is within you, but how are you going to meet It if you play around on the surface of the world with toys and baubles? Go within and meet the Christ which is the Spirit of God individualized. This Spirit of God was the intelligence and the love of Laotse; It was all that went to make up Gautama the Buddha; It was the life, heart, and soul of Jesus.

The message of Jesus Christ has given It to the world in words so plain that you cannot miss It. You cannot miss It if you once catch a glimpse of the truth that he is revealing an interior kingdom, an interior world that is more real than the exterior one. The interior world cannot be destroyed, and even if a bomb were released that destroyed this whole earth, there would still be as much of God as there was before. When there were only a few million people on earth, was there less of God than there is now with three billion? Will there be more of God next year when there are an additional one hundred fifty million on earth? Is not God always present in Its completeness and Its perfection even when there is but one? Is not the allness and the fullness of God represented in everyone?

You are that one. The fullness of the Godhead bodily is expressed as you. If you were the only person left on the face of the earth, you could live the monastic life—complete, perfect, and harmonious. If there were a billion around you not understanding and not believing, you still could lead the monastic life, that full and complete life in God, because you could always close your eyes in your office, in a park, or in your own kitchen, turn within, and realize, "Within me is the secret of the universe. Within me is the whole secret! The Holy Grail is within me; the word of God is within me, the Hebrew Torah, the Ten Commandments, the Bhagavad-Gita, the Hebrew Testament, the Christian Testament—all of these are within me. I can open myself to them, and let them flow out."

You go within and tabernacle with God, with the Christ, and with the saints and sages of all ages, and when you come out into the exterior world, their spirit will flow out through you to be the bread, the wine, the meat, and the water to those who come in contact with you in your family life, your business, your social, and your political life. They may not know the Source—they do not have to know It. That is your secret, and it is a secret you can divulge only to those who know how to respect and appreciate it.

To the many persons you meet every day, you are just a man or a woman in everyday clothes, and for the most part they are completely unaware that locked up in you is the secret of life, the kingdom of God, the healing grace of the Christ, the power to multiply loaves and fishes, the joy and peace of the universe. Locked up in you is the power to attract to the word of God all those who are seeking God.

To some extent all of you have demonstrated this, but not enough. To some extent I have demonstrated it, too, but not enough. I know, as you now know, that there is an interior world, a real world which is the Source of the outer world, the creative, maintaining, and sustaining Principle of the outer world.

You must learn to tabernacle with God, to commune with Him at the center of your being. Meet Him there every day. And there, too, you can meet all the other people that you have known on the spiritual path. Go within yourself and meet them there. You can never be alone—those you know on the spiritual path are always with you. They are as much a part of your consciousness as your own family, if only you will close your eyes and look for them there.

Every word of truth that God has ever uttered is locked up within you. Loose it and let it go, but never tell this secret except to those of your spiritual household. Do not expose your "pearl" to those who are not connoisseurs of pearls. Do not ever give anyone an opportunity to ridicule your inner life. Do not let anyone try to destroy your faith, your understanding, or your wisdom. You have a "pearl" for which the people of the world would sell their souls if they only knew what it could do for them.

This is the mystical life. This is the monastic life:

"I and my Father are one," and in God I find my Self-completeness, and then when I open my eyes and go out into the world, I

share the glories of God, the grace of God, the peace of God that passes understanding.

I of myself am nothing, but I can go within and there enjoy God's grace.

No man can take your riches from you; no man can take your peace. The world cannot find you when you are living inside because it knows nothing of an interior world, and if it were told, it would only laugh in disbelief. If the world strikes at you, it will merely be to take your money, your property, or your business. It does not know that those are your toys, the fruit that grows on your Tree of Life, the effect of the mystical life. And so that is all the world will ever want to take from you. If it does try to deprive you of this fruitage, you will remain undisturbed because you know that if this attempt should be successful, a process of spiritual multiplication is already in progress, and in due time there will be more fruitage on your Tree.

No man can take your peace from you after you have discovered the interior world. After you have discovered that within you is the substance of all form, the law of all effect, the divine Grace, never again can the world disturb you, never can it touch you.

The heart and the soul of The Infinite Way is its mysticism and its monasticism, a way of life that has nothing to do with leaving the world on the outer plane. It has all to do with leaving the world while you go within and eat of that inner meat, drink of that inner water, tabernacle with the saints and sages—the Christ—and then come out and enjoy every person and every thing that God's grace hangs on your Tree of Life.

Set in Linotype Electra
Composed, printed and bound by The Haddon Craftsmen, Inc.
HARPER & ROW, PUBLISHERS, INCORPORATED